ACTIVATING
the DIVINE
HUMAN

EMBRACING OUR SHADOW
AS WELL AS OUR LIGHT

ACTIVATING
the DIVINE
HUMAN

I.AM PUBLISHING

Cover art by Atousa Raissyan.

Cover design by I.AM Publishing.

Editing by Dori Harrell, of Breakout Editing.

Formatting by Colleen Jones, of Breakout Editing.

ISBN: 979-8-9912626-0-6 (Print)

979-8-218-46820-0 (eBook)

Disclaimer

The authors in this book are not medical doctors or licensed therapists. When viewing the content of this book, understand that the authors are not providing medical advice and not replacing conventional medical diagnosis or treatment that has been given by your doctor or medical professional. And if anyone feels they need help to seek and/or consult their physician, they should do so.

Front Cover

The front cover of this book is an augmented reality art, which means it will come alive and move. To see the augmented reality art, please search for and download the free Artivive App. And follow the app instructions to allow camera access. Once installed, point the back facing camera of your device to the cover. Make sure you have the volume turned on. Enjoy.

CONTENTS

INTRODUCTION

My experience with publishing has been through writing two multiauthor books, with different self-publishing companies, and a solo book mostly completed on my own. After seeing how most self-publishing companies went about publishing multiauthor books, I wanted to do it different. I started I.AM Publishing. I wanted to make sure that the writing and publishing processes were a healing experience for the authors, with a total collaborative energy. To ensure we all came together as a collective beyond this book. Writing in a group like this can be a triggering and at the same time healing experience. And what better way that we all help each other on this journey. And this book has done just that.

In late September of 2023, I set out to publish my first multiauthor book as a publisher. I invited only those who I was called to invite, which was about sixteen people. And out of those, eleven accepted my invite. Eleven was the magic number for me—my favorite number, a number I see at least fifteen times a day, and my life-path number.

In October 2023 the collaboration was born. And shortly after we came up with the title of this amazing book.

I invite you to close your eyes and hold the book in your hands so that you may feel the collective energy that we have placed in these pages. These magnificent eleven humans went through such a transformative process as part of creating this book, that it is beyond any words I can put into an introduction. They came together and helped one another write their chapters, through triggers with the writing and publication process and beyond it. Do yourself a favor and hold the book, gaze at the title, feel the cover, and allow the energy to come through. After a few moments of allowing yourself to connect with the power of these authors, begin to venture inside. You can read from any story you like. See which is inviting you first.

The authors share their stories, interpretations, and perceptions of what it is to be a Divine Human and embrace their shadows as well as their light. Each voice is different yet the same.

We hope that you connect with us and allow the guidance and stories shared to help you shift and see that you are beyond your physical forms, beyond your stories. We hope to activate the Divine Human in each and every one who holds and reads this book and help you find ways to embrace the duality of life.

With Love,
All of Us to Your Hearts

ACTIVATING THE DIVINE-SELF

By Atousa Raissyan

"Tell me the truth," I asked love,
"What are you?"
"I am the everlasting life,"
Love said,
"I am the recurring joy of living."
~Rumi

"The recurring joy of living" . . . Ask yourself, are you living or pursing? Are you pursuing happiness? Or living in joy?

Joy versus Happiness

Recurring joy of living . . . somewhere along the way, we mistook joy for happiness and happiness for love. Joy involves transcendence of ego/mind-self and is a condition of one's life, versus happiness, which comes and goes and is tied to accomplishments, receiving, keeping, and holding. Joy is the heart and unconditional love, where happiness is in the mind and tied to fear. The heart does not know right or wrong, good or bad, light or shadow; the heart only knows love. Where the mind is tied to duality, to identities, judgment, stories and therefore fear.

And when we start pursing happiness rather than finding/allowing joy in life and living, we allow our minds and fear to take over rather than the heart and unconditional love. We allow the ego-self to take over rather than the Divine-self or God-self.

This pursuit of happiness has led us to seek. To seek is an attempt or desire to obtain or achieve something or someone. Desire, obtain, achieve all point to something outside.

And the first line of the above poem, "Tell me the truth," is related to who we are in "truth" from the perspective of love and the heart and not from the perspective of the fear and the mind. And from "love's" perspective, the truth is, that we are God, we are life itself (without end or beginning) and recurring expression of joy in living and experiencing life.

Now why am I giving so many definitions? Because humans, in an attempt to express, understand, and communicate, tend to use words. However, our natural way of communication is more energetical than with words. Humans created words out of sounds and then gave meaning to these words, and then more words were needed to explain those. It's interesting to note that humans are still creating words, such as "cap," "bussin'," "sus," "drip," and so much more. Words, just like everything else, have energy attached to them, which bring out reactions, emotions, and thoughts. Be mindful of the words you use to describe yourself and others. And remember, your definition/perception of a word may be completely different from someone else's. Meaning, the word "smart" may feel good to you and get you excited, but the word "smart" brings out anger in someone who may have a trauma around that word. I may use the word "believe" to mean that through my own experience and knowledge, I have come to know and consider as truth, and for someone else "believe" is strictly used to mean faith in something or someone without experience or knowledge of it. Words we use have energy and power, depending on your experience and perceptions.

> " Words we use have energy and power, depending on your experience and perceptions. "

Which brings me to the word "God," which in every language, depending on your experience and perceptions, can either evoke fear, love, resentment, hate, joy, anger, and so much more.

Side note: Isn't it funny that we use other words to define a word, and people sitting together are constantly searching for words to say to break silence—not knowing that they are already communicating in silence and not consciously aware of the communication. Because the communication is happening on an energetical level.

I got side tracked. Now back to joy versus happiness.

Generally speaking, in the pursuit for happiness, everyone is looking for a quick fix, quick cure, and a magic bullet. Many people who come to me for my services want me to wave some magic wand or my hands, prescribe some plant medicine, meditation, sound bath, and/or somatic exercise so that they stay blissfully "happy," and the way that they will be "happy" is to manifest all or most of the things they have desired—perfect marriage, love relationship, perfect job, lots of money, success, and the list goes on. And sometimes "happy" is in the desire to find joy, life purpose, soul purpose. The emphasis being on "the desire" and "find," which point outside of self and urgency to achieve.

I was one of those people at one point in my life, desiring a better life, a romantic partner, marriage, money, success, and so much more. Desires came true. Some came true and then ended. As I walked a more spiritual path (being more forgiving, accepting, loving, trusting, and moving with the flow and being aware), some desires shifted and some new ones appeared. And at some point along this new path, I let go of the magic-bullet fix/cure because I knew that was not the solution. Along my journey I had also picked up a desire for spiritual gifts (sight, knowledge, hearing), connection to other realms and ethereal world, to be recognized as one with and to help people. I was waiting for someone, something in real life, or ethereal world, to bestow upon me gifts as a badge to mark my achievement and note that I had made it. And the fear came, of never receiving this badge or certificate and losing it all—losing the gifts, the communication to the spirit world, the magic. Again, desires came true, and some came true and then ended.

One important realization I had was my attachment to seeing my desires come true and attachment to keeping them alive (i.e., for them not to end.) My desire not to lose my gifts of sight, spirit communication (as something outside of me), and magic. As if I was going through a training and waiting for someone to say "you are done," and if I didn't finish, then all would be taken away. I had replaced my fear of loss with another fear of loss. And at the root of the attachments and associated desires was attachment to the desire to feel "good" and "happy." And anything that felt like moving away from this desire would bring out fear. My mind signaling fear would bring out resistance to anything that went against being happy. Every time sadness, anger, even fear would show up, it would feel as if an alarm had been set in a submarine, signaling all hands on deck to prepare to resist and eradicate. Why? Because if I was not happy, it meant I was not going to accomplish, receive, keep, or hold on to. I was going to lose everything and everyone, including the spirit realm.

We even form these identities around "I am helping people," "It's my soul purpose," and "It's my mission." Of course it is great to want to help people, have purpose and mission. What I am talking about is forming identities with desires tied to achievements and forming attachments around it. There is a difference between "I am the one helping . . ." and "I AM and helping is natural part of my existence and flow." The first is an action based on identity that wants to achieve and the latter has no identity or ego attached to it.

Soul purpose and mission is always a guidance to go inside and discover the "self" beyond identities, attachments, and desires. Beyond this human form. *And* embracing this "self-realization" with our existence in the human form. The wholeness of bringing the formless and form together in *love*.

Yes meditation, sound baths, yoga, breath work, ceremonies, and the like will help you find zen in your life. However, they will not lead you to find truth. Truth of who you are inside and life. Truth of discovering the peace and joy that will not be broken by the outside storms. Zen will not release the identities—it just makes them quiet for the duration that you remain in zen state. Sometimes these activities may even be a big part of an identity. At some point my ceremonies, drumming, and cleansing were part of my identity as a healer and shaman. I had made zen into a rule for being a healer or shaman, rather than allowing it to be part of my natural flow. I had to let go of my attachment to all of it. Sure, I still drum and use my sage—however, it is not as part of an identity attachment. I still play the role of healer and shaman, but I am not stuck in it. Which allows for me to be fluid in the moment and moving with the flow of what is needed at the moment for me and the client.

The truth can only be discovered through self-discovery.

No amount of purge from ayahuasca, micro-dosing, CBD-THC, or rapé/hapé will give you the freedom you are seeking in life. No amount of ceremonies, yoga, meditation, breath work, somatic work, or exercise will free your mind from seeking happiness. Because the approach with which you take these steps all starts from the fearful mind, with an attachment to desires, outcomes, and achievements. If right now you are saying that is not true, then great—I invite you to stay with me. Even if you agree, stay with me.

There is nothing wrong with any of the above practices. They are actually recommended, and I even prescribe meditations, mantras, and exercises. They are helpful, and if and when you are called to do any of them, follow that path. What I am speaking about here, rather, is the intention in which you are doing or seeking these practices. Is it based in fear or a flowing from heart space? Are you doing them to achieve or from a natural flow of life? If you stop doing them, does it bring out fear, anger, and resentment? Are you doing them to achieve feeling good and happy in the body and life?

Society has been addicted to feeling good and happy, manifesting, and living in duality by using the measuring scale of good/bad, happy/sad, right/wrong as a way to be. Living "in" duality, plus attachments to desires, is causing you to seek out these solutions in the first place. The battle with duality—seeking solutions from a fearful programming of the mind, judgmental programs of good/bad, right/wrong, and therefore the desire to manifest something different from what is there now—leads to staying in a place of fear and the mind.

Ask yourself this: If I was living in joy and peace in my heart and mind, would I sit in meditation? If my body felt joy and peace and moved that way, and I loved my body fully and unconditionally, would I do yoga or somatic exercise? If I felt joy and peace in my body, heart, and life, would I pursue plant medicines? It is not about doing or not doing but rather trusting the flow and process of life, without attachment. To know that all is for purpose and whatever plant medicine, exercise, meditation, and teachings that come to you will happen at the right time and place as part of existence. So let go of desire and attachment and trust that all that is showing up in your life has purpose.

Let's take them one by one. Plant-based solutions bring you the gift of you seeing you. You don't need the plant to see something unless you have been refusing to see it. Perhaps you have seen it and would rather unsee it or ignore it and say to yourself that *there must be another way to get rid of it*. Whatever the plant medicine shows you, then you still have to be willing to forgive, release, and heal it. You have to be ready to see it and let it go.

Most people meditate because "I heard its good for you, and I want to quiet my mind and gain the benefits of meditation." And therefore, meditation becomes an activity to escape and receive or get to a different place to manifest all those wonderful things your identities want to achieve. Not meditation as a way of living and being. The moment you say, "I need to quiet the mind and therefore I will meditate" (as an action) is the moment you have walked in duality and are playing with it. Meaning the desire to quiet the mind brings with it the attachment to quiet the mind to achieve peace, and an action by the mind has taken place from a place of fear. What if you can't quiet the mind? Then you cannot achieve peace? What happens if you cannot achieve peace? Then the fear really gets activated, to "OMG nothing is working. I have to 'do' more. I have 'to do' something." Meditation, seeking to quiet the mind, means that there is a personal identity that feels the need to meditate. There is a battle with mind. However, when these practices of yoga, exercise, ceremonies, etcetera, are part of the flow of life – natural and not forced or done out of some fear – then they are more joyful and peaceful. Rather if there is a doing, a seeking to achieve, a place, a status, or a feeling and not just for the fun or enjoyment of it, then you are in duality of the mind. With some of these practices there is a belief that to be spiritual and/or enlightened, you must be a certain way, do certain things, and achieve certain things, which adds another layer of fear and duality. Because now there is a spiritual/enlightened identity, and to maintain this identity there are certain things that this identity must do to maintain its status as spiritual/enlightened.

Ask yourself these simple questions:

> Why am I meditating? What is the purpose of it for me? Why do I want to meditate (or not meditate)? Is it for enjoyment of it, a natural state of my being, to achieve a certain state of being, or from my belief it's what I have to do?

> Why do I do tarot readings? Astrology? Psychic readings? Is it to seek an answer for what will happen in the future? Is it to get validation for how I am feeling or what is happening in my life to make sure it's right? Or is it just for enjoyment and fun? Or am I attached to it?

> Why do I do rituals and ceremonies? Is it as a must or should, in order to stay on the spirits' good side? Is it for me to not lose something? Or keep bad things away? Or is it just the pure joy and to honor the part of me that is connected to everything?

If you are seeing it, great. That means now you are aware of your intentions, desires, attachments. And from that awareness everything can start to unravel and release.

Because that is the golden rule—stay in awareness. Whatever you are doing, stay in awareness and see "who" is doing it. Because ultimately it will bring you to "I" beyond the identities.

Shift Your Perspective

Throughout my life, even as a young child, I was fascinated with prophets, gurus, healers, yogis, and so forth. And as I grew older, I continued to read and follow the teachings of masters and gurus for meditation and mindfulness as well as the teachings of prophets.

Meditation and mindfulness teachings always posed a big challenge, as I was fully into my traumas and associated identities that carried the traumas. And when it came to religion, I was terrified of the God, as depicted in the religions. At the same time, I found peace in a God I knew in my heart. And this God I knew to be true and what the prophets were pointing to.

Meditation and mindfulness teachings and practices point to a space where the mind gets quiet enough that you can let go of identities and stories created by a fearful mind so that it's easier to discover the true-self. And some of these practices involve quite "inner" sitting with self-discovery questions, such as Who am I? Where did I come from?

These practices posed a big challenge, since as soon as I sat with an intent to quiet the mind, the battle would start. And if I let go of the mind, the fear-based identities would be so loud and so many that it would be overwhelming to sit. Movement was my way to drown out the noise. But then the noise would also be there during the movement, and so blasting music in my ears solved that issue.

Until there came a time that none of it worked.

Even sitting with self-discovery questions of "I AM" "Who am *I*"?; and "Where did *I* come from?" posed its own challenge. Since fears would not allow me to let go of the mind long enough (if even) to feel that space of "I AM."

Some gurus' and masters' teachings point to self-love and gratitude to guide you to engage in the heart. And by moving in the heart, the more you become loving, kind, and compassionate with yourself and life, then the mind lets go of the stories and identities. But when you don't love yourself, you don't accept yourself and where you are at in life and how life has turned out, then these practices are more superficial, outward and fear based rather than blossoming from inside, as they are meant to be.

For me the path started with the desire to have the healing gifts of prophets, become mindful like gurus, and allow love to take over, like Rumi, who led me on my path. This was the path that led me to self-discovery, healing, forgiveness, self-love, gratitude, and full trust in the flow of life and doing the work I do today. (Which I share in my award-winning book *Change Yourself Change the World: Transform Your Life from Fear-Based Living to Choosing Love and Seeing Magic*.)

My mind noise was too loud, the identities too strong, the stories too real, and the fear too strong to easily quiet the mind that created it all and achieve self-discovery. I had to start with awareness of the identities and their stories, fully charged with emotions and programming that directed their choices. Once I was able to heal, release and let go of these identities, forgive, accept, and shift perspective, then I was able to change the programming of my mind to let go and allow more my heart and intuition to guide. This allowed for natural internal self-love and gratitude for myself, life, and the past. And the more my heart opened, the more I gained strength to trust in the process and flow of life.

The more we move toward the heart, then the mind releases its hold. All leading to letting go of identities along with their stories. This letting go is not a resistive letting go. The reasons you created these identities and then went along with their stories was for safety. When we move from heart, there is a natural trust—therefore, you feel safer, so it is easier not to be attached to the identity and its stories. And this is a natural letting go, since there's no desire to maintain the identity.

The core identities, such as "the judge" and being "alone," are much stronger, and in order to help me release them, my trust in life had to be much stronger. I had to trust and let go of control, which meant letting go of all fears. This trust and letting go of control then opened the heart even more and allowed the mind to settle in the heart. The more the mind settles in the heart, the more instances where you feel the space of oneness, unconditional love, and just being.

" The more the mind settles in the heart, the more instances where you feel the space of oneness, unconditional love, and just being. "

In *Change Yourself Change the World*, I mostly covered my personal healing journey, as well as the process and steps for me letting go of enough of identities and stories that I was able to realize I AM, I AM God, I AM Divine, I AM Life.

It's time to go deeper into this self-recognition and what it means to live life from this space. Living life as human and God in a world insisting on duality.

Changing Definitions

Before we get into this process, there is a need for re-defining certain words. Shift in perspective of meaning and concepts.

First let's look into the word "God." This is not God as it relates to religion. This is not God that does not exist for atheists. This is not God in the spiritual sense that is somewhere in the ether. This is not God that has a gender or race. This is not a God that can be described in words. It is a recognition of a space, of a state of being. It is a realization that takes place inside our hearts.

I believe the message of the prophets when speaking about God, it was a pointing to their own self-realization of being God. They spoke about there being only one God, that God is inside each of us, that God is love. They spoke about self-forgiveness, self-love, and ways to take care of the body and letting go of thoughts in order to discover God inside ourselves as opposed to searching for it outside. They talked about the power of God not as an outside God but the God that is inside each of us and our power to live a free life once we are self-realized. They spoke of God as inclusive and not separate. The teachings and practices were based on how they came to release the separation between ego-self and God-self and bring it all together as one and guided by unconditional love.

However, humans' perceptions and interpretations of these messages, practices, and guidance was from a place of a fearful mind. Humans that could not see this power and gift in themselves saw themselves as separate, and therefore their fear reaction was to either stand against the message and prove it false or to devote to it from a place of fear so that they would not be punished/destroyed by it.

Fear turned the word "God" into a word that carries lots of energy and carries duality, as in God is heaven, devil is hell, and there being good angels and bad angels. Fear was the origin of duality, and separation of self with God. Even duality in terms of gender as in God/Goddess, Divine Female/Male.

Fear of not having, fear of a traumatic time returning, fear of not being equal or accepted, fear of losing life and loved ones, fear of not surviving, fear of surviving but not having the means. Fear has fueled anger and hate, and anger and hate give a false sense of power. To this add "God" gave you this power, "God" wants you to do this, or "their God" is the cause of your suffering, which becomes the air that anger and hate need to become destructive. Or if you add there is no God, *you* (ego-self) are powerful, then this is also air to fear and anger and hate, to become destructive in the way that now this power is used to manipulate others, take from others, and destroy. If a person has too much separation from their heart and love and therefore their conscious, then fear-anger-hate power motivates them to act against their true nature, which is love. And the original intent of prophets, gurus, and masters has been to guide humanity to heal this separation and see themselves as one. One with God (inside), one with love, one with our heart, one with one another, one with universe. And from that place of oneness anger and hate have no space. Therefore, fear has no space.

In certain languages the word "God" does not have the energy of duality attached to it. It is more closely related to one/oneness and self-realized, as it is in the Farsi "Khoda" (I Am the Creator), Arabic "Allah" (the One), Sanskrit "Om" (Sound of God, One). It is important to note that the self in "self-realized" is not the ego-self but rather the true-self. I refer to the ego-self as the part of us that is attached to the birth-given name and the identities/personas that have been created as part of this name and his/her family and environment, along with their stories and perceptions. The ego-self is very much attached to a way of being in order to receive love and acceptance and to ensure safety. And the thoughts and emotions are entirely for the ego-self, as it becomes (takes on the role of) different identities/personas.

It's interesting to note that for the people to relate to God, they give it gender, skin color, shape, and form to closer match with their own physical bodies.

From a place of oneness, there is no masculine/feminine, no God/Goddess, because it's all in one human form.

Each of us carry masculine and feminine energies in our bodies. Each human form has testosterone and estrogen hormones regardless of gender. When these are balanced, we feel the oneness within. From a place of oneness there is no skin color, shape, or size because it's all viewed as one.

Our life, planet, and universe at this time are reflections of collective egos and the separation we have created in ourselves that has caused separation in our world. The more we recognize God as love in our hearts the more the ego shrinks and the more life, planet, and universe will reflect the God-as-love inside rather than the ego-mind and fear. The more we recognize the oneness inside, the separation disappears and we feel the oneness with the world. Therefore, we create from a space of unconditional love, peace, joy, and oneness.

Neutralize the word and give it a new energy

For many people and throughout our planet's history, the ego-created God has been used as the police and the judge. Fearing God, and God's punishment, therefore people will do good and right. Viewing yourself, others, and life through a lens of judgmental God, and therefore making sure to do good and right. And using this ego-God as the police and judge, creating fear, anger, and hate, humanity has gone against the true nature of love, peace, and joy, causing harm not just to themselves but others. And therefore, hate and anger toward "God."

If you believe in a God as something outside yourself, then neutralize it so it is not a fearful punishing God rather than a loving and forgiving God. Neutralize it so it is not a judging God of heaven and hell, but rather a forgiving and loving God helping all to find their way into love and unconditional love. Read the dos and don'ts of religion not as insights on how to find love in yourself and how to forgive yourself and others. Go back to the simplified version of God of religion and not a big book of rules of how not to be punished or how to punish others. Jesus, Muhammad, and Moses were all about love and forgiveness, finding your path to love, and living life devoted to love for yourself and others.

If you are an atheist, then neutralize the word God so that you release your anger and hate at the word. Forgive the ones who have used the word to punish others (and perhaps you). Forgive the people who have done unimaginable things using this word God. That forgiveness will lead you to find love inside your heart. It will allow you to discover the God-self and release the identity of "anti-God."

" Love releases, gives, allows, and flows. "

To let go of your mind's reaction to word God and Divine, neutralize them. Start by forgiving yourself and the version of the God you have been using to punish yourself and others and to judge yourself, others, and life. Start to recognize and feel God as love (unconditional love) rather than fear. Because it is not the outward God of religion that created suffering, judgment, punishment—it is the ego-mind of human operating from a place of fear. Fear desires power, safety, and security. Love knows it is safe and secure. Fear grabs and holds on. Love releases, gives, allows, and flows.

I had to neutralize the word God for myself. Even though there was a God in my heart that I knew to be love, there was a punishing God that society had said to worship. And this worship went beyond God, worship gurus, worship teachers, worship parents, worship elders, worship spirit guides. I despised worshiping, since it gave the subject of worship so much power over me and I was already feeling powerless as a child. Power of knowledge, being better, being greater than me that I could never achieve. Also, at the same time, I feared not to worship because of the presumed power I had given the subject.

Once I neutralized God, forgave, healed, and came to a place of joy, peace, and love, then worship lost its meaning and power. For me, worship has changed to being *one* with, and honoring and rejoicing in seeing/feeling the one in others as in yourself.

As you let go of punishment, then you can let go of judgment. Judgment is what holds the punishment in place. When there is no judgment, then there is no judge, which means no punishment or fear of receiving punishment.

It's interesting how if we go to remove the system of judgment/punishment, the mind automatically goes to fear—how will we be sure that people will do the right thing? Or how will we deal with people who are not doing the right thing? As if the fear motivation is not there, then everyone will either sit at home eating bonbons all day. Or that everyone will turn into monsters and start killing, looting, and stealing. If judgment, punishment, and fear are removed and all that is left is unconditional love, joy, and peace, will there be any killing, looting, or stealing? What causes those things in the first place? Anger and hate, caused by fear. What causes you to sit home eating bonbon's all day? Lack of joy, lack of peace in mind, and self-hate.

Greetings from my heart to you
who are always with me,
Hidden inside as the heart.
You are the compass of my life.
My course is your way,
No matter where I go.
You exist everywhere and in everything
Always watching over us.
My soul brightens in the darkness
When I speak your name.
Far beyond the body,
There is an opening from my heart into yours.
Through that opening,
I send you secret messages like the moonlight.
I polish the mirror of my heart
To be your reflection.
I make my ear the receiver
For the tenderness of your words.
You are in my ear.
You are in my mind.
You are in every burning heart.
What am I saying? You are "I."
This is my way to describe you!
I send you secret messages like the moonlight.
I polish the mirror of my heart
To be your reflection.
I make my ear the receiver
For the tenderness of your words.
You are in my ear.
You are in my mind.
You are in every burning heart.
What am I saying? You are "I."
This is my way to describe you!
~Rumi

The Judge and Attachment

This fear-based identity of "the judge" has created and carries many rules about how to be in life. It is a survival identity that not only judges self but judges others as well. And is one of the main ways to keep duality alive. Rules are based on good/bad and wrong/right, and therefore, a big part of duality and our reaction to life. And if you believe in good, then naturally you believe in bad. In order for good to exist and be experienced, there needs to be a bad, and vice versa. In order for triumph to exist and be experienced, there needs to be an obstacle, and vice versa. In order for push/offense to be experienced, there needs to be a pull/defense, and vice versa. In order for light to exist and be experienced, there needs to be darkness, and vice versa.

The physical form that has been given a birth name experiences duality and has developed identities with different story lines, with attachment to outcomes, results, past, future, and rules. And the judge identity interacts with all the other identities. These identities that we have created, including the judge, are the creators of our life experiences rather than the God-self. These identities are creating from a fear-based mind and attachment to the outcomes and experiences, as well as attachment to the survival of the identity. For example, if you have an identity of "savior," meaning someone who is always going to come to the rescue, help the underdog, and be there for every friend and family member in need, then in order for this savior identity to survive, it will seek out experiences to be the savior. Life responds to this identity by obliging it and creating stories and experiences to match this savior, *and* for you to see this identity and realize why you created it in the first place, why and how you are keeping it in place, to realize it is not needed, and release it. An identity like this is harder to release because the judge is always going to say you are doing good, you have to do these things, and when you don't, you are a bad person. It satisfies the need for "I am needed," "I am wanted," "I am a good person," and so forth. Therefore, to keep this savior identity alive, your life will create situations so that you can be the savior at home, at work, with friends, with family.

When you become aware of the savior identity, then you also can become aware of why it was created, how you created it, and why you require yourself to be needed, wanted, and viewed as a good person. And through this awareness, you can let go of the stories, desires, and identity itself, and along with it the need for good and bad. Some people get really hung up on the savior identity. Posing questions such as, "Isn't it good and right to be there for your friends when the chips are down?" "Isn't it good and right to help the underdog?" "Isn't it good to help people and rescue them?" There is a difference to follow the intuition and natural flow of life rather than feeding a need to be good, right, and viewed as good and right. There is a difference to be of service as a natural flow of life, without attachment, rather than being attached to the outcomes of the savior's actions, being needed and wanted, and seeking validation of being a good person.

Another example of identities and attachments is in my own life. I am an artist. In order for me to be successful, I have to create artwork that people will like in their homes and purchase. The artist in me that is attached to being a success and is fearful of failure then has all these rules of how to be a "successful" artist and vice versa. Because of this attachment to success and attachment to this identity of an artist, I get caught up in the stories/scenarios created by my mind and fueled by the judge that is constantly telling me what I am doing right or wrong. What I am doing good or bad. What I am doing to be a success or failure. What I am doing to be loved and accepted as an artist and rejected. Even judging the success. If I say, "I have done thirty exhibitions, won ten awards, and have been featured in twenty-five magazines," the mind-judge would come up with "That is great, but how many pieces of art have you sold?" If I say, "I have sold one hundred pieces of art," it would respond, "That is great, but how much money did you make this year?" The point is that the mind-judge will never stop. In this scenario, if I let go of my attachment to success and attachment to being an artist, I can just be as I AM. Meaning, if I am not looking for anyone to approve of me or accept me or consider me a success or not, then I can just be in the moment, follow what feels good in my heart and my intuition, and create from a place of joy and love, whatever it may be. There really isn't a moving or doing. Because there is no identity of an artist with its attachment to doing or moving. Just I AM in each moment, flowing and following what feels natural. I'll talk about how to allow the flow later.

The reason many people pursue trainings and certifications one after another, or feel they need the certification before doing anything, is due to the judge. The judge telling them, "You can't do this unless . . ." and "You can't call yourself this unless . . ." and "Who are you to call yourself this . . ." Then you get certified to show others that yes, someone told you that you can. You have the degree to show others yes, you can. Someone told you that you have made it, so you can. All to drown out the judge. However, the judge will come up with a new pursuit soon enough. I did not have a degree in art, nor did I have training or certification—all I had was what was flowing naturally from my heart. For the majority of the work I do to help others, there has been no formal training or certification—it is what flows naturally. It is who I am. I see people. I see inside them. Things that they cannot see themselves. The reason I see them so clearly is because I have cleared my mirror to be able to see them with eyes of love and compassion. The best gift is when in the first session at the end, they feel seen without saying a word, and their hearts open and tears come from their eyes. The joy from the heart. When you are of service to others, others are of service to you. It's not a doing, not an action. We are all guiding one another in different ways to discover this "God-self" in ourselves.

The judge, using the fearful mind and attachment to duality, brings survival fear thoughts and emotions. The attachment to duality is the same as attachment to life and surviving in life. The judge has a core rule that to survive in life, you need love, acceptance, and acknowledgment of others, and you need all that in order to have financial security. And all of it is required because of attachment to the identity that wants to survive. Identity of artist, engineer, lawyer, mom, daughter, son, sister, brother, Christian, Muslim, White, Black, female, male, heterosexual, homosexual, Asian, African, American. You want to be the best you can be in each of these identities, to be recognized as the best, as good, as accepted, and how you get caught up in the stories is

31

duality and ego-self. The judge, duality, attachment are what keep the separation alive. To feel safe and accepted, more rules, boundaries, and definitions are created. If you can find a way to identify with others or define others as something nonthreatening, then you can accept them and perhaps even love them. Or vice versa if you can identify and define yourself in ways that others can relate to or find nonthreatening, then you feel safe and accepted and will survive.

Identities in combination with the judge keep duality in life alive. Because for something to be true, the opposite of it must also to be true. For the savior to be the savior, it requires others to be the victim. And you play both of those identities (savior and victim) in different parts of your life. For the beginning to be true, then the end must also be true, because one cannot exist without the other. For the good to be true, the bad must equally be true. Therefore, the world we have created based on judgment and duality, and living life as identities we have created, and attachment to the experience, creates narratives that we repeat on loop—that is, you experience good times and bad times, and your attachment to good times makes it possible for you to experience bad times so that the good times can be experienced again. Let go of the identity, the attachment, the judge, and with-it duality, and experience life as a joyous flow of unconditional love that is all for a greater purpose, which you have had a hand in creating.

Ways to Release the Judge

To release this judge, we need to be honest with ourselves. Honesty in awareness of what, who, and why we are judging.

The judge is beating you with one hand, claiming that you are not good enough, you are bad, you are worthless, and in the other it's pushing you to do more, be more, achieve more. That is, you are not enough, do this to become enough, you are not good, do this to be better, you are worthless, achieve this to be worthy. And that is how it keeps you in the duality loop. So you feel good when you are being pushed to achieve more and bad when the same voice in a different tone tells you that you are not good enough. If you try to ignore the voice, resist the voice, then the fear gets louder, because all is attached to your survival.

People have found ways to drown out the internal voice of the judge (which has echoed outside as well, since others in judging themselves have judged you directly or indirectly) that is alleging you are being lazy, you will never make it if you don't do xyz, you will end up alone, you will end up on the street. You try to drown it by overachieving, being type A, being superhuman (supermom who does everything, super-friend who is always there and positive, superwoman who does it all), or by exercise, practical mediations (movement, sound), and so on.

The truth is that the judge has played an important part in your life to maintain all the rules that keep your life going and keep you safe. Some of these rules you may not even be aware of until you stop or change a behavior, pattern, or identity.

So now that you are honestly aware, now what?

A way to release the judge is to start by choosing to let go of the rules as you become aware of them. These rules can seem simple and silly to life threatening. Here are some examples from my own life. I had a silly rule because I was attached to looking a certain way. To achieve that look, I had to take a shower in the morning, either wet or shampoo and condition my hair, and let my hair air dry so as not to get frizzy. I needed to make sure if it was cold, I didn't go outside with my wet hair. And if I wanted to exercise, I had to do it in the morning before I showered, because I could not shower at night, since I had to wet my hair and it wouldn't dry in time for bed, and I could not go to bed with wet hair. Now all this might seem silly—it was even silly to me. However, when I moved to change it, there was so much attachment and fear that I had to break the rules in steps. First, it's okay if I don't take a shower everyday—I will not smell (childhood fear of my father telling me I smelled like a dog when I was in third or fourth grade); I will still be loved and accepted by others. Next, I can take a shower without washing my hair, and it's okay if it is frizzy. I don't have to work out only in the morning, and I can choose to take a shower or not after, and it is okay for me to take two showers in a day. There were several reasons tied to this, and those outside the US, Canada, and most of Europe may relate. First, we are always told water is something we should not waste and there is not enough of it. Second, the home I lived in until third grade did not have hot water, so we had to use the public bath, and that was not something we could do every day. And last, parents, grandparents, and others terrify you about going to bed with wet hair or going outside when it's cold with a wet hair. It is as if you are going to die. All these different fears, habits, and behaviors just around showering!

A more deep-rooted rule of mine was that I could not have life come to me easy, because I had to have enough challenge so the judge would see the value in it, since if it was easy, then I could not have value in accomplishing it, and if it was too challenging, then I would feel that I had no value, since I was not good enough to accomplish it, so just the right amount of challenge. This one I released by changing the definition of "self-value" and "self-worth" and choosing easy and allowing life to be easy.

You don't have to identify each rule and break free from it. I found, when the attachment was too strong, then it helped to dig deeper, parse out, and then release the rules. And after it would be easier to release the attachments and identities.

The way to release it all is letting go of attachment to identities and therefore their desires, outcomes, and expectations.

And when you do that, you don't get dragged into the stories the mind is creating. Staying as awareness. I am loving awareness. I AM.

How do you stay as I AM?

First, there is "no staying" (LOL), because staying implies an action, which implies an identity needed to take the action, and mind is needed to take an action.

So let go of attachment to even becoming "I AM," becoming self-aware. Because *becoming* is an action of the mind. You can *not* become something that you already are. Recognition is not an action—it's an allowing, a space, where the self-recognition takes place naturally and on its own at the right time and place.

And this time and space and the natural-occurring flow

take place by continuing to be aware. Aware of identities, aware of desires, aware of attachments. And in this space of awareness, the natural flow will initiate the release of these identities and their associated desires and attachments.

"At some point you will become aware of awareness."

At some point you will become aware of awareness. Recognizing that there is an awareness that has taken place from the mind and you are now becoming aware of this awareness.

Naturally you flow into this heart space.

All that is happening—even the meditations, yoga, and transformation works, in whatever form—is a part of the natural flow of you coming to this place.

When you say "I feel sad," "I am successful," "I am an entrepreneur," "I feel angry," or any statement or thought that starts with *I*, then ask, Who is feeling this way? Who is taking this action? Who is taking this title? Your response will probably be, "I am—the one sitting here." Then ask yourself, Is this the same *I* as yesterday?" Is this the same *I* as last year? Is this the same *I* as twenty years ago? Is this the same *I* as an infant? How far back does this *I* go? Does it go back to inside the time of birth? Does it go back inside the womb? Does this *I* belong to the sperm or the egg that created it? How did it choose which/whose sperm and which/whose egg is going to birth it? Or does it even go beyond the sperm and the egg? Can you find its origin?

These are the questions that at some point don't require

answering, but posing the questions to yourself will open you up to recognition of *I*—I AM and God-self. This space has no name. These types of inquiries are part of the teachings (or my takeaways) from Nisargadatta Maharaj, Mooji, and alike.

When you find it challenging to recognize this space and you are too much in the identity or what is happening, then use some of the tools in this chapter or the practice section of *Change Yourself Change the World* to recognize the identity. Then it's easy to see the attachment to desire or outcome. Once you are aware of the attachment, then it's easier to release the attachment.

Remember, there is no right or wrong way. We all have a different way to get to this space. Be patient and kind to yourself. Let go of even the attachment to finding this place. It will happen naturally as you follow what calls to you and what is part of the natural flow of life. Move from your heart. Move from place of love.

Answer the Call

There is a light, a beacon, inside each of us. This beacon is calling us home, to the realization that we are God. We are the creator of our lives and reality. We are one with everything and everyone. We are the unconditional love, joy, peace, and grace that holds no judgment and in it holds peace and joy.

The prophets, gurus, teachers, and masters all point to this place in different ways. As Rumi states so beautifully, "Let the beauty we love be what we do. There are hundreds of ways to kneel and kiss the ground."

The path and the way are not important. What is, is that we are all here for the same destination.

There is a part of you that is like a beacon, always calling you home. It is a feeling that there is more to life and this physical reality. The more you stay present for this inquiry, the more you realize that this home is a recognition that you are beyond the physical form and the person that at birth was given a name.

A part of you remembers the reason why it chose this time, this space, and this family, and that it set up everything to remind itself to wake up to the reality of this illusion of life—and all for a purpose. And that purpose is self-realization. Even if you do not believe in God (external or internal), reincarnation, Karma, or anything along those lines, there is a part of you, if you listen and go inside, that wants to be discovered. And that is this I AM, the beacon to become the "self"-realized. Which has nothing to do with religion, where you were born, your education, status, work, class, gender, anything. It is a common thread among us all us.

At some point we got lost in the identity we were given, our experiences with family, society, and what has been passed down from generations before. We got lost in the stories based on the perception of the identities that we created throughout our life. Identities in the family, friends, social circles, school, work, relationships, marriage, parenthood, and so forth.

We got lost in life as something to be done or achieved rather than to flow and be. There is a story "The Farmer and the Horse."

There was a farmer, in a small village, with a single horse who helped him earn a living for his family. The other villagers constantly told the farmer how lucky he was to have such a great horse.

"Maybe," he would reply.

One day the horse ran away. The villagers came to the farmer to express their sympathies.

"Your horse ran away. How unfortunate!" the villagers exclaimed.

"Maybe," the farmer replied.

A few days later, the horse returned home, with ten strong wild horses in tow.

"What good fortune. What incredible luck," the villagers crowed.

"Maybe," the farmer again replied.

The following week, the farmer's son was riding one of the wild horses in the fields, when it bucked him off and broke his leg.

The villagers arrived to express their dismay. "What dismal luck."

"Maybe," the farmer replied.

The next month a military officer marched into the village, recruiting able-bodied young men for the war. The farmer's son, with his broken leg, was left behind.

The villagers were joyful. "Your son has been spared. What beautiful luck!"

The farmer simply smiled.

"Maybe."

If we are not attached or stuck in the narrative and could see the big picture, or trust that everything is good and part of a bigger purpose, then we would recognize how magnificent are our lives. The beautiful tapestry that has weaved so many threads, and just at the perfect time and place, they all come together.

However, our attachment to duality, to good and bad and pursuit for happiness, causes us to not see or trust the big picture. Sometimes the attachment is to so called "bad." If you are someone used to things going wrong, you are fixing or planning for the worst to happen, the attitude of "shit is going to hit the fan at any moment—be ready." Then you have an expectation of things going wrong (because they always do at some point), which brings an attachment to fixing things all the time or preparing for the worst-case scenarios. All leading to lack of trust in the big picture.

It's okay even if you do, because as I said, you are getting all you wanted and it will leave you when it's time for something else. (I discuss more about trust and flow of life in *Change Yourself Change the World*.) The best way to state this is that all that you want, and even more, has been manifested already, and you are walking in time and space experiencing it. This is trusting life and flowing with life.

> *Mind interprets, The Heart Knows*
> *Intellect rationalizes, Love Knows*
> *Mind has stories and lives in duality,*
> *Heart knows all as one*
> *Unconditional Love.*
> ~Atousa Raissyan

Another great example was my recent retreat. Early 2023 I felt the urge to host a retreat. And internally I said yes. Meaning, I said yes, I am open to it. Saying yes means no story, no attachment of how or when or where. Simply whatever is going to flow to me, I am open to receive it. After all, how could I not—it has been manifested already. Late June 2023 a company in Bali reached out, and I loved everything about it, but something didn't feel right. Then August 2023 another beautiful soul, Lauren Dickinson from Orion Retreats, reached out to connect, to feature me on her site, and to see how else we could collaborate. It was an immediate connection, and I said yes to her. Part of her work was also to help put together retreats. Next thing I knew, I was selecting the location—Tulum, Mexico. And then she sent me several hotel options, and I kept feeling only one of them was best for me. So the location was selected—Kan Tulum. The retreat was ready, and we sent out the information. At first we didn't have the minimum number of people, and each time she would call me, I would say, "If it is meant to be, it will all come together."

During an online summit, I saw a post for this amazing photographer who did Soulography, Carlene Kanellis. Again, as soon as we talked, we connected on a different level. There are no words to explain it. I asked her to be a part of the retreat, and even before I had asked her, she had already wanted it, so it was an immediate yes from her.

Lauren would still reach out that she was putting it out in the universe as well so that she could come with us, and my response was, "Everything will work out the way it needs to be."

Finally, we had the numbers we needed. Carlene was coming, and now Lauren could make it as well. All set. Right before leaving, I kept sensing that Carlene was not coming to just take photos—she would be there to help me. At that point I had no clue. No resisting, judging, or attachment to outcome. To be honest, I had no plan for the retreat at all, just a general sense of what I wanted everyone to feel at the end when we were done, and some practices had come to me here and there. The first morning, as I walked into the restaurant with Lauren, one of my favorite songs started playing, and I paused with Lauren and said, "I love this song—it's one of my favorites." And a man's voice from behind said, "It's mine as well—this is my playlist, and this is my hotel."

The three of us started chatting, and he was talking about different events he hosts at the hotel, and I mentioned that I would love to be invited and that I would message my website link. He walked away only to come back two minutes later, showing us goose bumps on his arm and saying that his mom, from the UK, had recommended a must-read book to him, and when he opened my website, he saw the book that his mom had recommended: *Change Yourself Change the World*. We talked some more.

The next morning was the first day of the retreat and the first workshop. A few hours into the workshop, as I was helping a client and dancing, I hopped into the air, and midair there was a loud pop that everyone in the room heard . . . which came from my leg. I landed on my good foot, looked at the other one, and I could tell I wouldn't be able to put any weight on it. No pain though.

Carlene and I exchanged looks, and we both knew this is major. I told everyone let's get on with the work. And now I knew why Carlene was there. It wasn't just for her photos and to do her magic with the people. Also, she was there to be my legs during sessions where I would hop and crawl—I did the work, and where I could not, I asked her. It turned out that I had a full rupture of the Achilles. I continued with the flow of what was aligned with my heart, and that was to stay until the end of the retreat. I could not participate in the excursions as planned, but then Carlene and Lauren could go in my place, and the pricing worked out so both could take part.

I cannot describe the feeling. I knew the times I was left behind at the hotel was for purpose. To make the connection with the people there and to have my energy in that space. Also, space was needed for me as well. On the day we were all supposed to leave, at breakfast I was asking about where people got their candles from, since I needed some for my healing room, and Carlene told me to talk to Mauricio, the young man that I had come to know during my stay and who had taken care of me so well. Me and one other person were the last ones to leave, so when I went over to Mauricio to ask him about his candles, before I even said anything, he said he had a gift for me. As soon as he said that, I was tearing up, and when I opened his gift, it was a painting of a candle.

So why did I share this story? To show you when you let go of control, then you can trust and allow life to flow, and everything comes together in its natural flow, and it is more beautiful and magical than you could ever imagine. And the way you can let go of control and gain trust is to let go of attachments to outcomes and desires.

My injury was for a purpose, not just for me to see how much I had shifted, and also to help others around me to shift as well. I came home needing surgery and not being able to drive or walk—stationary. I love nature walks, hikes, and runs. Nature is my place of magic, that I take ten, twenty, thirty photos of sun, raindrops, morning dew, animals, and so much more. It has been the place of communication, receiving messages, and getting lessons. It's a place of meditation and relaxation. Now what? Beautiful spring weather, perfect time for my photos, process my injury, and just in general my go-to for feeling the magic.

However, this time none of that was needed. Because I had let go of my identity as a healer, shaman, and needing to be that for others, and with it all the attachments and desires. Sitting at home, and not even being able to move from the couch, I found a new way to play with the sun, discover magic, and take lots of photos. All my favorite animals came to visit me at my window.

Before, the way I processed information, received information, and communicated between my God-self and human form was by movement, running, nature hikes, driving. With my injury I could not do any of it. However, without an attachment to the identity that needed the movement, and staying in awareness, movement was no longer necessary. Before I would blindly follow that need for movement, but now I could see it was not needed.

Allowing the flow without attachments, life flows, and it's even more beautiful and magical than expected. It's not about being happy—it's about the joy and peace in my heart no matter what is happening. It's discovering you are a part of this flow as well, and you are one with the flow.

Even the forgetting of the beginning of our life is for purpose. We need to get lost in order to discover and find the truth of who we are. It is like we have left a treasure map to discover ourselves: "I Am Life Itself." The way to this self-discovery has already been set. This process of being lost and discovery is the duality that we experience in life. That duality that is needed to discover the wholeness. Ying/yang, light/shadow (darkness), love/fear, good/bad, beginning/end, birth/death, all encapsulated in a circle that has no beginning or end, no birth or death, completely whole, and through the experience of duality discovers its wholeness.

That feeling that many of us have, even as a young child, that there is more to this physical life, is that beacon, that light, that is guiding us to find the truth of who we are.

So who are we? We are God. Not the God that has power over everyone or everything. Rather the God that is love and is powerful and holds no power over anyone or anything. God that is pure unconditional love, joy, peace, and all knowing. Not the knowledge that is in books—rather, the knowledge that comes naturally.

One night I dreamed a dream.
As I was walking along the beach with my Lord.
Across the dark sky flashed scenes from my life.
For each scene, I noticed two sets of footprints in the sand,
One belonging to me and one to my Lord.
After the last scene of my life flashed before me,
I looked back at the footprints in the sand.
I noticed that at many times along the path of my life,
especially at the very lowest and saddest times,
there was only one set of footprints.
This really troubled me, so I asked the Lord about it.
"Lord, you said once I decided to follow you,
You'd walk with me all the way.
But I noticed that during the saddest and

most troublesome times of my life,
there was only one set of footprints.
I don't understand why, when I needed You the most,
You would leave me."
He whispered, "My precious child, I love you and
will never leave you
Never, ever, during your trials and testings.
When you saw only one set of footprints,
It was then that I carried you."
~Mary Stevenson

To me this poem is about that recognition of God-self. Those experiences that we have labeled as suffering and troubled times are just the ebbs and flows of life. Those are the experiences that guide us to recognize that God-self in all of us that is pure unconditional love—love for ourselves, love for life, everyone and everything in it. After all, if we cannot love ourselves, how can we truly extend that love to the outside? These are the experiences that help us forgive and let go of judgments, desires, stories, identities, and recognize we are beyond these physical forms. There is only one set up footprints because there is only *one*. Even those footprints belong to the body and not the God-self, God-consciousness.

And as you get closer to this recognition, then you recognize that there is "no one running the show" anymore and there is just ONE. And the one is not a person or a form with identity, story, desire, or attachments—rather, it is a space, a knowing, and an awareness.

When we become embodiment of this awareness, then we become one with life.

Without any identity that is attached to form, gender, birth, death, past, or future, then the emotions and thoughts lose their power and meaning because there is "NO ONE" with a story and stake in the story or its outcome. The suffering disappears.

The spiritual gurus' teachings have different names for this place and ways to attain this recognition with meditations, rituals, mantras, and other practices. The prophets' teachings call this place God, and to attain it with prayers, trust, faith, rituals, fasting, and other practices. Essentially no matter what religion or spiritual doctrine you follow, and no matter how you attain this recognition, it all comes down to the same.

There is no *one* (meaning no person) but one God, the God-self.

Life Is Calling You

All the practices (meditation, fasting, exercise, sound healing, movement, plants) and teachings are ways to move away from the mind and merging with the heart. A moving away from fear and surrendering to love. Life is calling you to come merge with me, be with me, become one with me. Wake up from this illusion that you have created based on these very personal narratives that are tying you down in the emotions, thoughts, behaviors, and rules of these identities (personal characters). They are not real—they are just characters playing a role in life. To each of these identities, their life stories feel very real and their birth and death feels very real. To wake up from this dream we call life and reality is to wake up and recognize we are beyond these physical forms and the stories we have told and characters we have played. That we are embodiment of life force that you can call God, Divine, Consciousness, Higher-Self, or Universe.

When we wake up, then we can truly see the magic, miracles, and beauty of this life. We find we are joy, peace, love (unconditional), and all knowing (not knowledge).

I am your Lover,
Come to my side,
I will open the gate to your Love.
Come settle with me,
Let us be neighbors in the Stars.
You have been hiding so long,
Endlessly drifting in the Sea of my Love.
Even so, you have always been connected to me.
Concealed, revealed, in the norm,
in the un-manifest. I am Life itself.
You have been a prisoner of a little pond,
I am the Ocean and its turbulent flood.
Come merge with me.
Leave this world of ignorance Be with me,
I will open the gate to your Love.
~Rumi

I invite you to say yes to your heart, say yes to the unconditional love that is you and calling you home, say yes to being free and no longer being a prisoner of the mind, the stories, or characters you have played in your life.

Creation is based in unconditional love, and heart is the center of it. Creating in its truest form and definition is about receiving in love and creating "new" in love. And when this creation happens in a space of nonattachment and nonjudgment, it is life flowing. There is no doing, because everything flows naturally from the heart. There is no manifesting, because there is no action needed and nothing needs to be made real.

Duality is experienced to find the way back to one, and that is healing. And this healing is a process of forgiveness, mindfulness, prayers, mantras, rituals, awareness, and so forth.

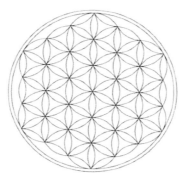

We are all ONE and part of ONE. "Flower of Life" is a beautiful representation of that. Space (outer space) is a marvelous representation of that. A place where there is no beginning or end. There is no real time and space, since it is relevant to perception of the origin.

As I am the creator, and God, and creating in my oneness circle, you are the creator, and God, and creating in your circle. When our two circles come together, we are cocreating. And to bring it to a higher level, we are all cocreators on planet Earth, including all its inhabitants. And you can go another level up, and then its cocreators in the solar system, including all its inhabitants . . . and so forth. This is the experience of oneness. There is nothing really outside of you, because you are a part of everything and everything is a part of you. Even the elements—water, air, fire, earth—are all a part of this human form, part of existence and coming together and flowing apart, life and death.

"And all of it for us to recognize I am ONE, I am God, I am Creator, I am Divine. Or simply I AM. I exist."

And all of it for us to recognize I am ONE, I am God, I am Creator, I am Divine. Or simply I AM. I exist.

Duality, shadow and light, are just tools used to recognize the oneness. Embracing the shadow and light is part of the healing, to recognize and become one with everything. I exist. For me, the symbol of a circle (that includes a dot) is the best representation and reminder of our existence as the formless God-self and human form as ego-self coming together as one love, a union of the two.

I always love Rumi's explanation of lover and beloved (ego-self and God-self), searching for each other, finding each other, and dancing together in one form.

A lover asked his beloved,
Do you love yourself more than you love me?
Beloved replied, I have died to myself and I live for you.
I've disappeared from myself and my attributes,
I am present only for you.
I've forgotten all my learnings,
But from knowing you I've become a scholar.
I've lost all my strength, but from your power I am able.
I love myself, I love you.
I love you, I love myself.
~Rumi

Living Life When You Recognize *I*

Disappear from your identities, and all that contributes to the identity (gender, race, sexual preference, place of birth, family, education, job). Releasing the identities and attachments and living only to discover the God-self. Allow the human form to be present only for recognition of God-self and vice versa. Be present in the moment and bring stillness to the mind. Let go of all knowledge and recognize the knowledge that comes from within. Recognize the strength and power that comes from within and not attached to the physical human muscle strength. Loving God, God-self, you love your human form. Loving your human form you love God, God-self. Loving yourself as one, you love all humanity as one.

When you let go of attachments, then you are letting go of desires and expectations. When you let go of desires and expectations, then you are letting go of identities. And when there is no identity to get triggered, all that is left is joy and peace.

> "When there is no identity to get triggered, all that is left is joy and peace."

To be human is to have desires. However, we need to change the definition of desire. We have taken desire to mean "I want something, and I want this something to come to me in a certain way, form, or direction and at a certain time." Even our morning coffee, if we have it as a desire with attachment, can be triggering when we do not receive it. Have desires, but let go of the identities that are attached to these desires. Let go of the outcomes, the how, and the when attached to desires. Treat desire as a wish that you blow onto a dandelion and let the wind carry—and trust that life is always ten, hundred, one thousand steps ahead of you and knows exactly when, how, and in what packaging to fulfill the desire that is even greater than you could imagine. At some point when we let go of identities and attachments, then desires are naturally released. Because you are just flowing with life and taking it all in. I desire my black espresso in the morning, but if I don't have it, my world is not turned upside down. I desire to open a healing retreat center, and I trust in the flow and process of life.

As soon as you start to let go of identities, desires, attachments, there is a natural fear that appears. Fear of What will my life look like if I have no desire? Isn't that same as being depressed? What is the point of life if I have no desires or attachments? If I let go of identities, isn't that same as dying? If I let go of my identities, how can I live and do my job, be a mom or dad? And the list goes on.

This happens because your personal-identity existence has been about duality of good/bad, right/wrong, light/shadow, good/evil. And the mind attached to the personal-identity fears existing without it. However, living life as God-self is not about rejecting or resisting duality. It is about embracing it as ONE. Both are an expression of ONE unconditional love. It's about seeing both clearly, recognizing in your own life the purpose it has served for your healing and self-recognition. Therefore, embracing it and moving away from the stories and identities and letting the heart lead you to the ultimate freedom of joy and peace within.

It's not about denying our masculine or feminine energies but embracing both and allowing both to be balanced so that we carry the masculine practicality and logic with the love and compassion of the feminine.

Recognition of "I AM" and living life from this space does not mean that we stop being human. Rather, we become Divine Human. That as feelings arise, they are seen in a space of compassion and love, as they melt in the truth of awareness.

In the midst of the darkness
A moon appeared with is brilliance.
Stepping down from the clouds,
It glanced at me.
Like a falcon that hunts a bird
And steals it away,
It captured me
And flew back to infinite space.
As I looked for myself,
I could not find me,
For my body had become all soul
In the tenderness of love.
The nine spheres of heaven
Dissolved in that moon
As the ship of my existence
Drowned in the sea of love.
~Rumi

Let go. Relax. You have already manifested everything in your life. Now all becomes aligned with the time and space to experience it. Meaning, all will come for your experience of it in the right time and space. All is for a purpose. Everything in life has value and is for a purpose. And that is to bring you to the recognition of God-self, Divine Human.

To become a Divine Human is embrace duality and become ONE. And to recognize we exist in everything and everyone. Allow unconditional love to be our guide.

To be part of the flow, with joy and peace inside that is not attached to anything. It is not about losing our humanness but rather embracing our divineness, our God-self, and becoming ONE in love and living a life from that place of oneness and love. Existing as one love. We are all God. We are all ONE. God is love, and you will find God and love in stillness, being of service, loving acceptance of your human form and human existence (life), and forgiveness.

I get up, have my coffee, be a mom, do my work, be with friends, and live life as if a "normal" person. However, there is not doing, since there is no one doing anything. I have plans but am not attached to the plans coming true. Emotions come, and they melt away, since there is no one feeling them. Thoughts come and go because there is no one thinking them. This is living as a Divine Human.

Be in This World but Not of This World

Self-discovery is our purpose. Discovering that we are the ocean. The water from Earth cycles in different forms and is given different names—air, cloud, rain, snow—and still it is water. We have taken Earth and taken it apart and given names to different parts of it, given it identities, and yet it is still Earth. And these identities bestowed on Earth created separation and further stories, creating wars.

You are like water, like the earth. The identity you were given at birth is just an identity with a story. The identities that you created over the years are just identities and not who you are, which is beyond all of it. The identity you were born into and the identities you created had a purpose. There is a need to be somebody before you become no one. A perfect meal takes time to prepare and cook properly—if it's not cooked all the way through, the taste might not be good or it might still be raw. The caterpillar needs time in the cocoon to become the beautiful butterfly. The time is the love needed for proper preparation. And the same is true for us. If we discover we are no one too soon, we will not get the proper preparation in love and understand the concept, and we might take on a bigger identity as a superhuman or powerful God that is not centered in love. The time that is needed for us to become no one is our grounding in love.

Time allows us to discover that we are the loving awareness of our life movie and the identities that we have created. When you watch your life from this place of loving awareness, then there is a natural gratitude for the beauty of this life, experiences, and the process.

This process of awareness, forgiveness, self-love, gratitude, and letting go of desires and attachments naturally allows you to let go of control and, therefore, naturally trust and be part of the flow of life.

At the initial stages of self-discovery, the awareness may be more of mind being aware. And that is okay, since that is still helping you to see the identities. This is especially true for those who have grown up with trauma and PTSD and the people who live with a belief that something bad will always happen, waiting for the other shoe to drop, things will be taken away, or fear of severe punishment. The mind is going to be strong for these individuals, and that is why there will be more of a mindful awareness, as it takes time to trust in love and in heart. As more trust and flow happens, the heart becomes more activated and then there is a heart awareness. And you can allow the heart awareness to be aware of the mind awareness. The mind always carries fear with it. Let the fear in your mind be met with the love in your heart. Be more heartful rather than mindful.

" Let the fear in your mind be met with the love in your heart. "

Mind will lead you to identities, judgment, attachments, and most of all *fear*. Heart will lead you to unconditional love, compassion, forgiveness, surrender, flow, and most of all to your God-self, Divine-self. Mind will use a measuring scale and judgment for everything. Heart uses gratitude and love. You are always being guided and supported—surrender and trust. It's all for purpose and part of a bigger plan that is beyond this physical form with identity. Let go of desires, attachment, and identities; let go of the mind. Love and accept yourself and all that you are as a human in this human exitance.

Heartfulness will lead to a loving awareness space where life is happening without any identity attachments—space of loving awareness of life.

I am sure you have heard this said by many gurus: "Be in this world but not of it," which means live in the moment, by being the loving presence and awareness of life as it is happening. Loving all that shows up. Even if at the beginning your mind will take it and run through fear programs. However, without any identity to follow it, without any desire or attachment, the program will stop and cease to exist.

Be still in your heart. Trust in the heart. Love over fear. You are the loving awareness existing in human form. Embrace both. You are connected and ONE with everything and everyone. This life is about unconditional love and heart. Embracing God and human as ONE love and recognizing all in life as part of same ONE. It all starts with the practice heartfulness rather than mindfulness. Heart over mind. Unconditional love over fear.

> *Put aside your clever schemes!*
> *O lover, be mindless!*
> *Become mad!*
> *Dive into the heart of the flame!*
> *Become fearless!*
> *Be like moth!*
> *Turn away from the self*
> *And tear down the house!*
> *Then, come and dwell in the house of love!*
> *Be a Lover! Live with Lovers!*
> ~Rumi

Practices

These are some of practice mantras that have helped me and I have used for clients. Hope one will resonate with your heart.

Mantras

Mantras are not just words to say. When you try any mantra, the energy of the words counts. The energy needs to resonate with you. Sometimes you may feel that you have a reaction to a mantra or a word. It could be that it is challenging to remember or brings about certain emotions. That is the time to be aware of the trigger. It is guiding you. Be in the awareness.

When you say a mantra, feel the words, as if you are eating or drinking the most delicious thing you have eaten or drank and it's going all over inside your body.

I give my heart permission to dance feely and openly. As I allow my mind to rest. Allowing the worry to float. Allowing doubt to float. There is no resistance. There no planning. I open and surrender myself and my heart and allow the dance with the divine and grace. All is unfolding with perfection in divine timing and miracle of grace. I surrender. I allow. As I allow and invite the change, the world around me is changing. (This mantra is great to make peace with change and life that is always changing and shifting. So that you see the beauty in change rather than the fear.)

There is nothing to solve. There is nothing to fix. There is nothing do. All is working according to divine time and divine order. I let go and let God. I surrender it all to the Divine. I am safe. All is well. (If possible, consider the God-self/Divine-self as you are saying this.)

My divine heart guides this human adventure. I let go of all my plans for myself, my life, and my plans for others in my life. I let go of all my plans and allow the divine-will. I let go all my plans, and I allow the divine time and order. All is well.

I am Divine Human, honoring this physical life and all that it contains, and with love, gratitude, and grace in my heart, I serve.

I am in tune with the divine in my heart. I am in tune with my own tune and harmony in life.

I surrender and let go. My body knows the way.

I receive life with ease and an open heart and in gratitude. I receive what is easy in at this moment.

I completely and fully and unconditionally release and let go of all control. I completely and fully and unconditionally release and let go of the gatekeeper and allow life to flow freely and without any conditions or desires. I allow everything to flow easily and freely without restrictions or limitations and according to grace. (You can replace "gatekeeper" with "judge.")

I am free from all judgment
I am free from all desire
I am free from all rules
I am love
And I receive all I love.
I forgive myself in this lifetime and past lifetimes. I am forgiven.
I am loving awareness

Meditation Focus

The items listed in this section are to bring you into awareness. To consider as you are going through the day or sitting in a meditative state.

"I am not needed," meaning there is no need for the identity. Atousa is no longer needed. There is just existence.

How do you live as Consciousness in human form? Be in the moment. All functions to flow from heart and not person/mind. There is no doing. Because there is no person or mind doing it. "In this moment" has no past because it didn't exist before today and has no future because it hasn't existed in the future.

Sometimes you have to lean into those statements that bring about sadness and fear. For example, accepting being bad at something allows for the good to be there as well. When you allow and accept, you stop the fight with the fear.

The more you focus on not breaking something, it breaks, because you have fear of breaking it. And the reason that "thing" that you don't want it to break, breaks, is to release the fear. Reminding you that you have everything that you need and want. This can be true for physical objects and relationships.

Stillness does not mean no movement. Stillness means that mind is not reacting with fear. Stillness is openness of a loving heart and allowing life to flow as you flow in life. Silence is not absence of noise—it is silence in the heart that invites the mind to be silent in love of the heart. And from this place of stillness and silence, the world happens, there is noise and movement and sometimes chaos, and you are still and silent inside this form.

"God is watching Atousa" (put your name) and is bringing love and comfort to Atousa. There are times Atousa is watching God and time when God is watching Atousa. (This an awareness exercise. To see the personal identity and the God-self.)

Practice being in "receive" mode rather than "protect" mode. When we are in receive mode we allow life to flow, and all that is coming is received in gratitude, love, and trust. Protection is separation, fear, boarder, defend which all blocks an ease in flow.

Quotes

These are quotes I have come up with. Short statements that will help you as you go on your journey. To guide you back home to you.

We are all growing at our own level and our own time. Don't compare your growth with others. We all grow at our rate in our own ways.

The space of "I exist," or recognition of the space of God-self, is like an anchor that is peaceful and comforting that draws you in. It feels as if it has reached out a hand and is grabbing you and asking you to "Come in— I've got you. It is going to be okay." It feels peaceful and grounding.

What I am rejecting, is where I feel rejected myself. What I am judging, is where I feel judged myself. Everything in life is showing you to you. The parts become aware so that it can release and find the space of love, divine, grace. recognize all of it in you.

Denying or rejecting something doesn't make it go away. Saying something is true doesn't make it true or make the opposite of it false. Everything can be equally true. Water from the ocean is still water. If you take water from the ocean and put it in the cup in your home, it is still part of the ocean. Just because it is in a cup and in your home does not make it "not" be part of the ocean. You are that. You are part of the universe. Just because you are in this human form does not make you not be universe.

Look back at your life and see how your needs have always been met for the highest good. Even in your most challenging times, all was working out for the best. Life loves you. Accept this as truth. Relax. Treasures reveal themselves to you at the right time and place and when you most need them. You are ready for whatever comes next trust in yourself, and trust life universe has your back.

Air and wind are the same. The wind can be present, but because you are moving with it, you don't feel it. You have to move against the flow of wind to feel it. That movement and moving against is needed to become aware.

You have to feel the pain to know the feel of relief of the pain. You have to feel the cold and shiver to feel the love and deliciousness of the warm blanket that covers you. You have to feel the thirst to feel the deliciousness of the water. Feeling the agony of not knowing, feeling the fear, so that the receiving of awareness is beyond delicious and satisfactory.

Impossibility is a possibility that you don't understand yet. To see something and bring it into your existence, you must really believe in it.

Darkest night will end. Life will come again. Hope and magic will come. Your true magic is your unique way of expressing the divine in your human existence.

When all else fails ... surrender.

There is beauty even in the pain. Everything in life has value and is valuable. Everything has purpose and serves a purpose.

We are all interconnected. Every single person, entity, being in your life has contributed to the identities, as well as helped to recognize the "I AM" space. God-self. All is a beautiful woven tapestry made of love, with love, and in love.

You may not see the immediate result of an aligned action. Trust that it is part of the bigger picture. Let go of the attachment to immediate results and outcomes. Everything has value.

Closing

Let's be heartful rather than mindful. Mind will lead you to identities, judgment, attachments, and most of all, *fear*. Heart will lead you to unconditional love, compassion, forgiveness, surrender, flow, and most of all to your God-self, Divine-self. Mind will use a measuring scale and judgment for everything. Heart uses gratitude and love. You are always being guided and supported. Surrender and trust it's all for a purpose and part of a bigger plan that is beyond this physical form with identity. You are connected and ONE with everything and everyone. Practice "heartfulness" rather than "mindfulness."

> *Put aside your clever schemes!*
> *O lover, be mindless!*
> *Become mad!*
> *Dive into the heart of the flame!*
> *Become fearless!*
> *Be like moth!*
> *Turn away from the self*
> *And tear down the house!*
> *Then, come and dwell in the house of love!*
> *Be a Lover! Live with Lovers!"*
> ~Rumi

About Atousa Raissyan

Life Alchemist: igniting passion in the heart and stillness in the mind

Atousa Raissyan is a shaman, transformational life coach, best-selling author, inspirational speaker, poet, and artist. She is dedicated to guiding individuals toward holistic well-being and life mastery through the magic of self-love. In her private practice, through her speaking engagements, and in the pages of her award-winning book *Change Yourself, Change the World: Transform Your life from Fear-Based Living to Choosing love and Seeing Magic*, Atousa guides people to release their traumas, reprogram their fear-based living, and shift to living a more heart-centered life. She's been referred to as a guiding light, life changing, intuitive, a gifted healer, and magic by her clients. Atousa has been a guest speaker on numerous podcasts, at summits, and in workshops, as well as featured in *USA Today*, *NYC Journal*, MSN, Trailblazers Women Leaders, *Potomac Lifestyle Magazine*, and *Entrepreneur Herald*, among others. To learn more or book Atousa for your next event, please visit Atousa Raissyan.

Websites:
atousaraissyan.com
soulysticartshop.com
Instagram: @atousar and @soulystic and @belove_seelove
Facebook: @soulystic
Youtube: https://www.youtube.com/channel/@
AtousaRaissyan
LinkedIn: https://www.linkedin.com/in/atousaraissyan

A LETTER TO FEAR

By Chelsea Bass

I think perfectionism is just a high-end,
haute couture version of fear. I think perfectionism
is just fear in fancy shoes and a mink coat,
pretending to be elegant when actually it's just terrified.
Because underneath that shiny veneer, perfectionism is
nothing more than a deep existential angst that says,
again and again, "I am not good enough
and I will never be good enough."
~Elizabeth Gilbert, *Big Magic:*
Creative Living beyond Fear

I entered this world consumed by you, Fear. A beautiful pregnancy turned into an emergency cesarean birth. Fear of an umbilical cord wrapped around my neck that would end my life too soon. I came out strong, like I always do.

I was born with the gift of being an empath, intuitive, intellect, and healer, which made me stand out from an early age. I could see and feel nearly everything family, friends, and strangers were battling. The good, bad, and ugly.

But everywhere I turned, you were right there. You made me uncomfortable, scared, tormented, anxious, and depressed. You had the ability to turn my emotions into physical sickness. I let you have so much control over me before I was even wise enough to know.

I would carry others' pain, trauma, and heartache without realizing it. This would manifest into chronic illness caused by living in a constant state of fight or flight that I would carry into my adult years. My God-given gifts were also the reasons I was bullied off and on my entire life. How could my intentions be so pure, yet the world around me was so evil?

I can't remember much of my childhood. But I remember the feeling of you in my subconscious, controlling my every move. I knew I was destined for greatness, but you would constantly dim my light.

From a young age, society taught me that hearing voices wasn't normal. I had a voice that wouldn't shut up. It was helpful when I was by myself to keep me entertained. I recognize now it was my spirit team helping coach me through life.

The more I repressed these voices, the more ear infections I would get. And the more I denied leading a life of God, another sinus infection chased with antibiotics over and over again. I would ask the doctors, "What is wrong with me, only to be met with more of you?"

But these voices were undeniable. I recall telling my dad and brother that my grandmother had passed, right before we got a call from Mom. Or lunch in the cafeteria and a voice would tell me to sit with the loner eating by themselves.

Unfortunately, society has a set of rules, and when you venture outside the norm, you also find yourself a loner questioning who your friends are—but really who *you* are.

I was so consumed by you that I repressed the feeling of you. I didn't want to sit with you because it was too uncomfortable. And the more I pushed you away, the sicker and lazier I got.

The combination of my ability to feel everyone's energy in the classroom alongside the constant voice in my head equated to overstimulation and crashes that led me to sleep through class, usually with my face planted on my desk. The fact that I was sleeping through class and getting straight As led teachers to question me. Math teachers accused me of cheating on tests because I didn't "show my work." This constant battle led me to become a chronic over-explainer and people pleaser.

I knew all along I held the power, a feeling in my gut that this too shall pass and I'd create space for a life I could only dream of. I had so much pain and suffering to go through in order to appreciate what's to come.

School was supposed to be the place you went to learn. But I felt like I already had the answers within—school came too easy. What I truly needed help with was how to find peace from within, learning how to set boundaries, for starters.

Or most critically, how to help people without carrying their baggage. I needed the mindset, skill set, and tool set to be authentically me—not who I was conditioned to become. Had I learned that from a young age, I don't believe I would be battling the chronic illnesses I've had my entire life—but I also wouldn't be the businesswoman I am today.

I was always trying to ditch you, Fear, by proving I

could take (calculated) risks. You would dare me to try something new, and I would fall for it. Literally fall for it. We went ski jumping on Valentine's Day while playing hooky from school with my family. I saw a young boy go over a two-story-high ski jump on icy slopes, and you told me I could do it too.

I ended up in the hospital needing emergency surgery and had to cancel my first Valentine's date. Quickly I learned I could never have light without darkness. I knew this fall would change the trajectory of my life.

I already had a birthmark on my stomach, and now I would have a metal rod, screws, and a big scar on my knee. I would forever be reminded of my choices. And just like that, I was consumed far too much by my looks.

I wanted so badly to fit in and have a big group of friends that I was willing to do anything. I would try to become a follower, when I was always meant to be a leader. Again, I was conditioned by my environment. There was right and wrong. There was good and bad.

My entire identity was wrapped in worrying about others' perceptions of me over my own perception of myself. This would ultimately be the beginning of the end.

And, like all toxic relationships, like attracts like and you, Fear, brought in perfectionism. I stopped myself before even starting if I knew I wasn't going to be the best. I had to protect myself so I wouldn't continue getting hurt by the outside world. I became highly controlling, critical, and definitely a know it all.

You taught me in college this was the quickest recipe for success. I was able to ignore my passions in exchange for becoming money and power obsessed. You helped me find jobs that could bring in more money than I dreamed of.

All it took was discipline showing up despite battling exhaustion. From a grassroots effort launching a men's Axe campaign on the University of Maryland's campus to simultaneously being a cocktail waitress (scratch that—beer-tub girl), lifeguard, and waitress, there was no shortage of cash and tips.

I learned quickly how easy life would become when I had money. I could buy anything I wanted whenever I wanted. I could keep friends around by paying for their cover, drinks, or food.

Society says if you want to be successful, get straight As, follow the rules, and commit to a sport, college, career path, and job to one day provide for a family. I would constantly question if I was on the right path—I recall overhearing my best friend's mother telling her friend I wasn't smart enough to become a doctor despite being valedictorian and interning at the National Cancer Institute, determined to cure cancer.

At some point after college, I was called to astrology, numerology, and human design, and it helped validate who I am at my core and my life's purpose. I'm a 4/6 emotional manifesting generator with a right-angle cross of contagion and a split definition. This means I was bound to be conflicted with my ability to make (accurate) decisions.

Combined with a Cancer Rising and Aries Midheaven, my purpose in life is to initiate, become an entrepreneur, find fame, and fight for justice. I'm innately a passionate leader with a bit of sass and bossiness. Always determined to get what I want.

Ultimately my insecurities from childhood fueled my spiritual journey. Without you, Fear, I wouldn't be evolving into the confident, bold, and independent woman I've grown into today.

Like a chameleon, my superpower is adapting to any environment. By simply focusing on my mindset, I'm able to manifest all the abundance in the world and have learned to shift my focus from the material 3-D world of luxury cars, handbags, designer clothes, raises, and promotions to a 5-D world in which I embrace the flow.

"A breakup with you Fear, was no longer optional."

I knew in order to get from the 3-D to the 5-D, I had a lot of purging to do, and a breakup with you, Fear, was no longer optional. I had to start from the beginning. In 3-D consciousness I'd be viewing the world from a purely physical state in a game of survival of the fittest—how I look, what I drive, what I do for work. Basically, the definition of FOMO. In 5-D consciousness we are all one and all connected. There is no good or bad, but recognizing we are all here to serve our God-given purpose. Love and compassion reign supreme, leaving no room for judgment.

It was through this process, I recalled having a bull's-eye rash behind my knee in elementary school, and the doctor told me I had ringworm. To this day I question if that was a tick bite in disguise, as I was recently diagnosed with chronic Lyme disease, triggering me to reflect on all my various ailments and how they're interconnected. While it started with chronic ear infections, strep throat, and sinus infections, it really became noticeable in middle school, when everything I ate would upset my stomach.

This led to full-fledge (undiagnosed) IBS by the time I was in high school and the start of a series of mysterious ailments. My OBGYN said birth control would help me manage my symptoms.

In college I would get painful stabbing pains in my stomach and would party with my friends to numb my chronic pain. But it could've also been triggered through a series of unfortunate events. Could it have been my first or second sexual assault triggering this or the fact that I'd had a gun held to my head while two men with warrants out for their arrest tried stealing my cash tips when walking home from work in college? I'm not really sure, but what I do know is that I didn't have the tools to know I needed space to heal—I wasn't superwoman after all.

After college my adrenals were shot. I started chronically vomiting and was diagnosed with Hashimoto's thyroiditis while simultaneously gaining weight, and I was so burned out that I would literally get sick if I went to a high intensity interval training (HIIT) class. I spent hundreds of thousands of dollars on a quest to get well, knowing the answer lay within me—I tried hypnosis, cognitive behavioral therapy (CBT), dialectical behavior therapy (DBT), eye movement desensitization and reprocessing (EMDR), but I was left with more questions than answers. I thank God every day I had the willpower and means to dive in head first on my quest to free myself of all this baggage.

My dad once quoted something I proclaimed to him a long time ago: "One day I'm going to do something really, really special." To my younger self: you've already made a mark on the world and will continue to do so!

" To my younger self: you've already made a mark on the world and will continue to do so! "

It was February 27, 2021—fitting for a one personal year in numerology—when I started down an incredibly fulfilling and life-changing spiritual awakening. My life leading up to this point can be described as chaotic yet boring.

Boring in the sense that I was groomed by society—I followed the rules I was conditioned by. I found myself surrounded by people who dimmed my light. I tried so hard to fit in, when I was destined to stand out and sparkle. Chaotic in the sense that I went through several traumatic experiences that I have come to peace with, knowing I would not be where I am today without them.

Entering what felt like the second phase of life, an intense period of withdrawal and introspection, my once extremely extroverted self became more introverted. This must be how the term *ambivert* came to be. For those people who have come in and out of your life, "it's not goodbye, but see you later." Each served a profound purpose at that exact period in time, for God has to teach us through connection with one another.

It is this profound period of reflection that led to monumental growth. I faced my childhood and generational trauma head on. I learned to embrace all facets of my being—the one who loves the spotlight, yet loathes attention. The one who loves to give, yet hates to ask for help. The one who preaches self-love, yet finds herself with limiting beliefs. The one who wants to be a superhero for others, yet can't save herself. The one who has endless bouts of energy, yet can't get out of bed the next day.

This shadow work allowed me to face the anxious perfectionist within me, who was controlled by Fear, and let her know she was safe and it was okay to relinquish control. There were massive periods of withdrawal as I shed the many layers of being conditioned by society—to the extent of vomiting daily for months on end—and again, no medical diagnosis or pill to cure me. Transformation isn't for the faint of heart, as its job is never truly complete.

Once I learned the art of unconditional love—and allowed myself to be guided by light—I came into my most authentic self. This manifested in a variety of ways:

- I earned the privilege of becoming a leader at work. It was during this period of time I changed many jobs, working my way up the corporate ladder in a variety of leadership roles that at the time made no sense to me. But now I realize that through these life experiences, I was able to channel my innovator leader energy that is fueled by extreme passion, purpose, and love. Yes, love belongs in the workplace because it fuels growth at the highest level. When we're all connected to a higher purpose, that's where magic happens.

- On July 1, 2023, my loving partner asked me to be his wife after a decade together, during which he'd patiently waited for me to be ready to take his hand in marriage. The saying is true—if they can't handle you at your worst, they don't deserve you at your best.

- Also, in a year's time, my soon-to-be brother-in-law welcomed a baby girl, and my brother welcomed a baby boy into the world, gifting me with another persona of becoming an aunt—though my sister says she calls dibs on being the "cool aunt."

But one of the most profound and recent life experiences I've gone through that has truly been a full-circle moment for me is when my dad allowed me to play a pivotal role in his healing journey.

Shortly after my engagement party in November 2023, my dad woke up one day unable to walk. He was in debilitating pain and unable to sleep, so he had to go on the Family and Medical Leave Act (FMLA), leaving him unable to work. His days were spent going from doctor to doctor, with more questions than answers. I watched my dad relinquish control—he had faith in God and his daughter that he would walk again.

My dad went from a walker to a wheelchair within a month. This posed a serious hurdle for me—a conflicted bride—do I put my wedding on hold with the hope Dad will be able to walk again, or do I plan the wedding not knowing if death is around the corner?

I went with the former and decided to use all the tools in my arsenal to help Dad fight. I promised myself and my family that if Dad had a comeback story, I knew my true calling in life. The calling being a patient advocate by listening to a disparate set of symptoms, conducting extensive research, and tapping into my network of partners I'd forged through my own journey to help others heal. My dad's journey began with what we'll call insanity. The same bloodwork and testing done by multiple doctors all came back with the same result—my dad was healthy on paper. I knew better after I was told the same thing for many years. The symptoms and speed of my dad's condition wasn't adding up.

I started coaching Mom and Dad on the fundamentals. The importance of nutrition, filtered water, and strength/movement. I had been mocked by embracing a gluten-free, dairy-free, and grain-free diet in the past, but unfortunately these foods are highly inflammatory, especially when your body is in fight-or-flight mode. I knew Dad needed a system reset, but I also knew the importance of testing, not guessing. I would connect him with a functional doctor who changed my life, Elsa Lam, at Golden Health Holistics. This was no easy feat, as Mom and Dad have always been rule followers, meaning they listen to traditional-medicine doctors.

By introducing Mom and Dad to the idea that inflammation and trauma drive disease and illness, they opened up to the idea that there could be a root cause that traditional medicine was unable to pick up on. Unfortunately, this avenue is incredibly costly, since insurance does not pay for certain types of testing that get to the root cause, including tests both Dad and I have gotten—GI map (stool test), tick-borne panel, micronutrient testing, MTHFR gene testing, organic acids testing, heavy metal testing, mycotoxin (mold) testing, and Neural Zoomer. The power of these tests unlocks your ability to understand how your body is detoxing and the specific foods you need to avoid that are fueling inflammation, as well as the specific supplements you need to meet your body where it's at.

My dad went from feeling defeated to having answers regarding the root cause of his symptoms, which was ultimately caused by a combination of the COVID-19 vaccine and a subsequent flu vaccine that tipped his body over the toxicity scale, and his system was beginning to shut down, as it was unable to rid all the gunk. In addition to the dietary and supplement changes, I educated Dad on using a pulsed electromagnetic field (PEMF) mat, infrared heat, and red-light therapy. My dad is now in less pain, sleeping through the night, and back at work walking on his own without assistance.

For those unfamiliar with these devices, the PEMF mat uses electromagnetic fields to jump-start and accelerate normal biological cellular reactions. Put simply, cells contain electrically charged particles, called ions, that govern all cellular processes. When the body is inflamed due to a variety of stressors, the cellular membrane becomes compromised and unable to do its job efficiently. Thus, using a PEMF mat increases cellular communication and circulation to decrease inflammation and pain, resulting in accelerated healing. I also recently purchased a Somavedic, which mitigates EMFs in the home and can structure water to help our cells chill out with 5G, Wi-Fi, smartwatches, and Bluetooth, which are killing our bodies. There are also wearable technologies that can counteract the technology we've come to love and adopt in our day-to-day lives.

Infrared heat contributes to improved oxygen and nutrient delivery to cells, promoting overall health. Infrared sauna is absolutely a game changer when it comes to detoxing the body, whether you're like my dad and have too much gunk in the system or like me, overcoming mold toxicity, Lyme disease, Epstein-Barr virus, and streptococcus A, or need to improve your cardiovascular health, pain, injuries, and even cancer. Just make sure you are taking binders and supplements to avoid getting a HERX reaction (too much of a good thing can quickly become a bad thing).

Red-light therapy, also known as photobiomodulation, works at a cellular level by acting on mitochondria. Natural sunlight has been used for thousands of years to promote health and healing. When you combine the correct wavelength of light delivered at the correct power setting, you are gifted with more energy, allowing other cells to do their work more efficiently. This results in curing neuropathic pain, like my dad had, as well as wound healing, post-exercise recovery, stroke recovery, reduced oxidative stress on the brain, and even at a deeper level to stimulate lymph nodes, improve thyroid health, and regenerate the liver. In my case it has been a game changer for easing Lyme disease and mold toxicity symptoms.

In the period of a few months, we went from planning for the worst with my dad, while hoping for the best, to watching a real-life miracle, thanks to a combination of therapies and nutritional tweaks. My dad is not only walking again but was able to go back to work when his FMLA was over after twelve weeks. While he'll always be on the road to recovery, I can't help but realize we walked this path for a reason together—one in which I was able to pass on what my mentors, guides, and coaches have passed along to me on channeling healing energy and loving vibrations to those in need. Selfishly, I'm extremely blessed to know, for now, that Dad will be able to walk me down the aisle.

None of this would be possible without shifting from fear-based living, or a life of darkness, into love-based living, one in which I make the choice to see the light every day.

When my life coach, Atousa Raissyan, reached out to me to take part in this multi-author book, my inner critic had a lot to say: *Who am I to be an author? What do I have to say that people care to hear? Will I be hurting my ego? Am I ready to take this step? You're supposed to be planning a wedding and preparing to start a family! You need to work on your next promotion and this book will distract you!*

Closing

My intention when I committed to this book was to help business professionals release the shackles holding them back from loving themselves and their families and to realize their job is just a part and not the whole, as well as having a ripple effect on corporate America to truly make better workplaces and a better world.

" We must do the work to clean out the gunk that we've carried down for generations. "

It's turned into so much more than that. Each of us deserves to live in optimal health, but we must do the work to clean out the gunk that we've carried down for generations.

I thought I had done all the work through my life transformations, but the work is never complete. You, Fear, will not be the reason for holding me back any longer. You will always be there in the background because I can't have light without darkness. I am removing the shackles from this day forward and living life on my own terms.

xoxo

About Chelsea Ann Bass

Chelsea grew up with a loving family in Frederick, Maryland, including her mom, dad, brother, sister, and two dogs. She was a competitive swimmer and lacrosse player. Chelsea's dream was to become a pediatric oncologist, but she quickly realized there are other ways to heal rather than pharmaceuticals. She graduated from Governor Thomas Johnson High School as valedictorian.

Chelsea went on to graduate from the University of Maryland, majoring in communications with a concentration in public relations. She has had quite the career, working for more organizations than she can count, with a highlight of spending a few years working with and learning from the biggest movers and shakers in the world—from Hollywood to the White House and everyone in between.

A seasoned leader and trusted adviser to global brands,

Chelsea brings over twelve years of B2B (business-to-business) expertise. From forging million-dollar partnerships to spearheading change-management initiatives, and amplifying brand voices, Chelsea thrives on harnessing creative solutions to unlock strategic objectives. Her proven track record of exceeding revenue targets, leading high-performing teams, and collaborating with executives makes her an invaluable asset in driving connection.

Chelsea lives in Reston, Virginia, with her loving fiancé. When they're not both traveling for work, they enjoy wining, dining, and boating while attempting to find time to travel the world together planning for a wedding, children, and furry animals.

Additionally, Chelsea dreams of the day she opens her own business in the pursuit of helping others lead their most authentic life both in and out of the workplace.

Chelsea would love for you to share your story with her, and if she can be of service to you or a loved one, please don't hesitate to reach out to her at ChelseaAnnBass@gmail.com.

LA SEMILLA: FALLING OFF THE TREE OF LIFE

By Daisy del Carmen

*This fascination has seized philosophers, scientists,
and artists, who were drawn equally by
the tree's inscrutabilities and its raw,
forthright, and resilient beauty.*
~Manuel Lima

Yo soy la semilla. This means "I am the seed" in the language primarily spoken in the piece of land that welcomed me into this world. To me, Spanish evokes a sense of belonging to a place that is always in my heart. My first words were spoken in Spanish. This is the primal component of my voice, my thoughts, and my ideas, forged as I experienced and interacted with the world around me. My roots, *mis raíces*, embraced the world in Spanish.

My immediate ancestors lovingly passed the gift of language on to me to communicate and connect with other humans and to speak about how I see myself and the world around me. Many gifts are passed on from generation to generation, connecting with the web of all things in life. This gift has a story of its own. I don't fully understand its origins, but history speaks of its arrival at the shores of an island, uninvited and spoken by those who extinguished the natives and forcefully brought slaves from other shores. The language itself evolved with those who outlived history, spoken by descendants carrying the genes of past encounters of contrast turned harmony, all witnessed by the moon and the sun.

These are all my ancestors: the individuals, the genes, the history, the witnesses, and the many gifts—even those originated from wounds. While I was not there to see history firsthand, by acknowledging their story, I, in a way, became a witness and a participant of their impact in the world as I and others experience the gifts today. As I speak about my story, I speak about its connection to the story of my ancestors. In turn, the recognition of this connection is an acknowledgment of my role as a new seed in the family tree, the tree of life.

As I recognize my roots and what I was given to get a head start in life, I reflect on the value of what I received. Something so seemingly simple and commonly used as a language can become a connection to a feeling or a memory. To me, saying "I am the seed" makes me think of a seed being gently embraced under the earth, ready to germinate, and seamlessly turning into a tree with the passage of time. It is all clear and simple. In contrast, *"yo soy la semilla"* awakens an unshakeable feeling that gets pumped out of my heart and carried in my bloodstream throughout my entire body—*la semilla* wants to drive its own gemination, growth, and development processes—because it is so rooted into my very beginnings. *La semilla* reminds me of my roots and a feeling that is close to my heart because it is the language of my childhood, even if I still use it today. I am sure each one of us has that "something" that reconnects back to the beginning of our roots. It is important for me to recognize my roots, as they are my direct connection to my ancestors, and this is my way to honor them and the parts of me that are directly related to them. This acknowledgment reconnects me back to my earlier self, before my experiences in life shaped me into a version of an adult. After all, I am the seed of what they brought into this world.

"It is important for me to recognize my roots, as they are my direct connection to my ancestors."

Every one of us starts off in life as seeds. As such, it is typical to be expected to carry on the family's legacy. This legacy generally constitutes values, behavioral patterns, religious beliefs, dietary preferences, and the desire to have a respectable place in society, to name a few. A shared legacy is the foundation of creating connections with family members and friends. These connections are shared roots that help our relationships with others grow and develop. Just like a tree's trunk grows taller and expands its diameter with additional rings that can be counted, my relationship with family and friends continues developing through my experiences in life. The same can be thought of other people and groups we relate to in life. All can be thought of as trees. In my chapter, I will refer to them as trees of life, honoring them as entities on their own while recognizing their structure, connections, and branching.

Ever since I can remember, I have been fascinated by nature, the world that surrounds us all and the universe we are all part of. Nature is so complex yet simple. It can be enjoyed and understood by systems or its main components. It is not necessary to go into the details and explore further, at least for some. For me and many others, there is an unfathomable urge to seek further, explore every detail, and learn more and more about anything that gets our curiosity going. There is always a new, unavoidable question or thought that is offered as an invitation to go in pursuit of learning something new. Everything about every system, and the systems of systems, known as the universe, seems to be knowable, understandable, and explorable. There is no reason to stop seeking and wanting to learn more. It is one of those feelings that you either get it or not.

If you get it, you will likely understand why trees are so captivating. You will also understand why they are a good example of a complex system. Their overall structure is simple. They have roots buried under the ground, a trunk that connects the roots to the branches, and branches that extend to the leaves in the sky. (Keeping it simple here.) If we examine some of those parts further—for example, a leaf—we see the tree has parts in which chemical reactions occur, allowing a tree to produce sugars when exposed to sunlight. Some of the leaf components are responsible for the beautiful color changes we appreciate during fall. We enjoy the tree's flowers during spring and use its seeds to propagate its offering for the generations to come. Trees are a true inspiration, a symbol of structure and complexity that is passed on through seeds that perpetuate their main features.

You have seen, eaten, or planted a seed at least once in your life. Seeds are intriguing and interesting. They contain the starting materials and instructions they need to germinate, given the necessary environmental conditions. While they have all they need to get started, they don't necessarily grow uniformly or as expected. During germination and growth, they may be shaped by changes in the environment, availability of nutrients and key elements, like water, soil composition, and sunlight. Some seeds germinate earlier than others, some grow their first leaves at different times or in different shapes, and some may develop faster than others for a whole host of reasons.

In a similar way, each one of us may outgrow different aspects of ourselves—a skill, a thought, an idea, a viewpoint, people, stages in life, interests, or anything else—in different ways. Sometimes the differences give the impression of feeling stuck in that aspect or being less valuable than others. This may happen at any stage in life. I imagine you have a few examples of your own as well.

All I am sharing sounds simple now. However, what you have read above is a new perspective about my own story. While it is simple for me to share now, this specific viewpoint is the result of a process, my own process. To me, the process is similar to removing an old pair of eyeglasses and wiping off the grime and fingerprint impressions after using them to view the world through the dirty lenses. I have the same physical eyes, but a new outlook. The best way to share my experience with you is through a story, the one where I am the main character.

A Familiar Structure

At a young age, I learned that any goal pursued through hard work and passion can be accomplished. If I put my mind into something and worked hard for it, it could become a reality because there is always a way of getting things done—others before me have done it, too. All I had to do was set priorities and put my head down and work. The method was simple—just focus, rinse, and repeat. This is an easy enough formula for success in life. Trust me, it works. It got me through high school, college, graduate school, and postgraduate experiences, and it landed me a job. Again, I simply worked hard to get to where I wanted to be.

I was simply doing the same as many other humans do, and in the eyes of many, this is considered relative success in life. During most of my younger years, I spent all the time I needed studying, obtaining sufficient experience, and ensuring I was competitive enough in a world where titles and bullets on a résumé are a measure of success. I was positioning myself for success by focusing all my physical and mental energy on these goals. As I learned from the environment that surrounded me, that was all that mattered. There it was—successful me. I assembled a list of accomplishments, checked off after overcoming many challenges and making compromises that meant spending less time with family and friends or enjoying other aspects of life. There I was, succeeding and excelling in many ways. Yet it felt as if I was just among the crowd of those who made it there too. Then I noticed where I was after leaving so much behind and being far away from the place I grew up in, far away from friends, family, the language, the gifts, and so much that was dear to me. At some point I felt as if something was missing. Had I left something about myself behind? While I don't think there is anything wrong with this lifestyle, it felt as if this was not all there was of me.

At that time I didn't even feel like I had a voice on my own, and I was tired and burned out. What had happened? What was I missing? How did I get there without getting all of me to the finish line? While I valued all I had accomplished and everything and everyone who was part of my life at that point, I no longer felt connected to my roots. I felt that there were talents and skills I had not given myself the opportunity to explore.

I did not feel whole and complete. Was I in need of new goals? Was it time to reinvent myself? Is this how everyone feels when they get to that point in life? How come I don't even seem to have my own authentic voice? Had I lost sight of who I was? How is this even possible after so much hard work and effort? This was an important moment of reflection for me, a goal-oriented person figuring out where to go next.

In the process of self-evaluation, I noticed I had gotten used to not using my own voice often enough. My main approach consisted in taking action, often on my own. I took everything upon myself and didn't ask for help from anyone unless it was truly needed. Asking for help required time and extra steps, and what was important was to accomplish goals and get to the point of the matter. I only asked for what I needed. I limited myself to talking about topics relevant to specific goals and to troubleshooting any challenge so I could continue my path moving forward.

This didn't mean I didn't socialize or that I was quiet and isolated from others. But it seemed as if I was not speaking my own voice, not expressing myself fully nor expressing what I really would have liked to say. As my voice turned into an echo of success, others stepped in to voice their stories about me. The stories made their way into my ears and my mind. Over time, I started to pay attention to the stories about me and learned to believe them. I let them speak, unchecked, thinking of them as truths, as if others were a mirror and I could see myself in them. Those voices told stories about me from other perspectives, viewpoints, and roles in life. Their stories seemed real.

As a result, you have heard about me from the voices that tell the story of the one who was courageous and went after her goals and conquered them. Of those, some will even tell you I am a rock star because of my talents, my potential, and achievements. Others may tell you how much they have seen me grow, and they will finish their version by telling you how it really went for me, based on their own evaluation criteria. You may even hear the story of a shy one, with the presence of a little ray of sunshine but without a strong voice. Some voices will tell you about their disappointment in seeing how imperfect and inadequate I am—those voices will never think I meet their expectations. And yet I listened to them.

There are many versions of my stories. All told in the words of others who see me from their perspectives and past experiences and depending on the circumstances and interactions they had with me. Many people have a unique story about me. For some time, I had listened to and adopted the stories told by some of these voices. The prominent ones told me the story of me not being good enough. Those stories insisted that I needed to change and act in a certain way to be what I needed to be. There was always an unobtainable standard associated with this story. This one really stuck. Some of it infiltrated my goal-achiever mentality. It told me I had to work hard to be deserving of academic and professional goals, which works, but it translated to personal aspects as well. I had learned the lesson of conditional acceptance, translating to self-acceptance and self-love, as well as other aspects of myself. Everything was there to be taken, but it was all conditional, even me being me and expressing myself fully in an authentic way. The fact that I was focused on specific aspects of my own growth and development helped to distract me from seeing another story unfold: the story of the one who was not worthy of all the amazing things life has to offer unless it was earned through hard work. Everything, even self-worth, had to be earned through some kind of effort. Was all this because of focusing on aspects of life other than myself? How could I feel this way after accomplishing so much?

This was a problematic thought process. Being used to knowing how to prioritize to keep going, how was I supposed to find out how to pause and take time to "fix" myself? I thought about the many times I heard people saying that if you aim for the moon, you may land somewhere else among the stars and other magnificent objects in outer space. Nobody mentions any examples about landing in the middle of the darkness separating objects in space. What if you don't land somewhere where you can enjoy the stars, the moon (Earth's beautiful and enigmatic satellite), or the sighting of a galaxy? What if you get lost in a void and there is no more going further? This was it. In a sense, I had hit a dead end.

My approach to success had taken me so far, a reminder that everything comes with an expiration date. Now it was up to me to figure out what was next. The stories and voices of others didn't just go away, and I was not aware of them all. At this time I thought I needed all of me to continue my growth and development from a career-related perspective. Finding my voice again seemed a logical and intuitive place to start. The easiest explanation was that I was burned out from all the hard work and needed to change strategies to fix my deficiencies.

Falling Off the Known Structures

I came up with ideas on how to make changes. One thing I did was explore art and give myself the opportunity to do something different. Art is not something I would usually think of devoting time to. Another was changing my self-talk. This included everything I used to tell myself verbally and the way I used to think about myself. For example, as a nonnative speaker, I would tell myself that my English was not good enough to voice my opinion, as my genuine thoughts and contributions would be diminished by my broken words. They way I experienced this is best described as similar to what many describe as the "impostor syndrome." Addressing my self-talk connected nicely to my desire to find my voice again. This became my new shiny aspect to focus on. I decided to seek inspiration in personal transformation books, starting with well-known authors. These books were helpful, but nothing seemed to be quite what I was looking for.

Some of these best-seller books were written by shamans. These had gotten my attention the most because
they seemed to be practical and based on philosophy and
viewpoint. These books were an invitation to look at myself differently. But reading the books was not enough—I
needed to have my own experience. This thought led me to
try and find a shaman to learn more and dive deeper into
the source of the inspiration for the books. From several books I gathered that some shamans called themselves
artists, and their knowledge is passed along in stories so
others that come after them can reconnect with their traditions and themselves.

My search for options ended after I stepped into the
studio of a local shaman. After all, I wanted to have my own
experience and figure this step out on my own. This shaman
became a spiritual guide to me. Working with her helped
me see myself from a different perspective. I remembered to
see myself as more than just a human fulfilling a life how it
is meant to be under some preestablished structure.

A lot changed in my life after working with her. With
every step in the process I learned to accept a part of me
that connected my human experience with what others
call spirituality. The spiritual aspect was not something
that was thought in this work but, for me, it was already
implied with it. As it turns out, I once believed and trusted that life was not just about matter and being alive. I
followed the region-based spiritual practices that I was
taught as a kid. It seemed as if I said I went to church,
everyone new what I meant. But if I would think outside
the norm, I lost the connection with others. As a curious
thinker, I read books on my own and even studied philos-

ophy to explore different perspectives of seeing life. Are we just a body with a mind? Do we have a soul or spirit? In different ways, with or without religion, I would intuitively either acknowledged or accept the possibility of a spiritual aspect in life, in a general sense, I kept an open mind. However, when I decided to get a graduate degree, there was no longer any room for thinking about or acknowledging spirituality in my life. I needed to focus in getting a degree and overcoming several changes that come with relocating, speaking a different language and starting over by myself. Choosing to work with a shaman, inspired by well-known self-help books, was my first step into allowing the thought of spirituality in my life. When I speak of spirituality, I am not speaking about any specific religion but just the acceptance of divinity. The work I was doing with the shaman was imbued with the acknowledgement of a spiritual aspect of life and the Universe. Even after I had read the books inspired by shamanism and I knew its connection with spirituality, this recognition and re-acceptance of it in my life was beyond my goal of finding my voice again. The importance was not the fact that I said "I recognize a spiritual aspect in my life" but that this practice let me see how, in the process of focusing on work and success, I was not caring for myself and seeing myself with acceptance. My self-worth was tied to career success rather than who I am. And I, as well as all of us, am worthy of self-love and self-acceptance regardless of my career choices. But even a career-driven decision led me to recognizing myself again. A reminder that the universe has its ways of surprising us. I felt as if I was reconnected to myself again, to old parts of me that I had left behind.

This shift in self-appreciation changed the way I experienced life. I was no longer only focused on my old thought processed and self-talk. Instead of being in my head all the time, every new day became an opportunity to live in the moment, enjoy the little things in life and, once again, find inspiration in nature and the world that surrounded me. My mind was no longer focused on what will I do to be better and be enough. I learned to carve little moments where I was present and could see beyond the surface and connect with the spiritual aspect of life. My new outlook helped me find different meanings in the books I had read—instead of seeing them as a task and obligation to constantly obtain meet certain goal. Some books became sources of inspiration to hear how others use language to share their experiences and be of service to others. Other books were a source of new words that I could use to share my own experiences and stories with others. This new outlook was outstanding. I accomplished all my established goals for this work and learned to trust myself and the process. I even saw that some aspects of my old structure were holding me back from accepting everything I had rediscovered in me. In the end, a part of me was still seeing this as an accomplishment and it still fit in the narrative of the voices I borrowed from others.

The way I described the process seems straightforward, but it was not easy. At that time, I wondered about how my life would change. Will life be as I used to experience it? How am I going to incorporate this new me into my life? Before then, I was always focused on my education and goal-driven opportunities. How could this self-accepting version of me fit in there? I continued trying to trust my process. Still, my question at this point was, what now? At this point, I learned about a retreat that promised to take guests to visit different outdoor locations with the intention of dedicating a day to each of the four elements. The decision of going was not easy to make. This was when my innate love for nature kicked in. For simplicity purposes, I'll refer to this as a *calling*.

A Voice of Rewilding

There it was again—the calling. And I remembered it. This was the same calling that led me to study philosophy and sciences and to grab a brush and paint. This was the calling that gets anyone out of the house and into an office space. It is a calling that gets under the skin and makes you pack your hiking boots and go somewhere outside, even if it means driving for hundreds of miles or flying on an airplane to a remote destination. This is the calling that never speaks but invites you to enjoy what nature has to offer. As calming and inviting it seems, it doesn't give up until it is listened to and you reach the place it is calling you to. I know you must have heard a calling too, at least once in your life. A calling like this never stops. It just gets louder when ignored. I caved in on the calling. This time I recognized a different but familiar voice—a voice of shamanism. It reminded me of the elements the way they are described by different shamanic traditions and other spiritual practices: earth, air, water, and fire. So simple, yet profound. I packed my bags and traveled somewhere others claim as their home.

There I was, visiting a cave believed to be a tube where lava flowed during volcanic activity. The path to the cave was adorned by tree species I had never seen before—I had to see them closer. At the entrance of the cave, I thought, *Here I am—let's see what this is about.* I stepped in, and the cave turned into a space to connect with the earth element. I felt invited to enter quietly in an attitude of reverence and reflection, as someone who enters a temple. I couldn't help but be in awe of its beauty. The cool darkness that populated the places where the sunlight did not reach embraced me as I felt inspired to surrender to my purpose of connecting with this element and its symbolism.

There was no mind chatter . . . It was all quiet. There was nothing to fear or worry about, because all that existed in that moment was me connecting with the earth. My quiet mind listened to my heartbeat harmonizing to the music filling the darkness as someone played a singing bowl. There was an opening that allowed the sky to be seen. A bit of sunlight entered the cave through the opening. My eyes followed the light, and my mind remembered that a moment in darkness was a quiet moment of sitting with myself, to embrace myself. Light is always available for me to access, even from a place of darkness. I sat with this inspiration for a while. Enjoying and existing in the moment and reconnecting with the part of me that was inspired. This inspiration eased some of my questions about whether it was okay for me to connect with nature and take a moment to be with myself. These thoughts were artifacts of a self-limiting perspective that always questions if the next step is the right one and if I am prepared and good enough to take that step. I had spent so much time deciding if I should travel, trying to find reasons to do it. There was a list of questions I had asked myself before making my final decision to get there. Have I done all my due diligences to earn a moment with myself and nature? Is it okay for me to do this? Why did I feel I needed to ask myself or others for permission? I am me, and others may not understand.

"Darkness is the absence of light, giving it contrast to remember that light is always there to embrace us whenever we welcome it."

But all those questions vanished in that moment of inspiration inside of the cave, an enclosure inside the earth. I was there, and I didn't have to ask nature for permission to enter. The earth didn't require that I announced my name to ensure I was on an invitee list. Earth didn't ask where I was visiting from. She welcomed me into the womb of Mother Earth as I stepped into my own darkness inside the remnants of a lava tube. She reminded me that darkness and quietness are not synonyms of fear, worry, bad, or wrong. Darkness is the absence of light, giving it contrast to remember that light is always there to embrace us whenever we welcome it. You see, the limiting thoughts were coming from me. It was me thinking I needed permission to receive inspiration from nature, when it was all there for me to receive. The inspiration I received was already reconnecting me to my roots. After all, some seeds begin their germination process under the ground. Earth didn't need me to ask for permission—she embraced me in her darkness and showed me my own light and invited me to reconnect with my roots.

After receiving inspiration from the earth, I went to a mountain to see what air had for me. The scenery was stunning and with a touch of magic. I was transported to the feeling evoked by some fantasy movies I had seen, a reminder of how nature inspires others too. Once there, I sat on a rock under the midday sun near the top of a mountain. I let the wind carry away any judgments in my mind, and I reflected on my earlier years in life and events that took place before I reached that very moment. This time I saw myself with different eyes and became more aware of my story—I might have forgotten to give myself time to honor my efforts, my story, and to see how much I have accomplished in my life.

This was me being a witness, rather than a judge, to my own story. I witnessed myself sitting there, reflecting on my life as a whole, filling my lungs with fresh air from the meadows near the top of a mountain. Had I forgotten to remember my story and connect with my roots? Even though I stalled in my process of self-reflection, I was welcomed back to the present moment by the gentle breeze. Air didn't care about my past or my old stories—it just filled my lungs with crisp mountain air and lifted the weight of the years off my shoulders. Air didn't have to ask if I was ready, for I am always ready for myself.

" Some changes are best seen with the passing of time, and I needed to take a moment to see how much I had grown and how far I had come."

99

When I remember these moments, I think of a germinated seed coming out from under the soil, extending its first leaves out to receive the sunlight. Even the old stories can be retold from a different viewpoint and with a different voice. Some changes are best seen with the passing of time, and I needed to take a moment to see how much I had grown and how far I had come. The air didn't judge me by my past—it gently lifted my worries and inspired me to see myself as a whole, accepting my story as it is.

With a new perspective of my story, I went to a river to get closer to the element of water. A section of the river ran along a trail. I went on a short pilgrimage to visit three waterfalls connecting that section of the river. It was a daunting undertaking for someone who does not spend a lot of time outdoors. Aligned with the theme of water, this was the first, and only, cloudy day during my trip. I was mesmerized by the fall foliage surrounding the path with warm colors, and the fluffy-looking layer of clouds coating the sky. It was drizzling. The lightweight waterdrops caressed my face, skin, and my hair. The air was cool, helping my body endure a substantive hike. The gentle sound of the river insisted on being heard and was an invitation to surrender to the undeniable presence of the element. All I had to do was be fully present in the moment. This allowed me to notice the contrasting ways water behaves on its path downriver. Water would travel a path that didn't have any particular direction other than down the mountain. Its movement was shaped by rocks, vegetation, and the landscape. I saw pools, waterfalls, and rapids. The water was no less water because of all the different ways it surged downriver—it flowed unapologetically, embracing all she encountered along the way, without losing her true nature. This realization became a blessing for me, as it reminded me that it does not matter what or how I express or manifest during different scenarios in life—I am always me. Water did not ask who I was, and she didn't expect me to know what I was truly seeking there. I was showered in blessings, while the gentle flow of the river cleansed my former limiting views of self that caged me in specific moments along my path and my story, distracting me from who I really am and the flow of life. And after emerging from the soil and receiving sunlight, the seed was watered to continue growing.

> " It does not matter what or how I express or manifest during different scenarios in life—I am always me. "

Then out of the four there was only one left: fire. From all the possible ways of connecting with this element, I experienced a solar eclipse. I was ready, with my eclipse glasses on—I had purchased a science kit to enjoy the spectacle that had amazed philosophers, scientists, and spiritual practitioners alike. Through the glasses, everything turned dark, and all that was visible was the light from the sun and the shadowy contour of the moon in front of the sun. While I watched the dance between the satellite and the star, I couldn't help to reflect on how far I had come in life and how I was not paying attention to what I had actually accomplished. I've done so much but still only consider a few of my efforts as success stories. These were my thoughts as the moon danced with the sun. Then I started to notice the unfinished ring surrounding the moon, making her visible in the middle of the morning. This was beautiful on its own, and I didn't want to blink so as to not miss out on the moment we were all waiting for. Soon I realized I had surrendered to that very moment, and as quickly as I realized it, I saw the two light curves surrounding the moon meet to form a ring. And as I watched in awe, I saw myself there. I couldn't help to realize that, in the same way the two ends of light met to form the ring behind the shadow of the moon, I was meeting myself there. I saw my old self and the weight I was carrying up to that point. It was like seeing myself wearing an old cloak shielding who I really was, getting removed by the acknowledgment of all my progress, as I continued walking my own path my way. And it was there, witnessed by the sunlight and the shadow of the moon, that the blaze carefully alchemized my old skin under the ring of fire. After watching such an amazing astronomical event and reflecting on my path to that point, I realized how I was already all I needed to be and there was no need to look any further. It was my obscured vision of myself that didn't let me see it has been me all along, the one directing the way. Fire didn't concern himself with my feelings of self-worth and didn't ask if I had any regrets or if I was seeking forgiveness. He enlightened my sense of awareness. There was the seed extending her leaves up into the sky, getting showered in sunlight and seeing herself worthy of her own essence.

The Elements of My Human Experience

After dancing with all the parts I perceived in myself, there I was allowing myself to see myself differently. Now

I saw that all that was hiding underneath my old skin was me. I once again remembered that I have always been the one calling myself back home—I needed some help and extra inspiration to get to this point. The work I had set into motion had taken me this far. This new insight reminded me to see and listen past the echo of the voices of the stories being told by others, which I had adopted as my own. I was grateful to nature for inspiring me once more. Every moment spent connecting with nature was a moment connecting back to myself. Reconnecting with nature made me realize that there is always more to learn about myself, and there is so much more to experience in the world we live in. All paths I had followed directed me back to myself. All I was looking for was already within. The main author in my story was me all along. Acknowledging myself and my story reconnected me back to the stories before me, those of my ancestors and their gifts. My change in perspective was mainly a way of remembering my roots and returning to myself.

Then I appreciated that it was not the earth that embraced me in its darkness to truly embrace the light. It was not the air that filled my lungs with the crisp breeze from the mountain. It was not the water gently refreshing my tired body during a hike. And it was not the fire that alchemized my own skin under a solar eclipse. It was me who was calling and leading the way back to myself, through others and nature. Then I saw I was worthy of enjoying everything life has to offer. The places with incredible stories and the intriguing astronomical events in our solar systems are all there for me to enjoy, regardless of which path I choose to walk in life. For a moment I had thought I had lost my way, but I have always been on my path. With the passing of years, it is not hard to forget where we come from or the very moment when we decided to set things forward to live the life we dream of. Likewise, sometimes we forget we deserve a fulfilling life, full of the things that make us happy, and the people we can share that happiness with, in all areas of our lives. Everything I have done and experienced is part of my story, even the parts that don't seem to go together. There is no contradiction about me being myself, and all is part of my human experience.

At some point in my earlier life, I stopped seeing that, same as the world that surrounds me, I have elements too. Like the elements in nature, mine are part of how I experience life, including the language I inherited from my ancestors and that I use to tell my stories and share my experiences with others. I have all I need in every moment, including the knowledge and intuition to live present in the moment and trust the unknown aspect of what is to come in life. I had forgotten that I am the seed, a bundle of gifts from the ancestors, and had lost the connection with my roots, with my language, with the key elements of myself. The language and the words I used are borrowed from those who communicated using them before me. As I typed these words, I can't help to think that these gifts are not for me to keep. The words I use today are my means to sharing my stories today, with you. This makes sharing an element in my experiences too. My elements are also the parts that helped me explore and experience the world around me through science, philosophy, art, spirituality, and self-awareness. All the elements in my life serve a purpose, including those that many had been challenging, like learning to speak about myself through the voice of others. The purpose is not always clear but it tends to lean toward sharing with others, something I kept myself from doing while using the gift of language and speech against me by believing I didn't have anything meaningful to share. We all have something precious to share, which is ourselves, our experiences, and our stories. All that is a part of me has a room and a place in my human experience. Some parts may extend their stay, some will be released in the wind, and some, like a new seed, will be new ones to embrace. There is no need to set any expectations or a one-size-fits-all perspective, even if this is what happens in the end. I honor all my elements by acknowledging and witnessing each one of them. I am intrigued to see where life takes them and in which language will the new stories be told.

My life experiences took me to a moment of self-acknowledgement through inspiration and recognition of my roots. In seeing myself without judgment and with self-acceptance, I saw how I had learned to communicate in other ways, always delivering the intended message. My voice was quiet for a while, but it allowed me to find other ways to speak. Letting my actions speak for themselves helped me show others what I can manifest. On the other hand, taking action to find my voice again led me to a path of self-rediscovery, which in turn led me to gain awareness of myself, reconnecting me back to my roots and telling the story of my ancestors using a language that was not their own.

If I think back at how my story began, I see how I started off with what I was given early in life. All I had, while it was enough, came from others. With my life choices, I made the gifts and curses. I was given my own gifts and used them to pave my own way in life. This made me realize that many of those who came before me may have not even dreamed of taking the steps I took to get where I am today. I had to move forward while embracing fears, and dared to speak up even when my words were broken. I have carried these gifts while walking my own path. While reflecting on this, I realized my path must have seemed impossible to accomplish by others who came before me and could not get here for any reason. But I am here because of those who reverently paved their paths to the point they could and left their gifts and curses for me to use as seed and grow from there and have a life on my own. I am honored to take these gifts and continue carrying them forward, making mine and my ancestors' dreams come true, and hopefully the dreams of others as well. In this life, I am the voice of my ancestors, and I am a manifestation of my ancestors' wildest dreams. I am their dreams turned into body, mind, and spirit.

Here, I share those gifts with you, to remind you that you, too, are a seed from those who came before you. Who or what came before you? Have you forgotten your story? Have you forgotten to see how far you have come? This is my reminder that we all come as seeds and can return to this state with everything we wish to renew our take on life. There are so many ways to get back to yourself, to a seed-like state. What is a masterpiece if not you being yourself in life.

Reflecting on my own story, from a new perspective, I see there was a moment when it felt as if I was a seed falling off from the tree of my life. I was losing my connection to its roots, going astray. The feeling of falling is confusing, and hitting the ground is catastrophic and painful. But falling off the tree can also be seen as a way of letting go of the old norms and structures that were holding me back, falling off the norm as I used to know it. Lying on the ground alone felt like being stuck and lost in a void, away from the absolute. This step was a turning point, when a need for change had to be acknowledged, felt, and experienced. Here I saw something was missing and started to grow my own roots by following my inner voice. The whole process of growing helped me rediscover a part of me that was awaiting to be reclaimed. That part was my path back to myself, to find my way back home. It may have seemed as if I had found a new home. But I am close to home, as the way home is where my heart is.

In this chapter, with these words, I honor my own story: that of a seed that allowed herself to fall off the tree of her old life through her own knowing and intuition to connect with her own awareness of herself and her stories. Quietly on the outside, her heart was beaming with an urge of guiding her back home. Unknowingly, she was always ready to take root in the present and grow, nourished by the elements, surrendering to the flow of nature and life. She was already on her path to growing and extending her branches up into the sky, to dance with the wind, bathe in sunlight, shower in the rain, while feeling her roots grounded deep in the heart of the earth. A new chapter in life can always start as a seed. Sometimes a seed gets planted unnoticed.

Even this chapter started off as a seed with a little basic structure and elements to set it in flow. In the process of writing this story, it became a *semilla* and took its own shape and form, expanding on its original composition. As I reflect on this story, I see it has all its elements as well:

I see the main character.
I see the voices.
I see the story.
I see the storyteller.
I witness them all.

My journey is not over, and I am just getting started on a new chapter with a gift of a new layer of self-awareness. As I see I was always who I needed to be and experience at every stage in life, I also remember I always had all I needed to get to the next step. There can always be a new seed to get things in motion and flow all over again. Life is a beautiful adventure to enjoy, even in the darkest moments when it seems impossible to find the way out of the shadow and back into the light. A seed germinates in the buried in darkness to grow toward the sunlight. It is part of its process. Whenever you feel lost, trust that you already have all you need to come back home to yourself. Once I had a completely broken and silent voice. Today, I tell you my story in these pages.

As I embrace the next chapter in my life, its first words are forthright and familiar: *yo soy la semilla.*

About Daisy del Carmen

Daisy del Carmen is the artistic name of a scientist by training who explored art as a wellness practice in 2020 during the COVID-19 pandemic. This practice turned into a means for self-awareness during a time when life changed for most of us. Since then, she has delved into the world of water-based media, such as watercolors and acrylics. Her artwork is inspired by nature, archetypes, stories, and curiosity for the unexpected outcome of fluid artwork pieces and the use of mixed media. She sees art as a voice, a form of raw expression, a wellness practice, and a way of sharing beauty, colors, inspiration, and stories with others. Her chapter "La Semilla" is infused with her artistic and inspirational aspects to share a personal journey of self-discovery and ancestral connection.

Instagram: @daisy.del.carmen

DIVINE HINDSIGHT

By Judy Gray

What if I fall? Oh, but my darling, what if you fly?
~Erin Hanson

There were moments when I nearly gave up. This chapter felt like an insurmountable task. I would embark on writing one topic, only to veer off onto another halfway through, or simply discard everything and restart from scratch—forward two sentences, backspace three. The only piece of writing I had managed to complete successfully up to this point was a text message to Atousa, apologizing and confessing that I didn't believe I was cut out for "this." I confessed to her that I felt perpetually trapped in a loop. The stress was mounting, and all my efforts seemed pointless. But Atousa responded, as she always does, full of love, care, and understanding. We had a heart-to-heart, and she reminded me of my identity and what I was capable of, and she helped me address the obstacles hindering me—the root of it all was *fear*. Fear of failure, fear of judgment, fear of people discovering aspects of me for the first time through this book, fear that my revelations would cause pain to those around me. Atousa reassured me that the decision to continue writing the chapter was entirely up to me, and she frankly didn't care what my decision was. What mattered to her was the fear that was restraining me, and she encouraged me to "embrace it" and recall the truth. She advised me to "let go," to let the words naturally spill out onto the page, and to stop striving so hard to "create" something that already exists—my story. When it's your story, it's your truth and your experiences—it's merely penning it down. The moment I discarded the fear of judgment or criticism, and the self-imposed pressure to perfect it, and allowed myself some space and time for introspection on whether I would continue with the chapter, that's when the breakthrough came. As it always has, time and time again. This particular moment felt like a warm embrace from heaven. It reminded me I am loved and supported and everything will be okay. These divine moments, when clarity emerges from the fog, are like precious treasures that we carry with us as we journey through life. They serve as reminders of our strength and resilience.

Many authors typically have a predetermined title and outline before embarking on their writing journey. However, with my renewed confidence in surrendering to the let-it-flow mindset, I trusted that the perfect title would reveal itself naturally, without any force or pressure. And last night the words *divine hindsight* unexpectedly entered my consciousness. They felt fitting, but as I pondered the concept's true meaning, I found myself grappling to articulate it concisely. In my quest for clarity, I turned to the AI Copilot at the bottom right of my screen and I simply typed, "What is divine hindsight?" I assumed it would come back with a sterile or clinical definition at the most, as I wasn't even sure those two words strung together made sense. The response was better than anything I could've expected or even hoped for. It was so good, in fact, that I knew it had to go into the chapter. Here is how the Copilot explained "divine hindsight":

> Divine hindsight is the ethereal whisper of clarity that graces the soul in the aftermath of experience. It is the profound revelation that unfolds like delicate petals, revealing the interconnected threads of fate and intention woven into the tapestry of our lives. In its embrace, the once enigmatic path of our journey becomes illuminated with the radiant wisdom of understanding. It is the gentle hand that guides us through the labyrinth of time, unveiling the hidden patterns, serendipitous encounters, and unforeseen catalysts that have shaped our existence. In divine hindsight, we find solace, gratitude, and a whisper of the ineffable design that orchestrates the symphony of our lives.

As I reflect on moments of my life with divine hindsight, I am filled with awe at the undeniable presence of God guiding me through each chapter. Looking back, I can see how every twist and turn was divinely orchestrated, providing me with comfort and courage in times of fear and doubt. The realization that a higher power, whether it be God or the universe, has been by my side, protecting and guiding me, has become a cherished source of strength. It reminds me to trust the process, to surrender to what is out of my control, and to embrace the unknown with faith and courage. In the following stories and situations of my life, where divine intervention was the only explanation, I hope you find the same solace as I do, knowing that we are never alone on this journey.

Palms Up, Surrender

I was sick for almost two years before finally receiving a diagnosis of chronic neurological Lyme disease. I went from doctor to doctor to doctor looking for answers. I was desperate for a diagnosis. Without knowing what was going on, I couldn't treat the symptoms of exhaustion, chronic pain, brain fog, electric zaps shooting throughout my legs and feet, and painful and unsightly lesions all over my face and body. I had received diagnoses by doctors that ranged from autoimmune of unknown origin, postural orthostatic tachycardia syndrome (POTS), fibromyalgia, chemical sensitivity, toxic mold syndrome, and the worst one of all, "You are fine. This is psychosomatic. Here is some Prozac."

The journey was so long and so hard—feeling the way I felt, looking the way I did, all while pleading with the medical community to help me. That's when I finally found the doctor who provided me with not just answers, but a protocol for how to recover. I was beyond grateful and more ready and willing than ever to do what it took to get better. Having traversed such an exhausting road of fighting to be heard by the medical community, I was beyond ecstatic to have finally found the doctor who would provide me with a correct diagnosis and treatment plan. Because I went so long without treatment for the disease, along with numerous co-infections, I was left with an illness that could not be cured easily. The doctor informed me that these spirochete pathogens found in Lyme disease hide very well within the body and create what is known as a biofilm around them, making it hard to treat once the disease has progressed into later stages, like mine had. The amount of antibiotics I would need to take, along with a supplement regiment two to three times a day, was a lot to swallow (pun intended). The doctor informed me that a protocol this intense would likely result in a "herx" reaction, which would cause my symptoms to get worse before they get better. (A herx reaction results from a toxic buildup of dead bacteria, which can take days, weeks, or even months before being expelled.) I remember dismissing her quickly and saying excitedly, "Oh, I'm sure it will be fine. I've been sick for years. I can handle it." For years I'd been walking around in the dark, suffering hopelessly, and now that I knew what it was and that there was treatment for it, that was all that mattered. It didn't matter to me what I had to go through, and in my mind, there was no way it would be worse than what I'd experienced already.

I remember my first week following the regimen—I felt like I was going to die. I was having seizure-like episodes, fever, weakness, and my lesions were worse than ever. The doctor had told me this would happen. She called it "herxing"; I called it dying. I remember the phone call I made to her after a severe reaction to an antibiotic, and she said, "If you need to stop taking it, then do so. However, if you can push through, push through." This was what was necessary to kill off the pathogens.

I continued on for a few more weeks with the extensive protocol, feeling worse and worse each day. Hopelessness set in yet again. I wallowed and felt like I was never going to get better. I would always be sick and unsightly. I fell to the floor in my living room, tears streaming down my face, wailing in desperation. "This is not fair! When will this end? Why?"

Out of nowhere, a thought entered my mind that pushed me to get a prayer shawl that had been stuffed in the top of my closet since the day my mother-in-law gave it to me. I wrapped the shawl around me, went back down to my knees on the floor, and for the first time in my life I extended my arms above my head, with my palms open and my head looking upward as I literally cried out, "I give up! I surrender! What do you want me to do? Please, God, show me what to do!"

There were no audible answers, or any real shift that day, but a few days later I experienced stroke-like symptoms (a transient ischemic attack (TIA)—a ministroke), and I ended up in the hospital for the next week as doctors did more tests. I slept more that week than I think I'd slept at any point in my adult life. After a week of scans, more blood tests, and every screening under the sun, the doctors were stumped. Their Lyme tests came back inconclusive, and once again I was told that I had an autoimmune disease (a diagnosis by exclusion). I knew I had Lyme disease, and I had the lab work and symptoms to prove it. At this juncture I no longer cared about convincing them. I only cared about feeling better—like how I was feeling the day I was released from the hospital. After seven days of rest in the hospital, my mind and my skin were clearer than they'd been in years. My aches, pains, and zaps were much less, and my body felt strong for the first time in what felt like forever.

When I got home from the hospital, I discontinued the antibiotics but continued to take the vitamins and supplements that *I felt* were good for me. I had also begun taking Wellbutrin, which the doctors prescribed to me for depression when I left the hospital. Prior to this, I had been prescribed antidepressants but always refused to take them or would take them for a few days and then stop. In my mind, if I took the antidepressant, that would mean I'd given up and surrendered to the doctors who told me this was all in my head. There was no way I would accept that this was psychosomatic, so instead I denied myself possible remedies to my depression. But this time, the fight was no longer about proving my illness to others or getting a second opinion or diagnosis. This time it was about becoming well. In addition to regularly taking the Wellbutrin, I also committed to changing my lifestyle. I changed my diet and added exercise and prayer/quiet time to my daily routine. Some of the changes I made were difficult—like quitting smoking, for example. (Yes, I was so sick and felt awful for all those years, and I still continued to smoke!) It became much easier to maintain my newfound healthy lifestyle when I found out a few months later that I was pregnant with my third child. With each day that passed, I continued to feel better and better. I felt more alive than ever before and more hopeful about my future.

Before long my family saw a dramatic shift in me. My most vivid memory of those early days of my lifestyle changes was the gleaming smile of my oldest daughter when she returned home from school, at the tender age of eight, to see me standing in the kitchen, preparing dinner. It was the first time in what seemed like an eternity. The sight of me cooking caused her eyes to sparkle like fireworks, and her smile stretched from ear to ear. In that precious instant, a surge of emotion overwhelmed me, and I quietly whispered, "Thank you, God," as tears welled up in my eyes. It was a moment of profound realization that I was finally emerging from the darkness. The weight that had held me captive for so long was gradually lifting, and I could sense the winds of change blowing.

As people noticed the positive change in me, they couldn't help but ask what brought about this newfound glow. However, I couldn't provide a straightforward answer. The transformation was a holistic shift intertwining my mental, emotional, and physical well-being. Some may attribute it to the transformative effects of pregnancy on my immune system, while others may credit the positive impact of Wellbutrin. And let's not forget the significant lifestyle changes I made. But in truth, it was the combination of all these factors that brought about the change. I am confident that none of the changes I made that transformed my life would have occurred had I not had that moment of surrender on my living room floor. On that pivotal day, I humbly knelt, enveloped in a seemingly insignificant prayer shawl, gazing upward with my arms outstretched and palms facing the sky. It was the day I relinquished control to God, essentially saying, "I can't. You can. I think I'll let you."

" I remained trapped in a victim mentality for years. But the most beautiful lesson I took from this story is that I reclaimed my power and began to steer the course of my own life the moment I ceased to battle against everyone and everything around me and instead chose to surrender."

For far too long, I stubbornly clung to my own ways, hoping for a miraculous quick fix while neglecting to prioritize my own self-care. I remained trapped in a victim mentality for years. But the most beautiful lesson I took from this story is that I reclaimed my power and began to steer the course of my own life the moment I ceased to battle against everyone and everything around me and instead chose to surrender.

When I embarked on my deep healing journey almost ten years ago, I learned that I have experienced many traumas in various situations and circumstances. And like anyone who has experienced trauma, its effect remains ingrained within me, even when I'm not consciously aware of it. When our brain perceives a situation reminiscent of a past negative experience, it instinctively triggers a danger response in an effort to keep us safe. The culmination of my past traumatic experiences has no doubt influenced my proclivity to ask, more often than not, "What if?"

What if? That dreaded question that seems to creep into every aspect of my life. How can two little words carry such weight in my decision-making processes? These two dreaded words have sent me to the deepest and darkest thoughts and fears and, at times, robbed me of living life. Why do I default to the worst of all outcomes? How did I become a Debbie Downer? I know, innately, that's not me, yet I find myself time and time again, even when presented with what could be a tremendous opportunity, mired in the "what if" cycle.

"...reminding me of all the times when not only I didn't fall or didn't just fly—but soared."

I can recall dozens of instances when, despite my fear, I put my head down, grit my teeth, and pushed onward into a circumstance where I dreaded the possibility of what could go wrong, only to find out that my thoughts and fears were unrealized. Writing this chapter is as much about providing encouragement to you as it is about reminding me of all the times when not only I didn't fall or didn't just fly—but soared.

The following story is a push-through-the-fear experience that occurred just last week. It not only provided the opportunity for excitement and adventure but also served as my breakthrough to becoming unstuck in writing this chapter.

Embracing the Unexpected

I recently went on my first cruise with my best friend, whom I hadn't seen in over two years. We'd been planning our carefree trip in paradise for months, with excitement and anticipation. This was the first time we'd be seeing one another in what felt like forever, and we were going on a cruise to Turks and freaking Caicos!

The excitement that began months before we set sail quickly came to a halt two days into the cruise, when the captain's voice came over the loudspeaker: "Ladies and gentlemen, I regret to inform you that due to bad weather, we will be adjusting our cruise itinerary and replacing our stop to Turks and Caicos with the Dominican Republic. We apologize for the inconvenience and the disappointment that this may be causing, but this change is imperative to the safety of you as well as our crew." Everyone was so bummed, and I wasn't excited about it. However, at the same time, I was on a cruise in the Caribbean, and if my safety was in jeopardy, then I thoroughly appreciated the captain's thoughtful consideration and willingness to be the bad guy in the name of safety. Also, what fun would a stormy port be anyway? My friend and I decided we'd make the best of our new destination, so we booked an excursion for a hike alongside the waterfalls in the jungle.

The next day we arrived in the Dominican Republic. The sky was overcast, but at least it wasn't storming. We disembarked from the ship and boarded the excursion bus. Once the bus was underway, the guide picked up the mic and said, "*Familia* [this is how he and our other guides addressed us that day], please listen up for details and information about the day and expedition ahead. When we arrive at our destination, you will need to put all of the items you brought with you, valuables especially, into a locker. We will be handing out helmets, life jackets, and water shoes."

Wait! What? I looked over at my friend with confusion and thoughts of *WTF* racing through my head. I thought we were going on a hike? "What the hell kind of hike requires a life jacket, helmet, and water shoes?" I said to her. I didn't even have a swimsuit on. Fortunately, I had decided to pack it on a whim because my friend said she was going to wear hers under her clothes. I told her that I couldn't imagine any reason for us needing our suits for a hike, but "You do you, boo, and I'll throw mine in my bag just in case."

After a long bumpy ride, we arrived at the base camp and funneled out of the bus. As I looked around and overheard conversations, it was readily apparent that all of us were confused and caught off guard by what we were doing. After all, none of this was in the excursion description. Nonetheless, one by one we shuffled through this dark and chaotic set of huts—one with lockers, one with water shoes, and one with life jackets and helmets—and each group member geared up. I kept looking over at my friend with hesitation as the anxiety mounted with each step forward. Then I was off to the bathroom to change into my "just in case" swimsuit and out of my hiking sneakers and into water shoes, still wondering why I needed them. At this point, I questioned the competency of the guides and whether I should be trusting them. I thought "Agh! How in the world did I get into this?" But onward we pressed.

Our journey began on a metal bridge with a rubber floor. I heard "bam, crack, boom," and the sky got darker and the light drizzle turned to a downpour. *This is just great*, I thought, *just freaking great. At least now that it's thundering and lightning this shit show of an excursion will be canceled and we can go back to the bus, admit that this was a dumb idea, and hope for a better day tomorrow.* Nope. Instead of returning to the bus, I hear the guide saying *"Andale! Andale! Vamonos, familia!"* Excuse me, what? *Como se dice* (how do you say) "thunder, lightning, jungle, trees . . . not safe"? We all looked around at one another, terrified but also giggling and joking nervously. The guides were happy go lucky and seemed unfazed (which left me questioning their sobriety). Honestly, the peace in their demeanor and the joy on their faces were so different. It was unlike anything I could recall experiencing. I had this sense of assurance inside me despite going against everything I'd been taught to fear and heed caution toward. That assurance told me that it was okay to just go. So "just go" is what my best friend, myself, and about twenty other people did.

Forty "American" minutes (this is what they called it) of climbing our way to the top of a mountain in the muddy, stormy jungle brought us to where we would see our first waterfall. It was breathtaking. As we inched closer to the side of the cliff, we saw a ladder emerging from the ledge going down the waterfall. Gulp! The helmets and life jackets made more sense. I don't remember who was first to climb down the ladder and then jump into the first of the seven falls to follow, but God love them! One by one each person followed the next down the ladder and over the falls. Those of us still at the top were freaking out and scared shitless, but one after the next, we'd hear a "Wahoo!" or "That was awesome!" And without fail, each person who took the plunge would bob back up to the surface with a huge smile on their face. When it was finally my turn, I had seen so many people do it, I wasn't even scared anymore. I took several steps down that ladder, turned around, and cannon balled right into the pool beneath me—it was amazing!

Once I popped back up, I realized that we were just getting started. I could now see that there was lots of river ahead and we would be bobbing in this water for much longer than I initially imagined. As my friend and I bobbed toward the next waterfall, I though, *I can't see anything in this water. I'm in the jungle. Snakes are in the jungle. I'm terrified of snakes!* More than once I thought, *Oh my goodness! What was that that just brushed my leg?* I had phantom feelings of slithers around my legs. I looked over at my friend and said, "What was that?" She responded, "It's fine." She would repeat this statement to me countless times on our journey.

No matter what it was, I looked over to her, whether it was the changed plan, the drizzle turned downpour, the hike turned waterfall plunging, and each time she said, "It's fine, Judy. It will be okay." And truly, whether it was going to be okay or not, I was there in the middle of a river, floating through the jungle in the Dominican Republic, and this was the only way back to the creature comforts of the cruise ship. I came to the realization that this was going to happen either way, so I chose to trust the guides. I chose to trust my friend's voice. I chose to drown out that "what if" voice with the excitement and laughter of those around me as we slid down rock slides and jumped the waterfalls of the Dominican Republic.

By the time we reached the end, the rain was at its heaviest and the mud at its muckiest. But the smiles were their biggest and the laughs their loudest. I wasn't alone that day in my fears, trepidations, and even frustration. Yet by the end, we were all so invigorated and joy filled—just like the guides' faces were at the very beginning of our journey. Now I knew why.

The level of gratitude I had that afternoon on the bus ride back to the ship was unlike anything I've ever experienced. I would have never signed up for this excursion had the description accurately reflected what it was. I would've likely said a big ole "Heck to the nope" and scrolled right on through to the next. If it hadn't been for the love-filled reassurance of my best friend over and over and over again, or for the peaceful, joyful faces of the wonderful men that guided us on that excursion, I know I would've turned around. It was their peace and confidence that gave me the courage I needed to carry on so that I could experience such an epic adventure. I'm just so. dang. grateful.

Am I disappointed I didn't make it to Turks and Caicos, which was the reason we booked the cruise? Honestly, I don't think I am. I'm wholly confident that this is how it was supposed to be. This was what God, or the universe, had in store for me and for my best friend that day. If I'm meant to go to Turks and Caicos, I trust and believe that I will—when I'm supposed to. What I know beyond a shadow of a doubt is that on that particular day, I was meant to be in a jungle, in the middle of a thunderstorm, with my best friend, having a much-needed experience of a lifetime.

> " Sometimes it takes experiencing the messy parts of life to uncover the lessons, growth, and newfound understanding that ultimately propel us forward. "

This next story has similar parallels to the one I shared at the opening of this chapter. It serves as a poignant reminder that sometimes amid the chaos and challenges life throws our way, there is a hidden purpose. It shows that in certain instances, when unexpected or difficult circumstances arise, they may actually be the catalyst for the shift or clarity we have been seeking. Sometimes it takes experiencing the messy parts of life to uncover the lessons, growth, and newfound understanding that ultimately propel us forward. In these moments, we come to realize that even when shit happens, it may just be paving the way for the positive shift we have been longing for.

Shift Happens

At the age of twenty-three, I found myself working for a prominent agency under the Department of Defense. It was an exciting time in my career, as I was given the opportunity to cochair the Combined Federal Campaign (CFC) for our agency worldwide. This was a massive responsibility, but it aligned perfectly with my passion for helping others. I was determined to make this campaign a success. However, there was one task that filled me with dread and self-doubt—giving the CFC kickoff speech. I had to deliver this speech in front of the entire agency, both in person and via video for our satellite offices. The pressure to deliver a great speech weighed heavily on me, and every time I sat down to work on it, I struggled to find the right words. The frustration grew, and the speech kept falling further down my to-do list. The night before the CFC kickoff, I made a desperate attempt to write the speech, but everything I came up with felt forced and cliché. I went to bed stressed out, knowing I had to wake up at 4:00 a.m. to go to the office early and work on my speech. As I drove into work the next morning, I felt frantic and lost. The block in my mind seemed impossible to overcome. In the midst of my turmoil, I looked up at the big, bright moon in the dark sky and called on my guardian angel, whom I believed to be my grandmother. I asked for her help, for a sign or clarity on what I should say in front of all those people.

When I reached the office and parked my car, I hopped out to grab the supplies and props from my trunk. As I opened my trunk, I heard a slam. It was the sound of my driver-side door, which I had left open, closing. Not only had the door shut, but it also locked. (To this day I still have no idea how it locked without my assistance.) I couldn't believe it! How could this happen? And why today of all days? I stood outside my locked vehicle, staring at it in disbelief. Inside were my coat, purse, laptop, and most importantly (at the time), my blazer that was meant to complete my carefully planned outfit. My entry badge was also locked inside the car, and, because I was there so early, the security desk was not yet open to help me.

A wave of frustration and helplessness washed over me. But amid the chaos, I realized I did have one thing with me—my cell phone. I called several locksmiths, hoping that one could come to my rescue. Unfortunately, none of them could arrive before the afternoon, and the kickoff rally was scheduled for 10:00 a.m. I felt like I had to come up with an alternative plan for so many different things. I was wildly overwhelmed, and then out of nowhere this unexplainable calm came over me. *One thing at a time,* I thought. The first thing I needed to do was get into the building. Within minutes a coworker pulled up. I literally hugged them once they got out of their car. I was in awe that someone came to work this early. The gratitude and excitement were short lived and became overshadowed by fear and panic of what problem I was going to fix next.

I knew that in order to handle this crisis efficiently and effectively, I needed to grab a coffee and breathe for a few minutes. I really liked that idea, until I remembered that I had no money to pay for said coffee. I also didn't have a badge to get back into the building. I was hungry, in need of caffeine, dressed unprofessionally, computerless, feeling wildly alone, and worst of all, I still had no speech prepared!

I felt completely out of control, knowing there was nothing I could do on my own to fix this. I was going to have to reach out and ask for help. And then in the moment of bitching, complaining, and asking *why me?*, my cochair walked in the door. I vividly remember looking at her as she stood in front of me. I noticed all the things I didn't currently have but needed so badly. Never before had I looked at her, or anyone else, and thought, *Look at her—she has her coat on, a complete professional outfit on. She has her badge and her purse with a wallet inside to buy coffee if she wants it.* She looked at me and could see that I wasn't okay. She asked me what was wrong, and I shared with her all that had taken place so far that morning.

With such warmth and compassion she said, "Oh, Judy! I'm so sorry for the morning you've had. It's going to be okay though. What do you need? How can I help you?"

I was so thankful she asked! I responded, "I really need a blazer or sweater or something to cover my shoulders," and just as I started to say "I'm not sure where I'm going to get one of those from," she said, "I have an extra blazer in my car. It's black and goes with everything. I'll go grab it in a minute. What else do you need?"

I graciously said, "Nothing. Thank you. A blazer is more than enough."

She repeated, "Seriously, what else do you need? Are you hungry? Do you want a bagel or pastry from the shop across the street? How about a coffee?"

I melted into a puddle of gratitude, knowing that if she hadn't offered, I would've never asked on my own. As she went to get our breakfast from across the street, I sat at my computerless desk and looked at the blank paper in front of me.

At this point, it was T-minus two hours before the kickoff and I still had nothing to say. I even drafted a text to my cochair, asking her if she'd be okay doing the speech solo, without me. Just before I pressed Send, it hit me! This shitty morning had just given me everything I needed to say! A prepared speech was no longer necessary. It was an opportunity to speak from the heart, to share my truth, my experience, and the lessons I had learned along the way that morning—the lessons that maybe wouldn't have been so poignant without the exact circumstances I found myself in.

During the kickoff rally, I stood before the audience, wearing a borrowed jacket that didn't quite fit, and shared my story of being locked out of my car and relying on the kindness of others. I spoke authentically, passionately, and vulnerably. I emphasized the importance of love, compassion, and generosity. The response from the audience was overwhelming. People approached me after the rally, praising the impact of my speech and admiring my resilience.

> " The true breakthrough was how the shitty start to my day shifted my perspective on challenges, the significance of human connection, and the power of asking for help from both our fellow humans and from God/angels. "

While the recognition meant a lot to me at the time, the true breakthrough was how the shitty start to my day shifted my perspective on challenges, the significance of human connection, and the power of asking for help from both our fellow humans and from God/angels. I also learned about the power of authentic storytelling, the impact our personal stories can have on others, and the importance of connecting with people on a deeper level. Since then I have continued to strive to speak from the heart and share my experiences, knowing that it can inspire, uplift, comfort, or validate those around me.

I do not believe all challenging situations are meant to teach us something, but I know that for me, this particular experience was divinely orchestrated to teach me valuable lessons that I carry with me to this day—to ask for help, find strength in vulnerability, practice gratitude, and trust in the unpredictable ways that our greatest breakthroughs can occur.

> " One of the most profound aspects of my healing journey has been facing my fears head on and learning to coexist with them. "

One of the most profound aspects of my healing journey has been facing my fears head on and learning to coexist with them. I am still a work in progress, but I have come a long way from where I once was. I now acknowledge my fears and validate them, but I also remind myself of the truth—I am loved, I am supported, and everything will be okay no matter the outcome. I am grateful for these unexpected opportunities to learn, grow, and heal, even if they are not the ones I would have chosen for myself. These divine interventions, appointments, and answered prayers have pushed me out of my comfort zone and provided me with the support and opportunity I needed to shed what no longer served me and become who I truly am. I have come to realize that the process of learning, growing, and becoming is never ending and constantly shifting. The more I learn, the more I understand how much I don't know. Rather than fearing the process, I try to embrace it and eagerly anticipate what lies ahead. And when fear creeps in, as it inevitably does, I try to welcome it and embrace it as part of the journey.

Trusting the Process

The phrase "trust the process" has been a constant presence in my life, evoking both love and frustration. It's easy to trust the process when life is smooth sailing and happiness seems guaranteed. But life doesn't always work that way. There are times when trusting the process requires long-term commitment and facing tragic circum-

stances beyond our control. It's about believing that there is a higher power, whether it's God, the universe, or something else, that is on our side and working for our good. It's about having faith that no matter what happens, things will be okay and that every experience will ultimately be used for goodness and love.

The greatest lesson I've learned about trusting the process comes from the season I'm currently in. It began seven years ago, during what I consider the darkest and most painful time of my life—betrayal and deception within my marriage. It shattered me, leaving me on my knees and crying out to God yet again. At that time, my family was just becoming complete with the birth of our fourth child. My health was thriving, and my connection with God was strong. But in my marriage, despite my husband's reassurances, I sensed something was off. I could feel the distance between us growing.

One sunny day in August, as I drove home alone in my car, I looked up at the sky and said to God, "I'm ready. When you're ready to reveal the truth to me, I'm ready to receive it. I know you are with me, Lord, and I know that I can manage whatever comes my way as long as you're with me." Little did I know that God would answer my prayer exactly as I had asked. I didn't have to search or beg for answers like I had in the past.

God was with me every step of the way. God was there when I asked for clarity and truth, and God was there when I received the devastating news. He stood beside me as I fell to my knees in my room, sobbing uncontrollably. In that moment, despite the pain, I felt an overwhelming sense of peace. I knew deep within me that this revelation was divine. As I continued to learn more about the betrayals and lies, something wildly unexpected happened. I had discovered a newfound access to the *real* him, stripped of the facade of perfection he had always maintained. I was so hungry to know all about my husband, and now that I was finally learning that he wasn't perfect and he was flawed too (just like me!), I was feeling a sense of relief and encouragement. This was the first instance of intimacy that I was experiencing with him. I had prayed for intimacy with my husband for years leading up to this point, and like all that came before, I could have never predicted how wildly God would answer this prayer. Now, please know that there was no "Kumbaya" sing-along around a fire with hugs and kisses and pillow talk. There was none of that. I was pissed off beyond belief. I was reeling in pain and plagued with the feeling that I can describe best as anguish. There were lots of tears, lots of cuss words, and more pain than the human heart should ever endure. I had experienced a lot of gaslighting and manipulation over the years (unbeknownst to me up until then), which I was left having to sort and grieve through. To this day I still find myself struggling at times. I still grieve. I still struggle to trust myself and others. I am a work in progress, and I will continue to trust the process of knowing that I am being stretched, enlightened, or refined with each experience that comes my way.

The rock-bottom place I found myself in as a result of betrayal led me to the painfully hard work of confronting my own shadows, as well as working to reach a place of accepting, forgiving, and loving myself fully. When I first met with my counselor, she told me that the recovery process from betrayal trauma would take three to five years.

I was shocked and resistant to the idea. The pain and un-answered questions seemed too overwhelming to endure for such a long time. I had a family to take care of and a life to get on with. There was no way I could wait three to five years to get on with my life and away from the pain I was feeling. But she told me to trust the process and to start learning how to be okay with not being okay. At the time, I wanted to scream at her, but now I understand the wisdom in her words. For years, so much of my life was about searching for solutions to, or ways to escape from, my problems. Today I know the life changing magic that occurs when we go through the trials in our life, rather than running away from them. My greatest healing was found in learning to love myself fully, finding comfort and safety from within and establishing healthy boundaries in all areas of my life. I'm at the seven-year mark, and I'm still in the process of mastering and consistently implement-ing these concepts. Healing, for me, has been a continuous process of three steps forward, four steps back. It's been long and exhausting. It has also required more courage than I ever thought would be necessary. But this journey I'm on has been worth all the fears, sadness, painful truths revealed, and setbacks experienced. I do believe, just like all the times before, that without the betrayal, the deep-est darkest pain I've ever experienced to date, I would not have made it to a place such as this, where I'm committed to heal, learn, and grow at such a profound level.

" My life's greatest "trust the process" fruit to date has been the realization of my deepest pain becoming my greatest passion. "

My life's greatest "trust the process" fruit to date has been the realization of my deepest pain becoming my greatest passion. Had I thrown up my hands in frustration and walked out the door of my counselor's office that day, I may have never realized the purpose and fulfillment I now feel today as I coach other women who have experienced betrayal trauma. Just like my best friend and the guides who helped and encouraged me along the way in the jungle of the Dominican Republic that day, I, too, am there to encourage and cheer on my client to take the next step in the direction that leads her closer to her values and to her true self. Always reminding her of her strength, her worth, and the courage that she has within to keep going. Do I have a handbook or magic formula that spells out how to navigate the tumultuous waters of betrayal trauma? Absolutely not. Everyone's journey is different, and there is nothing about healing that is linear. Even though there is not a one-size-fits-all approach, there is one thing that applies to the masses—the goal of reaching a place where she has hope for her future, unconditional love for herself, and safety found within.

Trust me, when I was a little girl completing my "when I grow up, I want to be" assignment, the words betrayal trauma coach did not show up. What did show up though, (after dolphin trainer lol) was a teacher or guidance counselor. Now, I may not be working at a school with students as either of those professions, but in so many ways I have become a person who does just that. I educate, guide, and encourage others daily, especially my clients, on betrayal trauma and all that it entails. Watching women's light bulb moments happen before my eyes as I explain to them the science and research behind all that they are experiencing is indescribable. It is like giving them the lyrics to the song they have been humming for so long, and now they can finally sing it out loud at the top of their lungs from the tallest of rooftops. That confidence and new-found trust in themselves and what they know makes way for groundbreaking realizations that fuel positive change and a deeper connection with others and most important-ly themselves. What a privilege it is to do what I do!

At a very young age I knew innately what spoke to me and what I wanted to do in my life, and while it looks a little (a lot) different from what my elementary-aged self was thinking, it has indeed come into fruition. This thirty-year process of unbecoming, learning, growing, surrendering, shifting, and embracing the unexpected has paved the way to my coming into a profession that compassionately teaches and guides others in the most fulfilling way. Friend, when things are bad and the world is crashing around you, trust the divine process and move through the rubble knowing that God is with you and directing your steps on a pre-determined path that is leading you to something greater than you could have ever imagined.

I have come to understand that our shadows are proof that light exists, and that without the bad we would not know to recognize the good we are experiencing. Looking back, I can see that the period between my illness and the discovery of the betrayal were the moments I needed to catch my breath and experience God's goodness. It was a time of peace, growth, and spiritual enlightenment. I'm so thankful for these serendipitous opportunities to learn, grow, and heal, especially the ones that I know I wouldn't have chosen to do or go through on my own. These experiences of divine interventions, appointments, and/or answer to prayers, where God gave me a strong push out of my comfort zone and provided me with the opportunity and support that I needed to trust and take part in the process of unbecoming all that I am not and shedding all that wasn't serving me.

If there is one thing I am certain of, it is that life will continue to throw curveballs our way, sometimes good, sometimes not. In fact, sometimes the hand we are dealt may be downright tragic. In those moments, days, or seasons of life, may we be brave enough to raise our proverbial glass and say:

> Here's to all the challenges that pave the way for transformation and to the fear of falling that magnifies the joy of soaring when you realize your feet are off the ground. When it all becomes overwhelming and answers seem out of reach, may you find peace in a mind that surrenders to changing its perspective, allowing the things you look at to change as well. And when the road ahead seems unpaved and rocky, remember to trust the process, knowing that there is light at the end of the tunnel and the destination you are heading toward is beyond anything you could have ever imagined.

I cannot close my chapter without first thanking Atousa for giving me the chance to contribute to this book and for the group of loving, caring, and beautiful authors I have come to know and love. I am so happy that I pushed through the doubt and uncertainty just a few weeks ago in order to see my chapter through to fruition.

About Judy Gray

Judy is an ICF professional coach member, certified professional coach, and APSATS certified partner coach. She is passionate about helping women and couples heal from sexual betrayal and the trauma it causes.

Judy has found strength and solace in her faith during her own personal journey of healing and transformation. She believes that there is purpose for the pain she's experienced and has dedicated her career to supporting others in their healing process. Judy offers supportive and compassionate coaching services that guide clients in rebuilding trust, establishing healthy boundaries, and finding a path to healing and growth that is centered around their own personal values and beliefs.

Judy lives in Southern Maryland with her four children and husband of fifteen years. Spending quality time with her family is where her greatest source of peace, joy, and gratitude is found.

You can reach Judy directly by emailing her at:

Judyg@gfycoaching.net

CREATED TO CREATE

By Lauren Dickinson

Can you see the light
Can you hear the sound
Can you feel this whole world turning around
~"Season in Hell," from the *Eddie and the Cruisers* album

John Cafferty and his repeating rift from Eddie and the Cruisers reverberated over and over in my ears as I stood in my kitchen mere weeks ago, grasping onto the edge of the kitchen counter. My body was equally struck and filled with a lightning bolt of light, love, and profound understanding of the meaning of life, the meaning of my life as I'd known it. Words that were spoken to me in a prophecy at the young age of twenty-one had just come full circle as I finally saw the culmination of its promise and ultimate purpose. To put this into words that can convey what otherwise would be considered a transcendental experience, I must start at the beginning.

"Lauren and her acid rain drawings." I chuckle, remembering what my friend said about my early colored-pencil drawings. It was my senior year in high school, and after all the electives and advanced courses I could take, I was left with a boredom that I felt deep within my soul. I wasn't consciously aware of the existential meaning this held—I just knew that nothing held excitement for me in school anymore, except for these art classes. My entire senior year was buried deeply in creativity.

This drawing was one I was obsessed with recreating over and over, using different colors—one of a road in the middle of darkness, winding slowly toward a doorway as the focal point that was shining a rainbow of colors, like the reflection point of a prism. Souls like water drops traversed the road toward the light, getting smaller as they reached the doorway. With each drawing, the road was different—it took a different path or the colors were brighter or the darkness was darker—but each held the same meaning of finding my own way through the darkness toward the light of infinity just beyond the darkness. Some drawings even had a beautiful mountain or meadow-scape through the doorway, somehow revealing to my soul a gentle promise of light and happiness after traveling the winding road, a welcome respite of following the path through the darkness, one faithful step after another.

The last drawing of this series stopped me in my tracks when I realized what it was conveying. It was a road again, high and teetering on stilts, again surrounded by darkness but leading to a doorway that was emanating more lilac and purple tones of promise and potential. In this drawing, out of nowhere, even in its creation from my hands, was a large gap in the road. Like a high bridge missing a section that gave any traveler a full stop. It couldn't be traversed. The other side of it continued on as normal to the doorway in the cosmic distance, yet it was otherwise unattainable. I stopped drawing these, as I was confused with what was coming out of me.

I was gaining skill with my drawings of all other sorts, from a John Travolta portrait to working on properly shading a still life of a pair of boots. Seeing my progress was one of the few things that kept me happy and content being in a school I was otherwise done with. My friends had turned their backs on me, I was fighting with my parents at home, and all I wanted to do was go away to college and leave this part of my life behind me. Would I be able to go to college? I had no idea what I wanted to study. I had excelled in English and the humanities, but what on earth would I do with a degree in either of those? All the career assessments I'd taken told me I would be good with working with my hands. Thinking back, I am reminded that my first panic attack came in the eighth grade when we had "career day" and I imploded on myself because I didn't know what I wanted to do with my life. I don't know where the pressure on myself came from, but I was stricken with a deep sense of an unknown purpose, one that I've carried into my adult life as I've searched for the meaning of this life with all it has presented to me.

One day in drawing class, a gentleman came to share information about his art school just across the pond of the Puget Sound and on the Olympic Peninsula of Washington state. I listened intently as this bubble of hope swelled in my heart. Art school? People could do this professionally? I made sure to grab a brochure and eagerly told my parents about it that night. I had previously had a pipe dream of going to Harvard, and this shift surprised even me. My existential boredom had made me into a bit of an escapist (and class skipper), and I'd lost my 4.0 status my sophomore year, and this only added to my self-defeating sense of angst toward not knowing what I wanted to do. I realize now that this was my soul's holistic way of setting me forward on a path of healing, service to humanity, and deep purpose and would eventually fulfill all my intellectual pursuits and interests. Yes, art school was for me, and I took to it like a duck to water.

Fast-forward one year, and I'm sitting in the guidance-counselor office at the art college I otherwise was thriving at. Five of the best teachers in the school had left, a dozen students had left, and I was stuck trying to decide my own fate. I didn't want to follow the crowd and leave, yet I knew I wasn't getting the artistic education my soul yearned for with subpar and uninvested substitute teachers. Being ever the diplomat, I decided to stay on one more year and signed the enrollment agreement that started the new term for me. I would see how it goes, I told myself. Looking back, had I left when my gut told me to, I wonder what my life and path would have looked like.

The first semester of this new term was dismal, and it became evident quickly that I regretted my decision. At the end of this first semester, I shared with the administration that I too was leaving and that I wanted to transfer to another school in Seattle. It wasn't until later in life that I'd found out that this was one of the best art schools in the nation, Cornish, in Seattle. All I knew at the time was that this would keep me on my path, and I jumped through all the hoops to get my portfolio ready for the big interview and artwork review.

"Well, you obviously have talent," my admissions portfolio reviewer said to me after looking carefully through my portfolio. I could hardly believe my own ears. "We would love to have you here." My heart dropped. My passion for art could continue. And after a year of being criticized for my creativity by one instructor in particular, I was shocked to hear someone appreciate or express that I had talent. I was on the right path!

After weeks of back and forth with the administration of the old school and that of the new school, a new reality had taken place—the old school would not release my transcripts nor transfer my financial aid until I paid them the balance from the "enrollment agreement" I had signed at the beginning of the term that put me on the hook financially for the second semester of the term I wasn't attending. My dream was stopped in its tracks. Had my family had the money to pay this, I wonder again what my life would have looked like. I was already riding my education on all the financial aid I could receive. It wasn't until later that I found out that this school also pocketed grant money and a Stafford loan for the semester I never attended, while reporting that I had received the payout myself. This one cold "business decision" made by the school would irrevocably destroy all my dreams of higher education with one fell swoop. Where was the heart, the compassion? I cried. It took me a long time for my soul to stop crying over this, and I did what any nineteen-year-old lost and scared young adult would do to survive in a

new environment in the middle of Capitol Hill, now with
rent and bills to pay—I got a job. And I haven't stopped
"working" since. My soul had bigger plans than the one I
buried in my heart, that I would find a way to get back to
school. I was a passionate student and just wanted to keep
learning everything I could about the world through my
love for creativity.

Fast-forward again another year and I was in Bellingham, Washington, and ecstatic that I'd gotten into the Fine
Art College at Western Washington University. I lived in
a studio right by the university, knowing in my heart I was
going to be there that autumn, back on my path again as
an artist. I just knew in my heart that a miracle would happen and the old school would change their mind, knowing that they did me wrong and that everything would be
aligned for me to start school again. I'd applied for other
financial aid and set the hope in my heart that my family
and father's business would have the means to help me do
this. I'd never been so certain in my life that this was my
path, and I would fight for it.

Autumn came and went, and my hopes were dashed,
being chipped away by the administration that refused to
budge. I needed a lawyer, but I didn't have the means to
hire one. I was lost in confusion, as I'd been so certain of
my purpose. I kept working and kept myself busy with
nurturing my newfound social-butterfly personality while
living in Bellingham in my early twenties. I kept it in my
heart that art school would once again be for me. I worked
hard and played hard and just kept my nose to the grind-
stone with a couple fast years passing.

One evening I was standing at the bussing station at

the restaurant where I worked, when a wave of lightheadedness hit me like a freight train. I woke up on the floor, with one of the servers putting a damp towel on my forehead. I was sobbing. I was cold. I had no idea what had just happened. "What, wha . . ." I stammered. "You passed out. Thankfully I was right here to catch you," said this angel of a server and coworker. I was confused, and I was breathing shallow and too quickly to be getting much oxygen, which only led to feeling more dizzy. Another coworker came and just helped me to breathe. I can't imagine what they were thinking. In retrospect, I'd been working two jobs and taking classes at the local community college to try to repeat my prerequisites so I could get back into the university, plus out late with friends when I could be. I was burning the candle at both ends, and my personal life was riddled with anxiety and this ominous and existential fear of the unknown and what I was doing with my life.

Within the next few days, it was clear something wasn't right. I nearly passed out a number of times more, except that I felt it coming, and though I didn't pass out, I was hyperventilating at the drop of a dime. One of these times landed me in the emergency room, to which the attending physician diagnosed me with generalized anxiety disorder, and I left with only more questions and a prescription for Xanax. I threw out the prescription after taking it only once, after it knocked me out a little too hard. All I knew was that I had to see my family, as they were concerned about me.

I left for Portland, and after almost a month of bloodwork and visits with our family naturopath, I had very few answers. I didn't know when I was going to go home, and the anxiety inside was growing every day that something bigger was coming that I couldn't put my finger on. In retrospect, my soul, as it had so many other times, knew why I had to be there and had orchestrated this invisible "illness" so I could be there with my mom and sixteen-year-old brother the night my father had a fatal heart attack. Had I not been there to give him CPR with my mom, it would just have been my high school brother home, the youngest of six, with everyone else out to college and their lives. I will never forget the terror in his eyes as he watched my mom and me, from the bedroom doorway, relentlessly giving my dad CPR until the medics showed up. Had he or my mom had to suffer this alone, I would have died even more than I did that night, when my heart shattered alongside those of my family's for having lost our rock and one of the dearest loves of my life.

The next few days were a blur. Weeks became months, and months became almost a full year that I lived in Portland to make sure my mom was okay. I got a job to pay her bills after my father's business collapsed, and just tried to stay busy. The rest of my siblings had also left their respective lives to be there as we hunkered together during one of the biggest tragedies of our lives. Eventually I would move back to Bellingham to try to live a life again, knowing that nothing was ever going to be the same.

The years rolled by, and I was autopilot with no sense of direction or feeling of purpose. My soul was giving me needed respite in this hibernation period, and my saving grace was soon realized as I found myself working in the wellness industry as a chiropractic assistant. Slowly my heart awakened to a dream again of going back to school, this time as a chiropractor. I didn't know this kind of doctor existed, and it seemed to fulfill all my intellectual ambitions I'd had in my youth. And go figure—it was working with my hands, like all the career assessments had told me I was designed for. My sense of destiny was slowly reawakened, and I applied for, and received, enthusiastic acceptance to Life West Chiropractic College in the San Francisco Bay area. I was beyond ecstatic. They would even give me credit for my prerequisites without the transcripts the art school wouldn't release.

Here was the moment of truth I'd been waiting for. I could start school, receive new financial aid, and transfer my credits, but not without one final, and denied, pleading request for the art school to have compassion and reverse their financial-aid scam that had kept me from getting the aid I needed to fund my dream. It was becoming clear I would need to earn the money myself. Had I had the money and full access to financial aid, I wonder what my life would have looked like. I kept working and working and working, all in wellness center administration, learning what I could about the business side of things and immersing myself in the healing industry.

Many of us know what life is like as a single person trying to support themselves and forge their way through life. I came to the gut-wrenching realization that higher education was financially out of my reach. I poked at the bear a few times to see what was possible, and each time was faced with having to pay back a loan I never received or hiring a lawyer to fight them, neither of which my single income could do on its own. I took my licks and continued forward, this time with a growing curiosity that perhaps my soul knew exactly what was going on in divine perfection.

When I let go of my death grip on art school, higher education, and the student I had dreamed of being, life took on a new sense of beauty. I had finally given in to the flow of life as much as my clever mind would allow, and I will forever be grateful for some of the best, and worst, times of my life that transpired when I let go of "the plan." I was led to visit beautiful places like Uluru, Australia; took a road trip through Oregon, California, the four-corners area of Colorado, Utah, New Mexico, and Arizona; and lived for five years in Sedona, Arizona, a place I truly still feel like is my soul's home, and another five in Dallas, Texas, chasing another pipe dream that didn't live up to its expectations.

I lived some of the periods with my family as we weaved in and out of our lives, some in partnership with someone I thought I would marry, and some on my own, all in attempts to figure this thing called *life* out. We lost my brother in Sedona, another family tragedy that would have reverberations in my still-broken heart for years to come. I worked, I hiked, and I obtained some certifications in a number of healing modalities to quench my thirst for education and to help others on their own healing paths. It hadn't fully dawned on me consciously that as wounded healers, we strive to give to others what we most need ourselves. Although I practiced here and there and always knew I wanted roots to have a full-time practice, my gypsy heart would keep this dream at bay as a far-off future, not yet tangible to my soul. Or, again, my soul was yet again in charge and guiding me, when my heart and mind were lost in the creation.

I was living in Dallas and working for an academy that taught a specific type of healing modality that I was also studying, as a work-trade opportunity that at the time sang to my heart. Here I could get the education I wanted and have the energy medicine modality I had been seeking to find for so many years. It became clear while studying bioenergetics that I was relieved to not have followed the chiropractic path, as I ultimately didn't agree with the inflammation process that a manual adjustment would produce in the body. I'd had some healing with chiropractic, but it was always with the energetic kind that concurrently worked with the soft tissue and energy body, like the Pettibon system, Network, and the Koren Specific Technique. Some days I still dream of incorporating aspects of these practices into my healing practice, but I know now that things will always come, and return, at just the right times and when they're needed.

"I know now that things will always come, and return, at just the right times and when they're needed."

One day I had a calling to create. I'd picked up the paintbrush a number of times over the years and could cognizably feel an insurmountable creative block that just wouldn't let me connect. I had kept my college toolboxes full of some empty and some full paint tubes, old brushes, and a few canvases, carrying them with me wherever I moved. Something in my soul just wouldn't let me throw them away. The joy I have now of seeing its higher plan is palpable as I see the thread of all the events of my life weaving a beautiful tapestry of life, experience, and adventures that has brought me to where I am now, which I have yet to share and will. In the meantime, this newest attempt to create would be the magic wand and proverbial brush stroke of luck I'd been waiting for. Had I not been healing my brain through the promise of energy medicine and holistic modalities, the day I picked up a palette knife and stretched an azure blue across an old canvas would have turned into nothing more than another futile attempt to reconnect with my inner wellspring of latent creativity.

What started with an azure background turned into layers of varying hues of blues, whites, and reds. I kept scraping the palette knife across the canvas in textured layers of vibrant color. How had I not known that you didn't have to use paintbrushes to create art? How had all my technical art training missed teaching this simple technique? I was hooked. No objective. No technical skills. Just pure, unabashed expression of color and abstracted emotions.

Night after night after work, I would create. And create. And create. I moved into an old Victorian house that gave me even more studio space in a second bedroom area. My soul rejoiced in its long-lost love for creating, color, and experimentation. I was fully immersed in the world of abstract art, and piece after piece was created as the joy flowed through my hands into whatever medium I was using, from texture to fluid and resin, to encaustic resin and wax. I would rise up early and create, go to work, and come home and create until late into the evening, night after night.

Eventually I was invited to art exhibitions and group shows in the Dallas Art Scene, and my life took on a whole new level of healing and creative abundance. I was healing all my heartache, loneliness, and the struggles of life from the inside out. It was a beautiful time in my life, one that also brought with it significant challenges from the business and rarely mentioned darker side of the art world, riddled with frauds, scams, and predatory practices by those looking to exploit the naivety of an artist's heart to just create and to be seen in the world. Some of my biggest life's challenges came from this time period, but also the most personal and professional artist growth I could ever have dreamed of. I left the healing world and spent the final three years of my Dallas life devoted to my art.

I have had the pleasure of sharing my art with international galleries and art fairs and have built a following of loyal collectors, whom I adore and am grateful for. I was commissioned for artwork for commercial clients and private collectors, and I have a portfolio of achievements I am proud of, including working with art associations as a board member to further the arts, a passion I continue to build. While I was nowhere near where my ambitious heart wanted to be as a professional artist, these early years of my art career were ones of a profound flourishing of my soul from the inside out.

In March of 2020 my soul once again took over, this time more adamantly and aggressively than it ever had. It was a time as if I had little to no conscious control of my life. COVID-19 had hit the world, and the announcement of the "fourteen days to stop the spread" global lockdown was about to start. Looking back at the collective fear of this time and the sheer uncertainty of the future of the world, I still feel the collective trauma that is still healing, as the insanity of this period will never be fully understood. For me, it meant packing up everything I could fit into my Subaru Forester, including my two cats and only the most essential personal items, and driving a white-knuckled twenty-eight hours to be with my family in Mount Shasta, in far northern California. When things get rough, we hunker together and always find a way to be there for one another. From my father's death and driving hours to each of my siblings' college life to share the tragic news, to being in Sedona together when my brother died and driving to Albuquerque, where my mom was visiting, to share the news in person, and now to coming together again with the global tragedies the world was facing, we are joined on a karmic soul level to do and be in this life together, with and for one another.

When I drove past the Mount Shasta City exit on Interstate 5, surrounded by beautiful snowfall and a crisp clarity to the air, I shed tears of relief that I could be with my family in the middle of this fear state the world had been involuntarily plunged into. When I arrived at my mom's house and my feet hit the pavement below me, I rushed to her with tears in my eyes that I'd made it . . . home. Home, again, was where my family was. My soul released all the stress of the years in Dallas and assured me it had a plan.

Over the next few months, I would eventually learn of my Dallas landlord selling her home and needing me to get the rest of my belongings, and with the world still on lockdown, I had no choice but to oblige. I stayed put in Mount Shasta while making arrangements to get my most important personal belongings and let her garage sale away the rest along with her things, in her own transition to a new place. It wasn't a decision I would have made on my own—the phrase "God does for you what you cannot do for yourself" is one that comes to mind when I recall this time. I surrendered to the higher power at work and did everything I could to make a home for myself in this cozy corner of northern California.

I did what I knew how to do best—work—and took the only job available during this shelter-in-place time, in the vacation rental business. I started earning money quickly, and eventually would get into my own place again after only a year of having to live with my mom and family. I stumbled into digital marketing with a dear soul I met here, who had come to this area only the year before, also from Dallas. My life blossomed again as I got my feet underneath me, continued making art, and grew accustomed to my new life in the beautifully picturesque city of Mount Shasta.

It's been four years to the day of this writing, and I'm grateful for the struggles and growth I've found in this sleepy small town. A seed I had planted in my heart for doing destination energy healing and somatic bodywork events in 2015 was awakened in this spiritual community. My interest and practice of nearly twenty years in the healing arts was now fueled again after learning about shamanism and the power of spending time in this sacred land. One single period of falling prey to the profound spiritual narcissism from a couple I was working with at a retreat center here spurred me on to actualize my vision of hosting healing retreats, which has grown exponentially in the three years since. There will always be a part of my soul that will turn tragedy into triumph and to take everything I've been given and transmute it for the utmost growth of my soul and those I have forever striven to help in my healing work, a deep sense of purpose of which has never left me. For all the times I doubted my purpose, knowing that I am here to help others has never left my awareness nor my ambition.

"Together my heart and soul cocreate a reality that is guided by the consciousness and divinity of the creator itself."

The healer and creator in me now knows that creativity and the connection to the divine is what heals us. Whether you want to call it the divine, God, Universal Source, or Creator, it is the God spark within each of us that is both the healer and the healed, the consciousness of the conscious, and the dreamer of the dream. The healer in me now knows it is a creator. The creator in me now knows it is a healer. Together my heart and soul cocreate a reality that is guided by the consciousness and divinity of the creator itself, because we are creators, made in the image and likeness of the creator, the created, and the creation. When we gain access to the higher states of consciousness that come from having profound access to our creativity, mountains will move and life will deepen in all its complexity and beauty, and the promise of human potential can be discovered in our very own lives.

The brain is a reality simulation vehicle that we can have conscious control over, instead of the other way around. When we're operating from our neocortex and human brain—the part of our brains that we have ever greater access to through the power of creativity—and get out of the reptilian brain and the ever-pervasive fight-or-flight response that keeps us locked in our left brain, we can access the latent gifts we are born with as creators. We can tap into the joy of existence, the healing of our hearts, minds, and bodies, as we're no longer living out of reaction but living into one of cocreation with the Divine, which is ultimately ourselves. If we have the courage to awaken to our divinity and ignite the God spark and the vastness of the universe inside ourselves, what kind of a new earth can we create together? What kind of a new earth can we create for our own lives and start living into the promised golden age of our civilization?

"We can be guided by faith alone and the conviction that life will once again resume on the other side of fear."

This isn't a far-off place in the future—it is the Shambala, the Eden, the Shangri-La that exists in our own hearts that we can live from and birth through our own lives. It has never existed outside ourselves, because it *is* us. It is the state of consciousness within us that we can choose at any moment once we get a taste of it and follow the road back home through our own hearts. Even if we must float blindly over any missing gaps in the road, we can be guided by faith alone and the conviction that life will once again resume on the other side of fear as we make our way out of the darkness and into the door of light that has been leading us home for time immemorial.

For as Sir Edmund Hillary so profoundly spoke, "It is not the mountain we conquer, but ourselves."[1]

What will we dream of next?

1 https://www.acethehimalaya.com/inspirational-quotes-sir-edmund-hillary/.

About Lauren Dickinson

Lauren is the visionary founder and CEO of Orion Retreats, a pioneering company in the conscious travel and transformational retreat industry. With over two decades of experience in the healing arts, Lauren has cultivated a deep understanding of alternative modalities for achieving holistic balance and wellness.

As an award-winning international contemporary multimedia artist, Lauren brings a unique creative perspective to her work in the wellness and retreat space. Her artwork has been showcased during Art Basel week in Miami and in numerous domestic and international exhibitions, attracting a global collector base.

With a firm belief in the power of creativity and conscious travel to transform lives and communities, Lauren is committed to creating containers for others to activate their brilliance and see their own divinity within. Through Orion Retreats, she continues to inspire and guide others on their journey towards wellness, creativity, and personal growth.

Where to find Lauren:
www.soulscapeart.com
www.orionretreats.com
Instagram: @laurendickinsonart and @orionretreats

MY MAGICKAL HEALING JOURNEY

by Lyra Silverstein

I have given up linear
time and linear distance.
We strain our eyes trying
to see in a straight line when the
world is all around. We strain our
minds trying to create linear history
out of time.
~Dr. Barbara Benary

A s I write this, planets are in motion. The energies of those who were, are, and will be all present. While we are in this immediate corporeal form, many of us are aware of only our current vessel—our bodies, minds, and spirits in this so-called container. When we dream, perhaps we see glimpses into previous lives or others intertwined with our own. Perhaps we see beings that are not human, such as faeries or aliens. Is dreaming, astral traveling, or remote viewing any less a valid form of energy exchange with other beings—human or nonhuman?

Of course not. The difference is that when we are in this state of consciousness, we are seeing things a bit differently. We are letting go of preconceived notions and programming from our conscious awakened state, allowing this energy exchange to happen freely, without exerting any kind of control.

There are some people, such as I, who have seen some nonhuman beings in a state of conscious awareness. As we grow older, it does become more challenging to see the Unseen—the realm inhabited by these beings. The realm of the Unseen is also the realm of the Divine— where Magick[2] and nature are intertwined and there are no limits to what we can glean from the insights offered by these beings. When we are connected, we are in tune with our deepest senses (beyond what we recognize as our five senses of sight, smell, sound, taste, and touch) and more able to receive meaningful messages (or "downloads"). Over time, our ability to connect to this realm can become diminished by all the programming, responsibilities, and distractions of adulthood that are pushed onto us through societal constructs and institutions. So how do we go back to a time when our minds were less programmed by these perceived structures or notions? How do we get back to that level of consciousness that allows us to be more open to these multidimensional senses that go beyond our perceived five? How can we get back that feeling of ease in connecting with this realm while opening to our own authenticity, embracing both the shadowy and light parts of ourselves?

---

2 *Magick* spelled with a *k* to differentiate from stage magic.

" By connecting with myself in a heart-centered space, I was able to build a better relationship with my authentic self. "

By connecting with myself in a heart-centered space, I was able to build a better relationship with my authentic self. I was able to connect mind, body, and spirit in ways that felt profoundly healing. It is an ongoing practice, and anyone can benefit from doing so. By learning to connect with your Higher Self in this way, you are already shifting your energy field and opening up more possibilities. Opening your heart and separating the ego in the form of self-judgment and low self-esteem is the beginning of shifting your consciousness, allowing yourself to simply *be* while learning to trust your intuition and your inner knowing. Through releasing the obstacles and working through traumas, you can allow space for a free flow of integration—the higher-consciousness part of yourself with the grounded, rooted, shadowy parts. Like a tree, the branches and roots mirror the patterns and connect through the trunk. The tree is a symbol for the process of connecting these parts in the Divine vessel that is you. The beauty of living in this space is that you become more open to receiving the gifts of Magick—interaction/communication with other Divine beings: spirits, deities, fae, or whatever form you perceive in this state of consciousness.

Although I have had many visions and what some might call "supernatural" experiences throughout my life, there was a piece that was missing. My internal narrative was telling me that yes, these beings are real in my version of reality. Yet somehow, I always felt different from everyone else because my child self always accepted this, but my adult self was taught to internalize and not be so open about my experiences. Why? Fear. Fear of judgment. Fear of being ostracized or rejected because I am a weirdo who believes in these beings. A part of me was holding on to memories of being bullied as a child for being "different." I was raised by musician parents whose lifestyles did not necessarily fit into the neat packaging of the somewhat conservative structure of the public school system and the families that already had relationships within that system. Part of the process of my healing journey was learning to shift my narrative by letting go of the inner voice that told me "I'm not good enough," or "I am not attractive," or "Compare yourself to others in their achievements." It is quite common for many of us to have that ugly internal dialogue that kind of punches us in the gut. As my partner, Miguel, puts it, if this voice was someone external, would you want to be friends with it? Would you want to hang out with it? If the answer is no, then it needs to be evicted immediately. (Picture someone who crashes your party and proceeds to get into disputes with your other guests. Pretty annoying, right?) And of course, that process is not always easy. It takes some time to let go. A lot of it stems from fear.

Fear is the catalyst that drives many of our decisions, including our inner dialogue. Many of us live with it in our daily lives, although we may not realize it. We hold on to it in many ways, including how we interact with others and how we treat ourselves. We bury fears and traumas by storing them in our bodies. It is not something we are necessarily aware of. It just happens. For myself, I did not realize just how much I was holding on to within my body. The fear and grief that I was unconsciously storing in my body translated into some health issues that I needed to address. But when I only focused on the physiological symptoms, it was not enough—I needed to go much deeper. Deep into my consciousness to holistically address the fear and grief to release those traumas and connect to my authentic self. It was only then that I was able to witness the power of Being in this state. When I was able to let go of fear and learn to trust in myself, that is when the Magick truly began.

There is an existing pattern I had only realized within the past few years—I was searching for this Magick externally. I was not turning inward and integrating or releasing the parts of myself that needed to be healed. Even though I had done some personal ritual work around this, there were much deeper layers of release that needed to happen. Thanks to my colleague and dear friend Sara Cronan, whose story is also shared in this book, I was able to connect with Atousa Raissyan during early 2023 and begin this type of healing work. After doing transformational trauma-healing shamanic sessions with Atousa, I have experienced a sense of wholeness and well-being that I did not think would be possible.

You are probably wondering what a transformational trauma-healing shamanic session might be. When I first started with Atousa, I was not sure what to expect. What I received was a wealth of empowering tools to help me manage certain thought patterns and ideas that were no longer serving me. I was able to peel back layers and get to a better place of trust in myself and my intuition. The work will be different for each person, since everyone is different. For some people it could mean healing generational-trauma wounds or reconciling and forgiving past versions of themselves.

In my sessions with Atousa, I realized that there were emotional and spiritual aspects to my wellness that needed to be addressed. I was able to connect with past versions of myself and heal some of the trauma wounds I was carrying. Experiencing these sessions has provided me with tools that will guide me through the rest of this lifetime and beyond. While I am no stranger to meditation practices, this was a bit different. This helped me dive deeper internally and face the wounds and traumas that I didn't realize were buried inside me the whole time. Some of these were not even mine to carry. In these sessions I was allowing the internal voices of myself that had been silent or repressed to speak up. If they needed comfort, I comforted them. If they wanted to leave, I let them go. If there were emotions or even feelings of physical wounds that I carried that were not mine to carry, I learned to release.

Part of the integration work is going deep within and finding these fragments of myself that were each a layer of identity—like an avatar or version of myself. There are also energetic layers I needed to experience to understand how they play a part in my wholeness. The fragments and layers needed to be dissolved or released or unified into my whole self. I was guided through these layers, and a sacred healing process of integration took place. There were some other meaningful integration and intense experiences I have had through other various guided meditation events. I want to share these moments with you because they were important steps in my integration of shadow and light, connecting to my Higher Self and the Divine. Before going into the stories of these meditative experiences, there are a few things I want to share about my healing journey. If I can help even one person by sharing my story, it will be worth it for me.

The story begins with my mother being diagnosed with Parkinson's. At the time, I was working for a corporate company in the fashion industry, doing web photo retouching. While I got along well with my colleagues, the corporate environment was stressful and not fulfilling—in fact, it was a soul-sucking environment. During this time, my body was trying to communicate with me. Literal physical symptoms showed me the impact of holding on to trauma. It was the beginning. There were no windows in our workspace and therefore no way to see the outdoors unless we took a break to go outside. The stale corporate environment and built-up trauma from bad relationships affected my body drastically. My gallbladder decided to stop functioning and was removed in 2015. The following year I met my partner.

By this time my mother's Parkinson's was getting to be more of an issue. She was a musician and always so independent that she insisted on driving herself to and from evening rehearsals in the city, which resulted in her having a car accident in 2017. This accident caused major spinal injuries on top of her existing osteoporosis. This event fast-forwarded her decline over the next two years. Between multiple spinal surgeries and recovering at more than one rehabilitation facility, she ultimately ended up at home in hospice care.

Witnessing my mother's decline and ultimate passing was like witnessing two deaths, one a slow version and then the aftermath of the final one. Existing in this world without her on the physical plane was and still is filled with an incredible amount of grief. I was carrying that grief not only for myself but also for my father. Witnessing his grief amplified my own. We shared that together, and I recognized that he was also carrying some of mine. Though I was not aware of how much fear I carried in my own body regarding what she went through, I could feel the heaviness in my navel area (sacral chakra region). At the time, I did not realize there was such a literal physical aspect to carrying trauma. Though I had experienced strong reactions in my body to stress in the past, this was different. This was a trauma like no other I had ever experienced. There was a soul weariness I could feel, as though I was looking at the world through the opposite of rose-colored glasses. Dull, depressing gray-colored glasses, you might say.

While processing my grief, I found myself being called in a new life direction. When my mom was still living in the house, she had been taking pain medication for her spine. The side effects were terrible. Some caused nausea and an upset stomach. The painkiller also made her unsteady on her feet and caused her to fall a couple of times. I researched herbal medicine and what alternatives there were aside from pharmaceuticals. While she was hesitant to trust in the alternatives, I felt it important to explore such options. It was like an awakening taking place, a calling too strong to be ignored.

The point arrived where my work needed to be fundamentally different from the career paths I had previously

taken. There was a deep urge inside for my path to become one that would give me a sense of fulfillment and purpose. I felt this deep desire to study herbalism and plant medicine. Especially after witnessing everything my mother had been through with her medical procedures and adverse effects of pharmaceuticals. My initial studies led to experimenting with homemade aromatherapy products as a creative outlet. It was a way I could process my grief over my mother's illness by working with my hands. Formulating was and still is a form of Magick to me. It is like how I feel when cooking. Gathering ingredients and creating something that offers comfort, satisfaction, joy, and/or beauty brings happiness to my soul and a way of connecting with my ancestors. For example, I can recall a specific moment in the kitchen where I got this ancestral whisper in my head, instructing me in a method of separating a clove of garlic from the bulb. I call it *ancestral* because it sounded like a grandmother/crone voice: "This is how it is done, dearie." It felt very much like the voice of a great-grandmother or perhaps even a great-great-grandmother.

Feeling this connection to my ancestors and to nature was something I always associated with my mother. She was always the glue in our family—the one who made sure to stay in touch with relatives. My adventures with her as a child heightened my love and appreciation for the earth. Answering the call of herbalism felt like a natural direction, as I had always felt this deep connection to nature, growing up where I did—near Harriman State Park in New York. From very early on, my mother would take me hiking and boating near the lakes there. She would talk about the native plants and trees. We would hang out by the dam and watch the little fish swim in the lake. I inherited her love of nature and plants. These adventures of ours also shaped some of my spirituality that developed in my teens, reading books on nature-based religions such as Wicca and books with spells and recipes. Reading these books and having wonderful moments in the natural landscape inspired some of my early experimentation with making herbal preparations.

During the time my mother was sick, I was formulating various products as a hobby that eventually turned into a small business. Spiral Moon Herbcraft was conceived in 2017 and became official in 2018. The year 2019 brought some of the lowest and highest points of my life so far. That year felt truly transformational as far as the path my life journey took me. It was filled with traumas, including an ankle injury, my own car accident (I was okay, but my car was rear-ended and totaled), and finally my mom passed away on my forty-second birthday. It was almost as if she waited until that very day to leave her physical shell. These events impacted me emotionally to the point where my life felt like it was in an upheaval. The tremendous amount of grief combined with the other incidents truly propelled me toward a calling that only my soul could hear at the time. It felt like a catalyst that pushed me further to my life path and hearing the voice of my Higher Self. It was the call to study herbalism. To connect more deeply with nature. To become a healer.

I was actively studying herbalism during this time and began working at a local botanical shop. Lata Kennedy, owner of Flower Power Herbs & Roots, hired me to be a part of the shop in Piermont, New York, and put her faith in me and my products. I am ever so grateful for that experience. Being in that beautiful space, surrounded by jars of many different herbs and spices, talking with people, sharing stories, and having some of the most intimate conversations was truly heart opening. I developed some wonderful friendships and connected with an amazing community of like-minded people who deeply love to work with plants.

Through Lata I learned about the Wise Woman tradition, a form of herbalism taught by her mentor Susun Weed. She takes a primal and spiritual approach to studying plants. This tradition is explained so beautifully in Susun's book *Healing Wise*. What I love about it is that it is centered on nourishing the wholeness of each person—there is no "curing" or "fixing." Each person is ever evolving and yet complete. As problems or symptoms arise, we can see them as gateways of transformation.

The symbol for the Wise Woman tradition is a spiral. According to Susun, "A spiral is a cycle as it moves through time. A spiral is movement around and beyond a circle, always returning to itself, but never at exactly the same place. Spirals never repeat themselves. Spirals remind us that life is movement, that each moment is unique, and that form is the essence of transformation."[3] The shape of a spiral is something I have always felt drawn to. Examples of some highly impactful spiral symbols include early cave pictograms, the mathematical Fibonacci sequence, and nature's gifts from nautilus shells to galaxies. One of the

---

3 Susun Weed, *Healing Wise* (Woodstock, NY: Ash Tree Publishing), 11.

oldest symbols containing spirals is the Triskelion, or triple spiral. The earliest pictograms of the triskele can be found in Malta and Newgrange in Ireland.[4]

The spiral has always stood out for me as an intensely Magickal symbol. It shows the interconnection between birth, life, and death and shows how our outer (ego) consciousness ties into our inner (soul) consciousness. The movement of the spiral shows how we shift in our consciousness as we grow, transform, and evolve. In fact, it was the shape of a spiral on a piece of jewelry gifted to me by none other than Sara Cronan that inspired my logo design and the name for my business.

One of the many blessings I found in being part of the local community of Flower Power Herbs & Roots is that I was able to meet some local foragers, including Paul Tappendan, who was a dear friend of Lata's. Before he passed away in October of 2021, Paul taught several workshops in Piermont at the shop and led some plant walks. I admired his dedication in educating the local community on the benefits of foraging. He identified and discussed local plants, sharing their medicinal properties and how they can be prepared in food and medicine. He taught me that it is possible to make a coffee substitute out of dandelion roots. I learned the immense value of the prolific plant *Artemisia vulgaris* (common mugwort), which is quite potent medicinally and magickly. It grows in big patches with deep-green leaves that have a silvery underside, reminiscent of the moon. Paul discussed how mugwort can be utilized in a variety of medicinal preparations, such as a tea to encourage sleep, a bath or infused oil to address

4 Wikipedia.

leg cramps, a ball of rolled dried leaves for campfire kindling or to smoke as a relaxing tobacco alternative, among others. Paul has an excellent book on foraging plants in Nyack, New York, called *The Edible Plants of Nyack*, with a primary focus on edible recipes.

> " If we move with the rhythms and cycles of nature instead of fighting them, there is a beautiful synergy that happens. "

The plant walks that Paul facilitated stirred up my curiosity and wonder at the innate intelligence of nature and how we can easily find medicine growing in our own backyards. And oftentimes what is available is precisely what we need. For example, in springtime there are purple dead nettle plants that pop up all over our yard. They are amazing for addressing some common upper respiratory symptoms that occur during that time of year, such as hay fever. One of the things I find so marvelous is that the plants grow and shift and change throughout the seasons, much in accordance with how we do. If we observe nature carefully, we will see that we are a reflection; we are part of nature. If we move with the rhythms and cycles of nature instead of fighting them, there is a beautiful synergy that happens.

During my plant studies, I quickly reached a point where I was interested in shifting further away from pharmaceuticals. Toward the end of 2020 I did some research regarding birth control pills and how they affect the liver. Because I'd had my gallbladder removed, I wanted to find more ways that I could support the work that my liver was doing. I went off the pill and consulted with a clinical herbalist. With her guidance I was able to gradually regulate my cycle without taking synthetic hormones. I built a wonderful relationship with plant allies and learned how amazingly effective they were. In addition to regulating my cycle and addressing dysmenorrhea with the clinical herbalist, I was also able to shrink a benign cyst in my breast through an herbal protocol by Lata that involved taking tea, tincture, and using a topical cream. Experiencing these physiological healing shifts was a profound confirmation that I was on the right path.

There are other forms of plant medicine that go beyond physiology. There are flower essences—a beautiful form of plant medicine that allows you to work with the divine energies of each plant. These essences address emotional, mental, and some physical healing, as well as soul development. Much of the power of these essences lies in how they are prepared. There is a clear energetic imprint on each one. I studied and worked with them, and they helped me to face some specific moments of fear, self-doubt, insecurity, and body dysmorphia.

Studying herbalism and incorporating preparations as a lifestyle go hand in hand. I take various tinctures and herbal teas or infusions to address specific symptoms as they arise. And I take others regularly to support certain organ systems, such as my digestion and my immune system. Working with plants in various ways, including tinctures, teas, and flower essences has demonstrated the healing powers they hold in ways I had not imagined would be possible.

Working with the plants during my personal health consultations made me realize that I wanted to further my studies and training. From 2021 to 2022, I took an intensive online training course taught by Sajah Popham, founder of the School of Evolutionary Herbalism. Through Sajah I learned the vitalist approach of herbalism, which takes the whole person and the whole plant into consideration in a holistic manner. My coursework in Sajah's program helped me to better understand the various body systems and how the actions and energetics of the plants affect physiology. This felt important, as I was working at Flower Power Herbs & Roots so that I could feel more confident in my ability to serve the local community. From the beginning I could tell that Sajah was someone I could trust in the way he communicated his passion for teaching and his love of the plants themselves. This made the coursework much more effective for me as a student. I found his videos and writings helpful as my studies progressed.

Speaking of nature and plant medicine, I want to come back to discussing my guided meditation experience. These meditations allowed me to connect with plant spirits as well as my guides. In a plant-spirit meditation workshop led by the angelic voice of Kendra Valentine, I gained a sense of what "the other side" looks like. It was the closest experience I have ever had to seeing that we are all connected to this Source (Divine/God/Goddess) energy. It made me less afraid of death and dying. At the time, I chose to work with microdosing a mushroom gummy (psilocybin) as well as ingesting a beautiful chocolate truffle infused with a myriad of plants. The plants in the truffle are typically not ingested, but the chocolatier is masterful at infusing these plants in a way that they are diluted to a subtle and safe. Examples would be belladonna and mandrake. The ingestion of these microdose amounts of entheogenic treats were part of what contributed to my overall experience. However, I want to be very clear that the most powerful channel of all was the voice of Kendra herself. Her low, soft speaking voice, rhythmic drumming, and singing would likely have been enough on its own. My choice of plant spirits to work with only amplified what I experienced. They served to assist in breaking down any barriers that separated my consciousness from connecting to Source.

I first paid attention to the colors inside my eyelids, as this is often the way I begin meditations. The colors I see, and the rhythm of my breathing are the two focal points that allow me to shut out the noise and clutter in my headspace. The colors started as a deep indigo to violet to purple (a color that often shows up for me in meditation in connection with the Divine). The color started to take shape. It became yoni (vulva) shaped. I entered a womb space surrounded by a warm pink energy that felt like a comforting hug, like being inside the womb. I moved from that space into what I can only describe as beyond astral. It felt like an ascension. Colors gave way to a divine being somewhere between an almond and humanoid shape that emitted white light with fractal prismatic rainbow holographic diamonds glittering all around it. At this point Kendra mentioned the plant spirit and the Being before me morphed into a tree shape—a white glowing tree with prismatic leaves. Then Kendra mentioned holding three seeds in your hand and planting what you want to manifest. The seeds from this tree were also white and prismatic. When I was dropping back into my body from the Divine realm, the colors reversed backward as I traveled back down into the womb space and then coiled back into the deep blue/indigo. The experience of this meditation was so profound because it showed me Divine love, Mother love, how love connects us, and how we are all the same energy, just in different forms. This experience helped me to shed some fears I held toward death and dying. It showed me what it feels and looks like to return to that form of pure energy and love.

Another profound breakthrough came during the experience of a wonderful cacao ceremony led by Masha Zolotarsky and Jeffery Tiger, where I met my spirit guides. Though I did not realize the significance at the beginning of the ceremony, I had picked two cards from different decks: the 3 of pentacles from the Wild Unknown tarot deck and the Village card (circular) from the Wild Unknown Archetypes oracle deck. Both decks are by Kim Krans. There was something important inside the imagery of both cards that I would not realize until after the cacao ceremony journey. The ceremony took place on April 7, 2023, and I had purposely chosen to participate to connect with my mother, since that would have been her seventy-seventh birthday.

I began the meditation with the intention to connect with her spirit on the other side. I visualized the fire in my heart as I felt the warmth of the cacao. The beauty of cacao as a plant medicine is that it is heart opening. In addition, there were other beautiful herbs infused in the blend. With eyes closed I journeyed across a field toward forests and mountains. My guide led me by the hand, and I traveled with her up into the mountains. We came to a bonfire. By the light of the fire, she looked like a combination of my mother and an indigenous woman, possibly Native American. She gave me the message that she and my mother were one and the same; she was her and she was also me—connected above, below, through, and tied into me. She, Her, We, Us: all the generations and ancestors combined. The Goddess: Maiden, Mother, and Crone. Everyone all at once like a matryoshka doll with all the layers melding into one. This was my trusted and secure source. This was my spirit guide. She made it known that I could choose to connect with her at any time. She also told me to allow my emotions to flow, not to repress any grief or sadness, and to allow me to be true to myself. She said that my mother (She) is proud of me. There was a mention of connecting with the elements, about making a deeper connection with each—particularly the air and fire for healing. At that moment it made sense because my mother's sun sign is an Aries. More pieces of wisdom flowed from this woman to me in this channel. She said that for personal healing to occur, I would need to trust in my intuition. The same thing for finding signs of her presence—trust my intuition. Follow what feels right in my heart as far as healing modalities.

The cacao ceremony allowed me to release some powerful emotions of grief and connect with that primal nurturing presence of my spirit guide that my soul needed to connect with. I only realized afterward that the two oracle cards I had pulled at the beginning of the ceremony both had mountains in the background. It was as though I was pulled right inside the cards in my journey to connect with my guides. They were like a portal or a gateway.

" Everything we go through is like a gift because it shapes us into who we are. "

All these spiritual experiences have led me to where I am now. They are like gifts. Even the ones that were not pleasant. Even the trauma. Everything we go through is like a gift because it shapes us into who we are. It shifts our perspective and really shows us how we are tested and ultimately how we evolve. How we become. The journey of healing doesn't have to have a clear end or beginning. It is trusting in ourselves, our inner knowing and the universe that allows the process to flow, allowing ourselves to choose the path that is right for us in our healing journey. It does not need to be defined or directed by anyone but us. We can choose with open minds and hearts. There is also an understanding and willingness to see that not all healing journeys are the same. When we see the Divine in ourselves mirrored in nature, we can start seeing the interconnected patterns. I love the example of how the bronchioles within our lungs resemble tree branches, or how the patterns on our fingerprints resemble the rings of trees. We can see this when we look at a piece of wood that has been cut through the center. We are intertwined. We are made of stardust. We are, in fact, cosmic.

One thing I am truly grateful for in terms of this work is how I feel like I am seeing the world from a shifted perspective. I'll go back to the example of looking through the opposite of rose-colored glasses, when I was feeling my lowest. Now I see through totally different lenses that are more clear, sharp, and beautiful than ever, like getting a brand-new pair of glasses that are the correct prescription, except these glasses are like third-eye lenses, which see beyond and through my literal eyes. All my experiences have led me to this point. My spiritual journey and healing journey are one and the same. It took me a while to realize this. I often thought of these things as separate. Earlier, when I was so focused on my physiological healing, there were points when I sought spiritual connection. Most major religions did not resonate for me. There was something about the structures or principles that felt the opposite of how I felt when I was outside in nature. Instead of feeling connected, I felt divided and rejected. By the time I was graduating high school, I was reading books on witchcraft and occult. Something became clear to me. There was a path for me where connecting to the Divine in nature was something to be accepted and encouraged. These truths weaved and spiraled together for me in a way that resonated deeply.

Exploring this interest in witchcraft and nature-based religion, I found a sense of community when I met other people who were equally interested in these aspects and wanted to form a coven back when I was an undergraduate at Bennington College in Bennington, Vermont. For those who are unfamiliar with the term "coven," it means a gathering of witches. While the term is typically applied to groups of witches who are practicing Wiccans—Wicca being a religion—one does not have to be Wiccan to be considered a witch. In this coven we shared what we were learning with each other and bonded over books, movies, and crafting our own ritual ceremonies to honor certain times of the year that are considered sacred seasonal transitions, known as "sabbats." That first coven was my introduction to working with a group.

After graduation I shifted away from my focus on spirituality for a while due to forming a relationship that became a marriage. This marriage was one in which I felt my spirituality and uniqueness as an individual were not in alignment with that relationship. Although our marriage did not work out, we were able to each mature and grow as individuals. As time went on, we arrived at a space of mutual respect and compassion. My interest in spirituality did not necessarily wane during the marriage. I certainly visited some metaphysical stores and attended a few workshops, but I did not have an altar set up or try to connect with any covens or circles. There was a clear pause with my outward expression of spirituality.

After my divorce and almost ten years after graduating college, I was at a point when it was time to seek that spiritual connection again. I sought community and found myself attending workshops at a wonderful store called Brid's Closet, named for the goddess Brid or Brigitte, owned by Bernadette Montana and located in Cornwall, New York. Bernadette instantly felt like home, like a mother/guardian/mentor. Being in her presence, I instantly felt welcomed. Her coven and community accepted me, and I felt like I belonged. I mostly attended workshops and rituals open to the public, not exclusive to the coven. I felt like there was work I needed to do for myself as an individual that did not fit into a coven format. However, the open sabbats helped me to fulfill the part of myself that yearned for community and connection. I am also grateful to Bernadette for being one of the first people to really stir up my curiosity about studying herbs. Through her I also made deep connections with other folks who truly shaped me both in my spiritual studies and herbal studies.

I began to also study some astrology. It was not until much later that I learned that there was a connection between herbalism and astrology called "medical astrology" and "astro-herbalism." The difference between the two is that medical astrology is a way of using astrology to assist with diagnosis and treatment of illnesses and diseases, while astro-herbalism connects the study of astrology with the study of plants, seeing how they connect with the planets and how they affect our bodies here on earth. It includes the dynamic of connecting these areas of study while also observing the elemental patterns and energetics of each.

In studying astrology, I learned that my chart has a lot of watery elements to it, as far as planetary placements. Therefore, it makes sense why I tend to avoid being cold, why I prefer spices that are warm, and perhaps why I tend to dye my hair red. These energetic patterns are like the opposite of my body's constitution. In the vitalist approach of herbalism, the energetics of the person are paired with the balancing properties of the plants. If a person's overall constitution is out of balance in one way (or more), the plant can shift its physiology through its actions and energetic properties.

The energetic patterns that I mentioned earlier are also conveyed well by the Ayurveda concept of doshas. Doshas describe three different body constitutions. There is Vata, typically characterized by someone who exhibits dryness in the body, with symptoms that fluctuate. They tend to be colder and thinner. Pitta is characterized by someone who tends to run hot, with a flushed face. Someone who tends to get angry easily and is averse to being hot. Kapha—the category I would be in—has a slower or sluggish metabolism and does not like being cold or damp. If I were to look at myself through this lens of Ayurveda, I would want to balance out the slow metabolism and the cold and dampness (again, lots of water in my astrological chart, which influences my physiology) with warming, stimulating herbs and spices. It makes sense why I gravitate toward ginger, cinnamon, cardamom, and hot peppers. Conversely, someone who has more of a hot Pitta constitution would likely prefer to work with herbs and plants that have more cooling properties. Learning about energetics is one of the key parts to understanding how plants work on our physiology.

Other key aspects in studying the medicinal properties of herbs:

- Taste—it communicates to the body how the plant will affect physiology through its phytochemistry, medicinal properties, and organ affinities.

- Affinity—which body organ systems are affected. For example, if an herb has an affinity for the respiratory system, that indicates that the herb will be supportive of the organs and tissues that belong to that system, such as the lungs and the sinuses.

- Actions—descriptions of how the plants shift our physiology. For example, "diuretic" indicates that the plant influences our urinary tract in that it will encourage more urination.

- Unique qualities—key to understanding how plants work is to examine if they have any special or unique qualities. In Ayurveda this is known as *prabhava*. One of my favorite examples of this would be how rose has a special quality of supporting the heart through difficult moments when we are feeling emotions such as grief or heartache. Rose can be heart opening and address these moments in a gentle, nurturing way. I have included rose in some of my formulas for this very reason.

These key aspects of plant study are a great place to start when you want to understand how a particular plant works medicinally. You can go even further with it into magickal properties by researching and exploring bioregional and cultural folklore, foraging, astro-herbalism, folk Magick, and recipes for spellwork.

For those who are reading this and feel called to work with plants as part of your healing journey, but have no idea where to begin, be patient with yourself. There are many books on these subjects, and it can easily become overwhelming. My personal suggestion would be to research and connect with the plants that are local to your bioregion first, unless there is a plant you feel strongly connected to (and that you have access to) that does not grow in your bioregion. A lot of information on herbalism is available in books, online, through courses, and through your local botanical shop. Start with one plant at a time. Study the plant. What are its actions, energetic properties, and preparations? How would you work with this plant? Would you take it internally or topically? Is it safe to ingest, or would you work with it as a spiritual totem? You can burn certain dried herbs and resins in smoke cleansing as part of your healing practice. You can anoint yourself with infused oils. Whatever plant you choose to work with, be sure to research if it has safety precautions and whether there are any contraindications if you are taking prescription medications.

If studying plants feels overwhelming, the simplest way to experience healing with plants is to spend time with them. This could be walking in the woods, being in the garden or a park, visiting a plant nursery, or even sitting with potted plants indoors. Sit with the plant and feel it. If it had a voice, what would it tell you? What properties does it evoke through your senses? How does it feel or smell or taste (if ingestible)?

" Choosing to live in a heart-centered space and releasing any fear that is present inside is a journey that takes time. Be patient and love yourself."

When you observe nature through this heart-centered lens, you will receive all kinds of messages. They could take the form of plants, animals, shapes, colors, and sensations. You might notice patterns or numbers that keep popping up. The Unseen might reveal themselves to you in various forms. The more you allow an openness and willingness to learn, you will receive the information, guidance, and healing that nature and the Divine have to offer. You will come to know that you are always supported by the universe. Choosing to live in a heart-centered space and releasing any fear that is present inside is a journey that takes time. Be patient and love yourself. Remember that fear is what makes us vulnerable and impacts our health: mental, physical, and spiritual. When we allow life to flow in this way, we develop this beautiful trusting relationship to the universe and ourselves. We develop our inner knowing and intuition. We learn that anything is possible and become open to receiving it.

Writing this and sharing it with you is also a part of my own healing journey. Finding my voice and being open to sharing my story has a Magick of its own. I can feel the embrace and support of my guides in sharing this story with you. That is what I would call a worthwhile journey.

With love and gratitude,
Lyra

About Lyra Silverstein

Hello! My name is Lyra Silverstein. I grew up in Rockland County, New York, and have lived in Vermont and New Jersey for brief periods of my life before returning to where I was born. My children are both furry, with four legs and tails (I have two cats). Miguel and I have a lovely garden, and we live in a stone cottage that borders Harriman State Park. He is the green thumb around here and a wonderful steward of the land. I began Spiral Moon Herbcraft in 2018 in my pursuit of crafting magickal herbal products for self-care and wellness. My love of herbalism is what drives me and has provided a path that has been extremely rewarding in serving the community. My products are currently sold both online and in reputable botanical and

metaphysical shops. Follow me online for events and up-
dates with the links below. Many blessings!

Linktree: https://linktr.ee/spiralmoonherbcraft
Website: https://www.spiralmoonherbcraft.com/

TO SEE THE CHANGE, YOU MUST BE THE CHANGE

When I Heard the Whispers of My Wild Heart
By Mielle Fox

My five philosophies about living your best life:

1. If you want to see the change, then be the change.
2. If you can just listen to the whispers of your heart over the cacophony of your mind, you will hear what your soul is speaking to you more clearly.
3. Transformation is an inside job.
4. You only have this very moment to be fully present, so make the most of it, regardless of what it looks like.
5. Life is a gift.

It has taken me decades to really integrate and embrace these five transformational components in my journey. I am forever grateful I have a wild, untamed heart that never lets me down and has shown me some of life's most beautiful and joyously expressed moments, but I will say it has taken me quite some time to understand this. How and when it all began . . .

For you to get a better sense of how critical it is to heal generational trauma, let me share how some of my conditioning and carrying my history of shame, guilt, and trauma came about.

As a child and young teen, I heard many conflicting recommendations for maintaining independence, success, acceptance, and love. Most of these tales came from my mother, an only child who, at a young age, was sent to live with relatives. She was raised by her grandmother during difficult times (1920s–1930s), living on the outskirts of Edinburgh, Scotland, on a small farm. Times were lean, and scarcity of resources was commonplace.

Wartime is difficult regardless of the geography. For my father's family, it was a time of upheaval. He was a Jew, and the atrocities of war forced his family to leave Vienna in the dead of night to escape Hitler's invasion of Austria in the late 1930s. My father was the only son in his family, raised during a time of hatred, war, and antisemitism. His entire extended family were gathered and killed in the concentration camps in Europe. His immediate family— his parents and sister—escaped to England. With all the fear and political upheaval, my father was told to deny his heritage and culture. He was to follow the path his parents declared for him as a career. So he became an engineer and enlisted in the British army to fight in WWII.

My mother chose to run away from home at sixteen, lied her way into the military services during the time of enlistment for WWII, married young, widowed young, and married my father after the war. They relocated to America without family, connections, or community and started their own family. My father changed his very ethnic name to a more Americanized version so his heritage and culture would be less noticeable in a new land. My mother berated everything about America, from politics to culture, but obviously enjoyed the gifts of accessing the more that were available in her new country.

Back in my mother's day, it was expected that women would stay in the home to raise a family. It was the cultural norm to be dependent on the spouse for everything—transportation, financial security, protection, a home. To say it was a difficult transition coming to America would be an understatement. Add to this starting a family, with generational and cultural expectations of how society and family units should work, as well as their own unaddressed traumas, well, as you can imagine, it left us kids with a lot of conflicting information. Neither of my parents had a good sense of family life, what parenting really meant, how to raise children, or how to show, express, or receive love.

On one hand, my mother would admonish me and advise that I needed to always have a skill to support myself so I "would never have to depend on a man or anyone else for my needs and wants." In the next breath, when I told her I wanted to continue to college and develop my own career, I was told "that's such a waste of time and money. Why would you do that when you can just marry up and be supported?" Needless to say, she was merely projecting her issues onto me, but I didn't see that at the time. You only know what you think you know at any given moment.

I was athletic, a small but sturdy kid, smart, witty, and sometimes vocal, but not in a positive or constructive way.

I was told it was not a good thing to show people, men especially, how smart you really were because "men don't like to feel like they're not important or all knowing." I was told "men don't like strong, muscular women because that's ugly, intimidating, and not ladylike." However, I was also expected to work hard like a man, be strong and independent, and not to ask for help. You can see how this could be so confusing to a growing teen female in a very stereotyped environment. I learned to stay quiet most of the time and do my best to try to fit in.

When did I build the wall? When did I close the door? When did I lose the innocence and trust of a child? How did it all seem so wrong, so hard, so unfair, so cruel?

I tried to dull my shine, not stand out in class, struggled to fit in when I really didn't. As many of us were and are, I was a child of a dysfunctional family. I share this not because my trauma is any greater or less than anyone else's, but it was my trauma and my experiences through my filter. Of course, what wasn't immediately clear, as a child, was the reality that I would be imprinted and carry not just their trauma but also the generational trauma they had also been "gifted" with in their lifetime from ancestors. How could I know? How could any child know?

My parents were both born in the 1920s and immigrated to America in 1956. I was a young first-generation American kid raised with old-school European expectations. We were raised that to have anything (food on the table, a roof over our head, a chance to go to school, new clothes once a year) was a privilege. Both my parents lived through times of extreme hardship and scarcity of life's basics. Punishment was swift and severe, none of this "you're grounded," meaning you can't watch TV for a week or play with your friends. I'd have been thrilled to just lose a playdate versus the physical wallop that was the standard. I would have been thrilled to just "not have a dessert" as punishment versus "You'll finish what's put in front of you, hot or cold, until it's gone—there's starving people in Africa who'd give their right hand to have what you have, so don't be so ungrateful," or "Well now, how could you be so greedy after eating your food that you think you deserve dessert?" Again, the concept of privilege to have what others considered normal was elevated to new heights. While it did teach me the value of being grateful for basics, it did strike me odd as a child that my friends didn't receive the same discipline and rules that I did.

I had a weird name, weird parents, weird siblings . . . I believed we were always on the sidelines and not included because of all our weirdness. We were "that family." I didn't believe I was pretty and "cool," like the beautiful-girl clique. I was intimidating to the boys. I was the oddball kid with the strange name and foreign family that didn't fit in anywhere.

I was not raised in a lovey-dovey environment. There was little physical comfort in the form of hugs and kisses. There was little confidence building and safety in acknowledging the try or effort in being a human learning new things. My parents considered emotional neediness to be a sign of weakness. In my child's view, it was clear that the path to being approved, wanted, and loved was by being a good girl, not creating waves, going with the flow, fitting in, getting good grades, and not making any scenes privately or publicly.

My home life and my outside of the home presentation didn't match; that made for a lot of problems. Of course, this led to a lot of rebellion and defiant behaviors as I struggled to find my way. I was brassy and defiant on the outside, while scared and feeling unloved and unsafe on the inside. At a young age, I learned to stay under the radar to avoid getting caught, but I smoked, I drank, I consumed a lot of unhealthy foods, and I tried to hide my body. I was a curvaceous, well-endowed young female teen, which came with its own problems. Man, kids are so cruel to one another at times. It left me feeling vulnerable, defensive, and anxious. So much so that I leaned on physical habits to try to calm myself. I injured my body with repetitive cuts and scratches. I chewed my nails incessantly and basically was a miserable human. My adolescent years were, quite simply, a living hell. I lived in a household of screaming, yelling, drinking, physical abuse, emotional abuse, shaming, blaming, and who knows what else I'm not even remembering clearly.

I think, in their own way, my parents felt and believed they loved their children but certainly didn't know how to express that, each having been raised in difficult upbringings with physical, mental, and emotional abuses of their day. Without having any tools or an understanding of their own programming and their own fear-based beliefs, they raised their children as most parents do—wanting better for the next generation than the one in which they were raised. As you can imagine, in their world that meant achievement, success, obedience, deference, keeping up with the expectations of the community, and leaning on external validation for what it meant to be "okay."

I actually didn't realize how damaging these conditioning patterns would be for me. I saw it all too clearly for my older brother—the only boy of a Jewish father, with three sisters in an historically and culturally rigid European upbringing embarking on a new journey in the new world of America. As the only boy, he typically would have been raised in a Judaic household as the golden child, but since my father was raised by threats, criticism, and bullying, he brought these child-rearing skills into our family. My brother took it hard, as the only son. He was a bright, funny, athletic boy but suffered bullying and ridicule not only at the hands of schoolmates but also at home. My parents were demanding, expecting, and hard on him, the only male. He was constantly demeaned for not being "enough," for not "doing it right," for not showing up in the world the way in which my parents expected him to show up. His needs were always put after the needs of his elder sister, who was fawned over as the perfect child. Emotional expressions, voicing opinions, and shining too brightly was not only not encouraged but was a source of punishment. He was expected, from a young age, to "suck it up," "act like a man," "take care of your sisters," and basically deny any and all the normal feelings a small child might experience in a multi-sibling family. The impact on my brother would not only be a contributor to shaping his future but also mine. It was difficult to watch and not be able to shield my brother from this treatment. More on this a bit later.

After twenty-eight years of a marriage filled with all the types of abuse that can be imagined, both to each other and to the children from the marriage, my parents filed for divorce. Sheets to the wind, as we were all scattered to different living arrangements in our teens. Remember, the European standard was for a child to remain at home until marriage, so moving out was a new concept to both my parents. My older sister (twenty-one at the time) had already moved in with her boyfriend (which didn't go over well at the time with my parents) and his parents (later to marry and divorce). My brother, two years younger than the eldest, moved out on his own. My younger sister (just nine and terrified of my mother) chose to live with my alcoholic father rather than suffer the abuses of our current home life. Honestly, what nine-year-old should have to make that kind of a choice? My mother didn't even fight for her, but I was too scared to intervene. Again, I didn't understand the ramifications. Her future would also take many twists and turns after the divorce. I was afraid and assessed what my safest route would be—no option was great, but I chose to stay in the home with my mother.

I was around fourteen at the time. When you're a young teen struggling to just get by, looking for love and acceptance and guided by guilt and shame, you make choices from a different place than what you know later in life to be the truth. And so I lived with shame and guilt, fear of rejection, and sadness for my mother's plight of becoming a single parent in a time of stay-at-home mothers and her financial insecurities on top of perceived judgments from others. I allowed myself to feel sadness for everyone at what seemed so unjust. I couldn't have described it then, but losing all my immediate family felt like a living death, with grief I didn't know how to handle. I didn't have communication with anyone other than my brother, who drifted in and out. I didn't speak again to my other siblings for another thirteen-plus years and probably as long to re-establish a connection with my father.

I soon felt obligated to fill the roles of daughter, spouse, friend, confidante, financial supporter, and personal assistant, twisting my mind and emotions around *how could I be all the things to please people and fix this mess and show her how much I love her, despite all the horrors?* Because I didn't understand what it was to give and receive unconditional love that, in my mind, this contorted perception made sense. It was just me left in our household, which was once four children and two parents. I wanted to believe my mother wanted me and loved me enough to insist that I stay in the home for my own good, but it was really for her own good. I would find out clearly within a few years that my choices were made for someone else, not for my highest good. Again, huge upheaval, disruptions, destructive patterns, blaming, shaming, guilting, manipulation of head and heart escalated to a whole new level of twistedness.

Combine the stressors of divorce with the stressors of school life, fitting in, peer acceptance, and peer pressure, and as you can well imagine I was a mixed-up, defiant mess. I was angry and shutdown, closed off, and continued with the emotion-numbing behavior patterns of smoking, drinking, and superficial and narcissistic, manipulative relationships. This went on for years because I didn't believe I was enough, worthy, loveable, or a kind human just as I was. I leaned on my close connection with my brother a lot. He was my lighthouse in an otherwise dark existence.

These changes in my life brought to me a belief at the time that my only way out was to be independent and successful. I was pretty sure as a late teen that I needed to "be somebody," and I had to do it on my own in order to escape the prison of dependence on someone else for anything. It clearly didn't seem to have worked out for my mother or my siblings. Again, the blindness of youth when we don't know any differently. I digress. Let me continue . . .

By the time high school was over and it was time for college (that was my perception as the way to success back then), I had forfeited a full scholarship to one university in lieu of commuting to a local college at great personal expense. I made this choice in order to stay home and be available for my mother. I took out many loans, as there was no financial support from either parent. Once again, I believed she needed me and loved me, so I didn't believe I had a choice. How chivalrous and martyr-like of me to believe I could save her. She basically had guilted me into this by offering up, "I have nothing to live for if you move away." Please keep in mind, I was so shutdown and disconnected from myself that I didn't realize I actually had a choice to meet my own needs. So, with the burden of her suicidal threats weighing on my heart, I lived at home until age twenty-five, when the bottom fell out.

This was one of my turning points, my wake-up call from what had made me believe at the time that love was a commodity. It became clear that I had taken on her trauma and now had to deal with the consequences. School was an easy space for me. I was always a good student and of course enjoyed the accolades of achievement. I was so accustomed to defining my worth by academic achievements that continuing in school was a no-brainer. It was not only a path to perceived freedom but was also the perfect escape from my life. I didn't really understand the degree to which that kind of financial debt would shift my future life, but it didn't matter at the time. I was desperate to make something of myself. I was in postgraduate school to advance myself for a career in oral health care and desperately needed to live closer to the university to complete my studies and dedicate myself to completing the course of academia.

At twenty-five I was still living at home at the time to be available to my mother. She had already disowned the other children, refusing to see or converse with any of them. I had watched her remove herself and shut people out as quick as a blink of an eye. She basically pushed everyone else away—her other children, her ex-husband, her previous friends (which were few and far between). As you can imagine, while I knew I needed to dedicate myself to my studies, I also knew I could not continue the pace of emotional caretaking, babysitting, and managing everything in my mother's twisted world and succeed in school. I held a difficult conversation with her about needing to be closer to school, which would mean moving out on my own. Her response was far from what I expected. (I must really have been in denial, as I had already seen her

MO with my other family members.) Despite attempting to reason with her, she was adamant. Not only did she advise me that if I moved out I could never return, but she also advised that I would be disowned and she would never speak to me again. Because I was so wrapped up in the fear of rejection, the people pleasing, and the guilt and all that it represented to me, I felt overwhelmed, helpless, alone, and deeply hurt. This was crushing, but the piece that stuck with me and had been the hardest to come to terms with was her venomous statement, said with pain and *her* perceived truth at the time: "You're dead to me—I wish you had died in the womb."

As you can only imagine, I was devastated. I knew deep in my core this was no threat. I had seen her disown her other three children already, so I knew she wasn't kidding. In that moment I realized I had hinged my power, my heart, my soul, my truth in what I believed was a pathway to be accepted, approved of, and loved by my mother, on the one woman a child is closest to and trusts instinctively at birth. I had learned and created the belief that love was a commodity and had conditions if you were going to be deserving of receiving it. I felt like my entire life to that point had been a lie, a fabrication. It was emotionally wrenching and psychologically destructive. I simply could not fathom that a parent could wish such a thing, that she could turn love on and off like a light switch, that she could throw away twenty-five years of experiences, memories, and feelings in a moment. The truth of how the purity of love for another human, especially a child, had been distorted and used as a negotiating chip in an emotional war zone overwhelmed me. I was devastated and determined not to allow myself to be so deeply hurt again.

I tried to reason with her, explaining I would be available to see her and spend time with her, that I just needed the space to dedicate my energies to schooling. My mother was absolutely an all- or-none vessel. There was no negotiating, no discussion, no compromise. I did move out, and she refused all my calls, my letters, my cards for birthdays and holidays. She was true to her word—I was dead to her.

As an aside, what I found so interesting now, in twenty-twenty hindsight, was her capacity to emotionally manipulate people for her own needs. She was horrendous to my father yet maintained contact with him until his death for every little detail of life management (health care, moneys, legal issues, etc.). Rest his soul, he fulfilled all his contractual commitments from the divorce, even as he moved on with his life. She'd perpetuated her lifestyle of excessive drinking and gambling (addicted to horse and dog racing, scratch tickets, etc.), basically bankrupting herself, and lived the remaining seventeen years in a state-supported nursing facility, ultimately passing without any family members nearby after many years of degenerative dementia. She was assigned a legal representative while in the nursing home, as none of her children agreed to take on her legal needs after her mental status rendered her incapable of living on her own. I realize this sounds unimaginable, but to me, after a lifetime of lies and deceit, I simply wasn't interested in picking up the shit that was left over. I would ultimately come to a place later where I could forgive that version of myself all those years ago. I have forgiven those younger versions for just doing what they thought needed to be done at the time, but still have a ways to go to integrate and embrace the love of self that needs to be available to me so my soul can express itself as purely as it is meant to express. If you've never received unconditional love from another human, it's hard to grasp how to build that for yourself. It is a process like anything else. Trust and faith in something bigger than our earthly selves, God, the Divine, Spirit, whatever name/phrase you use—it is *love*. And there it is—it's not learning love from your humanness, but it's learning and owning the love of who you are as a soul in a human body. From love, to love, we are love. But please allow me to continue the story.

> " It's learning and owning the love of who you are as a soul in a human body. From love, to love, we are love. "

As cruel as it sounds, my mother basically told the universe what she wanted through her actions and behaviors. I can recall her saying to us as kids, "You've made your bed—now you will lie in it." Interesting that her words would become her reality at the latter part of her life. It took me a few years after her passing to really understand her pain and torture through her own stories, her addictions as her means of numbing her pain, her own upbringing, and her lack of tools and choices to make it a better life for herself and her children. I can see now that everything I had endured was serving as the breadcrumbs to lead me to where I am presently. It was rough, but I can see the blessings in disguise for me through all these experiences. I wouldn't know what I know now or have the capacity to understand how much choice I have in creating and redirecting my life.

Without realizing it, that day of deciding to move out was also the beginning of how I fiercely defended my tender heart. On the outside I was as polite and friendly as always. However, on the inside I had vowed not to be so foolish again as to allow my heart to be crushed and tossed aside like yesterday's trash. Not only did I have a poor sense of relating to others on a deeper level, but managing intimate relationships in a healthy way was totally off the charts. The handful of relationships I engaged in as an adult were all manipulative and narcissistic in nature. I couldn't see it at the time. I continued to use addictive patterns to try to cope with the isolation and rejection. I continued to drink excessive amounts of everything from coffee to alcohol, chain smoked, and ate poorly. I was, and still am, an emotional eater (recovering emotional eater!). I was basically conditioned from early on that food was the answer to everything. If you were happy, you ate to celebrate. If you were a good girl and succeeded or got a good grade, you were rewarded with food. If you were not well, you were fed to soothe the discomfort. If you were sad or lonely, a sweet treat would help with that. So basically, it didn't matter what the emotion or activity was . . . the answer was food.

Combining the reward system of food with the clean-plate-club mentality of feeding children, I felt destined to have a life of constant eating crises. Even though I came from a home of alcoholism and addiction, this didn't stop me. I did it anyway. And it didn't make an ounce of change in my level of unhappiness. I punished my body while hiding my heart. I was the poster child of everything a human does to hide from pain, to numb from feeling, to avoid looking at the *why* behind the triggers. I had *no tools* at this point to even begin to understand how this cascade of events was deteriorating my being and trying to kill my soul. I decided right then and there that I would never marry, would never have children (I certainly wasn't going to promote those genetics!), and would dedicate my energies to others, to try to serve and "fix" in my best capacity. By diverting my energies externally, it meant, in the moment, that I could hide from my own hurt and brokenness. I dove deep into my academics, my career, and switched my geography to start anew.

I had chosen to work in oral healthcare, as I felt it gave me a way to serve and provide care to those in need without having to really commit my heart to anyone in particular (apparently, including myself). And while I developed a beautiful career, offering much-needed services in my rural community, I still felt broken and empty inside. All these habits continued for many years, until I shifted my understanding of self-value and self-worth from within versus trying to gain it from outside myself.

I believed my career direction was basically dictated to me by choosing a career perceived to bring me success and honor. My father's career was chosen for him by his parents. So here it begins with the handing down of generational traumas, patterns, beliefs, and stories. I didn't know there were other avenues. I was so busy justifying, validating, and belittling myself for not being enough or being more that I wasn't able to hear the whispers and tap, tap, tap of my heart trying to get my attention.

It's so interesting that while I serve as an oral health care provider in my day career, the same issues of shame, guilt, demands, expectations, and projected blame I lived with as a child have followed me through interactions with patients. There is a tremendous amount of projected issues with clients as they come in with their own burdens of patterns, fears, and beliefs. In order to show up for clients in a compassionate and open way, it requires the capacity to have personal emotional boundaries, understanding what energies are my own versus the client's and still be able to execute the mechanics of the services needed. It requires a compartmentalization of my thoughts, triggers, and emotions. At the same time, I use these moments as learning experiences as I see mirrors or reflections of patterns from my clients that I had also experienced.

I love my job for what it has allowed me to do—serve my community and feel good about my service (can you say "external validation again"?), but early on it wasn't doing anything for my need to tap into my real issues within myself. Choosing not to own and see your own beliefs as contributors to your overall wellness was, again, simply not on my radar at the time. It took a few more knocks to my health, physically and mentally to make me wake up.

So l back to the story. After graduation from college, I moved in with my then partner. Big mistake. I left that manipulative, narcissistic relationship and moved several states away. I had basically traded the manipulation from my mother for my lover, but it was still emotional and psychological abuse.

It felt shameful that for being such an independent and clever woman, and well respected in my profession, that I was a scared, small girl searching for acceptance and love. I never felt enough. I was still subconsciously willing to be used as an emotional doormat if it meant I would feel wanted or needed. I was a perpetual people pleaser and gave away my own sense of power and self. I had no real awareness on a deeper level (a.k.a couldn't hear my heart whispers) or any cognitive concept that I was responsible for my own well-being. It simply wasn't totally clear to me that I would not and could not achieve peace and happiness by looking for it outside of myself. The idea of starting over and moving seemed like a fresh start, but really, it was just a geographic shift. My internal turmoils followed me to the next location, only to show up in a different version of the same problem. Despite being well educated and working hard, I still did not understand how all my past and my stories and choices contributed to my overall poor mental and physical health.

As such, I would continue to speak harshly to myself, berating myself for not knowing better, for not doing better, for allowing myself to give my heart away and have it crushed again. Instead of leaning into how I could make changes, I chose to shut down. On the outside I was funny and social, but on the inside I was crying with emptiness and defeat.

In my thirties, I was exhausted from the previous twelve years of rigorous schooling, moving, my career, my struggles, my unhappiness, my constant disappointment in relationships, my constant disappointment in myself. I had spent more time being angry and crying than enjoying my waking hours. I was in total adrenal fatigue, in an emotional downward spiral, and felt that I was at the lowest of the lows, rock bottom.

I thought taking a small break for a long weekend would help. So I took myself on a little journey to a retreat location with a marketed mission statement of "getting in touch with yourself" by learning mindfulness techniques. Sounded so New Age. I was all in for that. Or so I thought.

We all know that you can run, but you can't hide. On this trip (I know now that the universe guided me there), I discovered modalities of mindfulness and meditation and the gift of time spent with the energy and acceptance of horses, which served as a mirror for me to take a look inward.

Everything at this retreat was centered around the concept of being in the moment—from meditation to eating a meal. I felt embarrassed that I was not able to slow myself down enough to grasp the value of meditation, let alone do it. I beat myself up as I failed at doing what seemed so easy and obvious to everyone else in the classes. I was again existing in external validation, self-limiting, and inner-critic mindspeak, berating myself at every turn.

While there I participated in an equine session to learn about energy and communication. It was early on in the equine facilitated therapy world (1990s). This was my aha moment of how my energy, my actions, my thoughts, and my emotions were not only mirrored back to me (horses are the ultimate mirror) but also how I was reverberating that energy out into the world.

205

No wonder I was repeatedly attracting poor connections, undesirable relationships, lack of fulfillment, and abundance of joy in my life. I was a disaster on the inside despite how put together I appeared on the outside. My facade was transparent to those horses. They read my energy and my lack of grounding in an instant. Those horses changed my life. That short vacation was my pivotal shift. I came back from that trip determined to shed my fears, my baggage, and my stories and really discover myself.

I was determined to learn as much as I could about horses, their energies, their way of communicating, and mostly how unconditional and forgiving they can be. This was echoed, of course, in my natural attraction to animals. I get along better with most animals than with people. I never really understood why then, but I do now—it's about the unconditionality of their beings. They don't hold grudges and don't judge. They show up in the present moment and have a willingness to trust and try far beyond what one would expect, considering how frequently we knowingly or unknowingly act in such a way that would cause distrust and avoidance of humans. They are the epitome of unconditionality in the moment. Those horses represented everything that was missing from my childhood and my adult relationships. I had been conditioned from very early on that acceptance, peace, and the exchange of trust and love was conditional and attached to an expectation of some level of performance or success. My time with the horses was such a clear wake up to the possibilities and reality that love is unconditional, not to be bartered, bought, or sold.

The journey that started with that three-day getaway continues to this day. I made a decision that weekend that there simply had to be more to life, more than what I was living, more than what was around me. I hadn't understood then the extent of the lack of alignment between my mind and my heart. I had no clue then that I was running from myself and my problems by keeping busy and doing all kinds of things—I am an extreme doer, overachiever, overthinker, all common traits of avoidance. I proudly labeled it as ambitious, motivated, type A, analytical, multitasker, hyperactivity, etcetera. What I didn't understand was that it was my mind trying to protect me by keeping me from really slowing down to look at myself, my feelings, my beliefs, how I saw myself mirrored in the world. Gratefully, I was guided (I know now) by Universe to choose that particular destination vacation for a pivotal shift in my very being. Funny what you don't know until you do. That trip had cracked the door open ever so slightly to see there was more than what I had lived with up to that point.

Why hadn't I learned any better as an adult after all the suffering with the same feelings I had experienced as a child and a teen? I was so sure as a grown-up and a professional that I had outgrown all those things. Oh, I was so wrong!

Following that brief getaway, I returned to my home, my job, and my living arrangements and saw them differently. I was able to recognize how extremely toxic my environment was for my spiritual and emotional well-being. My work and living situation took an extreme turn, and a downward spiral of my world began again—professionally, personally, financially, and of course emotionally.

I had another pivotal point in my journey when my then business partner made some choices that doomed the business. After fifteen years of trust and hard work with this person, I found myself without a job and in a position of bankruptcy. It culminated with needing to leave it all—sell everything and start over *again*.

When you live by the approval of others to define you, it is hard to own up and be accountable to yourself for your own choices that led you to give away your power. That owning and acknowledgment brought up shame. Shame that I had once again fallen prey to old patterns of earning and trading for acceptance, love, worthiness. I felt shame, embarrassment, anger, frustration, loneliness, defeat. I berated myself for not knowing better, for allowing myself to be duped, for not being successful. After years of schooling and working in an esteemed career path, here I was again, forty and feeling crushed—crushed financially, emotionally, psychologically, and spiritually. The shame of how I let myself down and all the expectations I had set up for myself was defeating. Except this time I had a much clearer idea as to why my life was in shambles—*because of my own choices*, because of my giving of my own personal power to someone else, because of external validation being more of a priority than my personal well-being. I had confused trust in someone else versus trust in myself and the Divine. I was riddled in all the low, disempowering energies, but also with a determination and resilience that this time I wasn't going to get sucked into another manipulative situation.

"What is clear to me now and I didn't know how to express then, was that my wild untamed heart, my soul, my truth, my Higher Self was always whispering to me."

My saving grace, which I called stubbornness or resilience, was in my constant belief that I would be okay. I knew I had the stamina to keep going, rebuild, and start over. Yes it was exhausting, but I refused to believe that I was put on Earth to just suffer it out in such an unfulfilling way. What is clear to me now and I didn't know how to express then, was that my wild untamed heart, my soul, my truth, my Higher Self was always whispering to me. My heart encouraged me to stay the course and hold on to life. I would be okay. I would be safe. My heart encouraged me to break free from the conditioning and trappings of my mind. I innately knew I needed to hold on, to persevere so I could hear my heart speak louder than my mind could speak.

Fast-forward, I rebuilt my career, my finances, and my social circle, but I hadn't rebuilt my personal confidence and self-awareness or addressed the long-standing lack of coherence between my head and my heart. I questioned if all the unhappiness in my life was really external. How could I be so addled with bad luck, bad relationships, and unfulfilling experiences year after year? Perhaps it was me. This came as an epiphany. I did all the outside things, the bodyworkers, the spiritual path, but it was lip service. I hadn't really looked within, deep within, and addressed those blocks to my heart and soul.

I read books and learned about spiritual practices. I visited with alternative bodyworkers trained in Eastern medicine to try to help with my obviously clogged-up life force energy, my chi, my chakras. No clue what all that meant back then, but I knew something wasn't right. I cleaned up my nutrition (for a while) and exercised like a fiend. But yet, deep down things were not improving (because I wasn't really managing and dealing with the crux of the matter—*me* . . . my ego-based thoughts, my beliefs, my patterns, and my learning to love and forgive all my personas). Despite making many healthy choices and changes and absolutely creating more happiness for myself, I still hid my heart and avoided looking at my past, my past emotions, my younger versions of myself, and my inherited traumas from generations behind me.

I connected with a course that really walked me through the root causes of my beliefs and how I could shift the rhetoric, how I could learn to forgive myself and others, how I could learn to be nonjudgmental about all my wounds. This made an enormous spaciousness where I have been able to continue to realign my heart and my mind. It has taken decades for me to have the awareness and insight to see the truth for what it was and is and to peel back the layers hiding my heart, which had been built by *me*, my stories and experiences. I know now that every human has the capacity to own their power, to shine their light, to express joy and passion.

> " The lull of complacency to believe you've done all the work that needs to be done and it's a completed task is another lie your mind tries to tell you. "

It's so interesting that I believed I had healed well. That was, until the next layer of emotional triggering and ego-based stories I had held on to rose up. Here again I was being shown another layer, by mirroring through experiences the places where there was more work to be done. The lull of complacency to believe you've done all the work that needs to be done and it's a completed task is another lie your mind tries to tell you. Here's how I discovered this for myself.

If you recall from the beginning of this tale, my brother was the only son to a man who was also the only son. After moving to America and having his own children, my father unfortunately applied his family's conditioning on his own son. The expectations for achievement, success, masculine superiority, strength in the perception of society and family weighed heavily on my father. These same tactics of emotional abuse and manipulation were passed along to my brother. He was constantly berated for not being enough, achieving enough, showing up in a way that showed my parents anything beyond failure. It took a toll on him starting as a child and ultimately, in my opinion, led him to his early death. The brother I knew and the son they wanted were two different people. My brother was brilliant, the most kind and warm expression of compassion, love, and support any sister could want. We were four and a half years apart, and I worshiped him. He was always supportive of me and was my champion. There was never a time that I couldn't call on him to stand by me unconditionally, holding space while I processed my difficulties.

Despite him being able to be present for me, he was completely unable to be present for himself. He was tortured by his stories and unable to let go of the rhetoric his ego-mind repeatedly told him. He never grasped the awareness of the journey versus the destination. He used to ask me how to find happiness, and I would say, "It's not on a shelf labeled *H*." I would encourage him to try different things, create, express, experiment in his world, but he was not able to leave the uncomfortable comfort zone of his acquired emotional and psychological prison. His emotional unwellness, in my belief, led to his physical unwellness. Fast-forward, he had an acute physical breakdown that led to his final trip to the ICU. I remember the day I received the call from the ICU physician. I dropped everything, flew across the country, and stayed by his side 24/7. Even in his debilitated physical state, with the inability to verbally communicate, the exchange of love from his soul to mine was all the conversation we needed. Our hearts spoke to each other without the cloudiness of the mind involved for much of the last few days. I will have to admit that explaining the severity of his condition and holding the space for him to make his own choices for his time left on Earth was undeniably the hardest thing I've ever had to experience. There's nothing harder than to tell someone you love that you cannot help them or fix them and there's no more time to stay on this earth—it feels like a piece of your soul is being sucked out of your being. He passed in the ICU. My sister and I took care of what needed to be taken care of, and we left to return to our respective lives. In addition to learning the lesson of not being able to fix a situation that had always been my strength, I now learned a whole new level of grief. I hold grief as a perpetual companion and have learned to cohabit with it in a manageable way. Some days are harder than others, but I know deep in my soul that my brother's essence is with me, as I believe we are all ONE, we are all sparks of love from the Divine, and we will return to such when we leave this earth. My human grieves, but my soul knows.

That event was another pivotal turn on my journey. It pushed me to prioritize myself, my visions, and to get serious about following my journey to have better head and heart alignment and to live more in the moment. No one knows how long their time is here on Earth. It catapulted me to dig deeper and recognize the ways in which I had built roadblocks to being able to access my essence, my core, my heart, and my truth. It showed me that we can grow, can find the happiness and joy in our day to day while still working on the old stories. It showed me that grief becomes a piece of your soul, your heart, your makeup, that ebbs and flows on any given day but never leaves. If you don't find a way to make peace with grief, it can and will destroy you. Choosing how you will dance with darkness to move from dark to light and choosing to find joy in the depths of sorrow—these are lessons I have shown to me on a daily basis.

All this would come with deep soul searching and stepping beyond my uncomfortable comfort zone, but mostly the shifts occurred when I could acknowledge, without judgment, that those younger versions of myself were simply doing the best in the moment to survive. When I was able to see those different expressions of myself, the younger versions of me, and forgive those versions for not knowing any differently; when I could offer kindness, grace, and compassion to those versions of me, that was when the bricks blocking my heart and my truth tumbled.

" As I continue to discover more of my heart, I am able to expose the brightness of who I am."

As I continue to discover more of my heart, I am able to expose the brightness of who I am, the sweetness of Mielle (honey), the grace of God in this body to offer me opportunities to show up in the world as a mirror of what love can look and feel like. I never understood a lot of things that, as a child, seemed so out of sorts—including why I was the only child born in the spring, why I was the only child with a non-Scottish name, and so much more. Universe, however, in its infinite wisdom, knew more, knew deeply that my soul had chosen a resilient, compassionate, chatty little girl to bring forward the message of love.

Here's the story of how I came to be called Mielle and why that matters. My mother, being from Edinburgh, Scotland, was proud of her Celtic heritage. When we were all kids, I used to wonder why my siblings all were gifted with Scottish Gaelic names and I had a French name. All my siblings were born in the fall, while I was born in the spring. It struck me oddly as a kid. I was a weirdo, but

I didn't really think about it until recently. Through my transformational healing journey, I've discovered a lot of things about myself, my birth, my name, my numerology, and divine coding—which in twenty-twenty hindsight, make all those earlier questions make sense.

So here is how the story began.

Apparently, after my birth, the nurses brought me to my mother in the hospital and stated, "Oh, Mrs. Fox, what a *honey* of a baby." My mother, in her infinite wisdom, decided she would call me Honey, but since she was watching a French vocabulary show on television at the time, she chose to name me Mielle, which is the feminine version of the masculine noun Miel. Miel is honey, as in bee honey. As a child, I was so indignant to have been named after *food!* Little did I know just how very special my name is for *me.* Also interesting is that I carry a ruling number / life path of more dominant/masculine type energy as well as a heart-centered, heart-chakra-based contract energy . . . Stick with me—there's more.

I hated my name as a child. It was torturous in schools, and I was called every variation of Michelle, Meow, Miellie, Nellie, etcetera, throughout my years in academia. I was angry that I had a weird name that created bullying and criticism. Why wasn't I honored with a traditional cultural name from my ancestral country of birth—Scotland? I hated explaining why my name was what it was and even tried to come up with a catchy nickname. (That didn't work.)

Fast-forward—not only do I now understand more clearly why I was named Mielle (thank you, Universe) but also why I was not born in October like all my other siblings and why my path is so distinctly, divinely described by my numerology. Of course, I believe I am a piece of God's masterpiece experiencing this lifetime on Earth. I believe it was no coincidence that I was born in the spring, sign of Taurus, divinely coded in numerology as a ruling number / life path of 7, with a universal contract card 5 spades. I am a combination of science meets spirit, grounded and spiritual at the same time, heart centered and always evolving and pivoting to grow forward for the betterment of the collective. This is clearly destined by powers greater than myself (or my parents)!

> " I am a combination of science meets spirit, grounded and spiritual at the same time. "

But wait, there's more. In Celtic tradition, honey is associated in cultural folklore, as the honeybees were believed to be intermediaries between this world and the next, acting as conduits between humans and the dearly departed. The Egyptians embalmed the deceased in honey. Honey has been symbolically associated as the symbol of love and affection since ancient times. It is associated as a symbol of happiness. The goddess of honey is the Roman goddess Mellonia, the Greek goddess Melissa, the Norse goddess Beyla, carrying a strong connection to fertility and the earth. Honey is also known for its sweetness, healing, and magic.

Pleasure, sweetness, truth, and knowledge. Honeybees are responsible for over 50 percent of annual pollination of crops, produce, flowers, trees, shrubs, and fruits in Scotland.

My father's side of the family was Jewish. In Judaism, honey is the Jewish symbol of hope, happiness, success, and health.

Now, as an adult, I realize that there was a divine intervention in being named Mielle. My mother was naturally intuitive but assumed, as many Scots do, that the "knowing" of things (a.k.a. intuitive knowing) and having an aura of connecting to the "fey" (spirits of the universe—e.g., faeries, sprites, etc.) was commonplace. I don't think she made any connection between the timing of the nurse's entrance, her declaration of the new baby's temperament, or the happenstance of the TV having not only a bilingual education show but to be on the word *Miel*—honey—in that given moment . . . Well, if that isn't synchronicity in its finest, I'm not sure what else it could be. I too have learned to trust my knowing, to follow the guidance of my Higher Self, to understand the connection between what we think is real in our 3-D world and the availability of other expressions of energetic presence in the dimensions beyond this earth.

Through removing the barriers to my heart space, I am now able to shine my light more brightly, understand why I am here, share my journey to help others, and know that the best way I can be of service is to be in my truth of who I am. I am here to be creative, to share, to express, to use love as a mirror to humanity for the awareness that we are all connected and ONE.

I am a channeler of Divine Love. It's that simple. I am here to serve as a creative essence to help others find their heart and their truth and bring that forward for humanity. I am here to help other humans one heart at a time by helping to expose the layers of conditioning that block us from hearing the whispers of our heart. This is what I know to be true now, but in the earlier years, with all the social conditioning and generational grievances I carried,

I didn't feel loved, let alone to acknowledge that I am a channeler of Universal Love. I didn't feel sweet like honey (even though I AM as my truest expression of myself).

Perhaps the biggest awareness I am discovering in my journey back to myself is that love is my birthright; it is everyone's birthright. I understand so much more clearly that I have choice and I have abundance to create and exist in any experience I choose, with as much joy and love as I was made to express.

" Love is free, wild, and untamable. "

Love is free, wild, and untamable. It is not for sale. It is not a commodity to be purchased or sold physically, emotionally, or spiritually, and it comes to us as we are sparks of love created by the Divine. We are all love, we are from love, and we will return to love. The drapings of shame, guilt, and fear are merely shackles to which we have always held the key for opening and removing them—forgiveness, to give and receive love, to be held in love. By returning home to our heart and removing the roadblocks to our true self, we are clearing the path for future generations to have the capacity to live in a more aligned, harmonic, unified experience.

I am grateful for all my experiences—the good, the bad, the joyful, the painful, the gains, the losses. They are all serving to provide me with the tools my human body and mind need to walk my way home to my essence, my heart, my soul . . . all that I AM.

About Mielle Fox

I consider myself to be a multidimensional being with varied talents, passions, and interests. I can tell you what I do, but to really understand the crux of who I am, that is tough to describe, but here we go . . .

I am an energy-awareness navigator, an aligned wellness coach, a certified EFT practitioner, an advanced numerologist, a podcaster, an equestrian, a health care provider, and an all-around sciency, spiritual geek.

You can find me on social media in many places and spaces including:

www.foxdenenergetics.com
Podcast: *Energy of the Untamed Heart*

IF I CAN, YOU CAN

By Paula Lemos

Know it shouldn't have happened.
This was not a lesson you needed to learn.
~Jordan Pickell, trauma therapist

I was born in a small town in Portugal and moved to the United States when I was a teenager. To say the least, it was a complete culture shock. I did not know English yet, so there was also huge language barrier. Soon after arriving in the US, I started high school and went to ESOL (English speakers of other languages). There I met many friends from other backgrounds and loved it!

Also, it was there that I met a guy who was handsome, and he came to my "protection" when I encountered a weird situation at school. Soon after, we were dating and hanging out a lot. He was nice and good to me . . . At least, that was what I thought then.

Two years later, at age sixteen, I was pregnant. I didn't know what to do. I felt ashamed, and I worried about what my family would think and say. So I kept it quiet. I was in denial that I could even be pregnant. Months later I felt a stabbing pain. My boyfriend's sister told us to go to the hospital. It was then I officially learned I was actually pregnant. We had no choice but to tell my parents. The news was rough on them, and I felt terrible that I was disappointing them. So we decided to get married.

My nightmare started on the day of our civil marriage. That was when he started pushing and shoving me. With time, it escalated to more and more physical and psychological abuse. I left him many times, stayed in shelters, ran to my parents, even moved to another state to get away from him. Somehow he would always find me and convince me to go back to him, usually by threatening me— he slashed my tires or threatened to kill my loved ones. I was scared and did not want my mistake to hurt my family. He was clever and made it so that I could not prove to the police that he was acting out on these threats. The only thing I was able to prove was the abuse because of the evidence he left on my body.

By now I had two daughters, and this abuse would continue on and off for a long time. I did not want my daughters to endure this level of abuse, nor did I want them to grow up thinking they deserve less from any man, or any relationship. I decided to end it for good. No more abuse! I wanted to show my daughters that this is not love, and I wanted to be a better role model for them. I filed for divorce not long after that.

" No more abuse! "

And as I suspected, it was not easy. The court system failed me as a victim and victimized me all over again. The court system allowed him to make up lies, and the court listened to him without hearing me. An investigation was opened against *me*. My daughters were appointed a court attorney, and investigators came to my house to confirm or deny his allegations. During this time, we were asked to see a mediator, regarding the children. I remember that first day sitting in the mediator's office. I was so scared to be in the same room with him. I also feared that he would most likely follow me afterward. Luckily, I got there earlier than him and told the mediator my story. She listened attentively. She heard me. At last, I felt safe and knew that she understood and validated me. She prompted me to leave, promising to keep him inside the office for a while to give me time to get away.

It was a grueling process, but finally after about three years later, I was able to finalize the divorce. This time, the judge saw and heard from the investigators and attorney for the girls what had actually happened and how much I had gone through. The judge apologized for allowing this to happen in his court.

" There is a way out, and you are not alone! "

I am writing this chapter of my life to share with so many of you who have been or are victims of violence in the world. I hope that my story will give you a glimpse of hope and strength to fight and move out of the cycle of abuse. There is a way out, and you are not alone! It took time for me to process that this was not love, that I deserved better, that it was not my fault. It was abuse. It took me several attempts to get away from my abuser. All I wanted was to be a role model for healthy relationships and real love for my daughters. Ultimately, I did find my way out. There are resources out there, and if you're facing a similar fate, remember it is not your fault; you are not alone, and there is a way out. Please research all the potential resources to help free you from your abuse.

If I could escape this nightmare, you can too. Better to live in love with yourself, be a happier version of you, than to endure what so many of us have. I send you love, courage, and empowerment so that you can escape your abuser and live the life you deserve—a happy fulfilling life with love.

For a list of resources:

National Domestic Violence Hotline 24/7: 800-799-7233
Languages: English, Spanish, and 200+ through interpretation

About Paula Lemos

Paula lives in Rockville, Maryland. She is a reiki master, certified hypnotherapist, and spiritualist. Paula loves to walk in nature and spend time with her daughters and granddaughter. She wrote this chapter in hopes that her story will help other women in domestic violence relationships to know that they can leave their abusers and live happy lives—it takes courage, but if she can do it, so can you! She hopes her chapter touches your heart and resonates with you.

EXCAVATING MY
ANCIENT SELF

By Sara Cronan

*We are all in the gutter, but some of us
are looking at the stars.*
~Oscar Wilde

As I am writing this, I am feeling the power of the word, the power of creation and destruction. This is a moment for me to present myself fully naked and honest. There is no shifting of perspective without looking under every rock, every nook and cranny inside yourself. And my story is naturally intertwined with that of my parents, who adopted me at birth; my family; my friends; and my ancestors known and unknown. I write this as not just a form of healing for me but to send love and healing to all those connected, and to those reading these words. This is my personal truth of experience, and by accepting, understanding, and healing various aspects of myself, I have reconnected with my highest self and live each day guided by my true nature. My wish is for all humans to set themselves free from their self-imposed prisons, connect to their Divine Humanity, and live from the heart. To embody the love we already are.

My story is about so much more than just addiction and recovery and, in turn, learning how to truly love myself. More than learning that self-love naturally translates into connecting to and helping others. It is about learning to acknowledge and heal all the wounds I carry: the shame and worthlessness common in those who were adopted, healing the generational and societal baggage of gender stereotypes, finances and making money, success, beauty, the feminine and masculine. All of it. Learning how to live in the world and follow my own heart instead of trying to fit within a prescribed system. Knowing and trusting in the support and guidance from the universe, nature, God. Learning that by just *being fully myself,* I am helping others and living a blessed and beautiful life.

Love is always the answer. The ancient wisdom of Rumi, of the Toltec people, and of other indigenous cultures connected to nature and the Divine all speak to this. If you peel away the fear that humanity injected into the major world religions, they all also point to this truth. John Lennon understood all we need is love—but how does that translate when we live in a world ruled by the mind instead of the heart? A world that is ruled by fear and violence? A place where money is king, and power corrupts? A literal hell on earth. As the late Jean-Paul Sartre, a French philosophist, bemoaned, hell is other people, and there is no exit.

It is about learning to love oneself, connecting fully

with the body, and living in your heart instead of your mind. Seeing the fear that we all harbor and choosing to face it head on with open arms and open hearts. When in doubt, choose love. When you're angry, choose love. When you are sad, choose love. Choose to accept and understand all the parts of yourself without judgment or reprisal.

Your reality is dictated by how much you love and accept all parts of yourself. This is why I had a physical imprint of my mind being blown, of not being able to handle the truth I was handed, the truth I uncovered. Because in the face of that reality, *all I had left was my fear.* The world was ugly and cruel, harsh, and unforgiving. It took immense joy in fucking with me. My sixteen-year-old self believed that we were being governed by alien overlords and were surrounded by people who were working for them. Some humans, some aliens, but all designed to create this torturous hell on earth. My life was a joke, and I was a plaything.

Recently, I communed with an alien/higher dimensional energy and discovered that it was an old friend. Even before I could comprehend what I was seeing as a child, it came to me to help me heal spiritually and also physically. We had met each other in the before time. The time before I was born into this life.

Lately I had been experiencing a physical and real energy pulse that was trapped in my stomach. This is not too unusual, as many of the energies I hold on to are visceral—you can see the pulse in my flesh when they are quite strong. They are trauma and fear.

This one had been evading me for a few weeks. I would

feel it, I would place my hand on the spot I felt it, and it would disappear, only to show up in a new spot a few minutes later. I could sometimes feel the energy moving around as it tried to hide from me.

Then a few nights ago, I had an intense dream. One moment that stood out was seeing the outline of a small creature pushing from the inside toward the outside of my stomach. Yes, like in the movie *Alien*! I was trying to catch it so I could remove it, but it was too quick every time.

When I woke up in the morning, I could feel that same energy in my side, upset and freaking out. I finally calmed it down enough to have a chat.

It was my sixteen-year-old self, raging and that "all of my life is a lie! My understanding of the world is completely wrong! Nothing is the way I thought it was!"

I finally realized what was happening.

At fifteen I had started using drugs—mostly cannabis and alcohol—and around sixteen started doing mushrooms, LSD, and opiates regularly. I tried anything else that came around, but they didn't feel good, so I didn't continue using them. I was constantly high, and I tripped so often that I didn't hallucinate anymore. I was living in my new reality, and I was a character in a play. Unfortunately, the cast of characters I surrounded myself with were just as depressed, confused, angry, and self-hating as I was. I began to see the wheels turning in people's heads, the social and mental calculations that we all were accustomed to making before we spoke, before we would make a move. I became quiet and observational in social situations, just trying to understand this new scene I was experiencing.

Trying to understand why people hung around me, what they could possibly want to do with me, want from me.

And herein lies the issue—I had zero confidence in myself. I knew I was intelligent and not ugly. I knew I had physical strength—I would spar and play-fight with any man to prove I could whoop his ass. Beyond that, I was depressed, anxious, and borderline suicidal. Life didn't make sense, and I had given up on the possibility that God could exist. I wasn't even certain a soul existed. All the Christian ideals I had been taught conflicted with one another, and there were multiple interpretations of Scriptures I found not just confusing but infuriatingly inconsistent.

That inconsistency was mirrored in society, with its dismissal of stay-at-home mothers and hatred of working women. It's giving to the poor with one hand and snatching it back with the other. The mind-boggling culture clash of White and Black America playing out in my very divided town in Missouri. I became obsessed with discovering the truth. The truth about God, about the universe, about our souls and why we exist. I told myself, "Timothy Leery says LSD is the gateway to enlightenment—to expanded consciousness—so I will continue using it until I understand." And so I did.

Using LSD or other hallucinogens on a regular basis leads to an intense reality for that person but a disassociation with what most people refer to as "reality." I preferred to dress nearly the same each day—I liked to think I was a cartoon character, and, therefore, had only one outfit I would wear. My car was my spaceship, and I was the designated pilot during our group trips away from the basement of my boyfriend. I had extremely intense dreams: I would wake up laughing, or talking, or screaming, or crying on most nights. As I have connected to my soul more and more, I have reconnected with guides and spirits who were with me during those years. I apologized for not being ready or able to handle the truth . . . They laughed and said, "This was the path! You [as a soul] like big challenges with big growth and are learning patience. You needed to forge ahead and fail and have the experience of being lost, angry, soul sick, addicted, and suicidal so you would have the fertilizer you needed to grow into the brilliant flower you are now."

I would talk to everything—my car, a tree, the cat digging in the alley dumpster—but I felt extremely uncomfortable talking to people. None of these other things were trying to defraud me, to take advantage of me. But people always seemed to have an agenda—to get my drugs, or use my car, to get in my pants, to get . . . well, whatever people want out of teenagers.

I started dating a thirty-two-year-old when I was sixteen. I distinctly remember feeling at the time that it was cool that someone so "mature" was willing to have hours of conversation with me, found me interesting, found me attractive. When I was thirty-two myself, I was confronted with the disturbing reality of that situation. I now wonder what trauma he was carrying that it was okay to have a sexual relationship with a child? If you are asking how my parents were willing to allow it, it is simple. I had threatened, and fully intended, to completely disown them if they pursued legal charges. They knew me well enough to know I was serious, and grudgingly allowed me to have my experience. Now, I look back and am grateful for all the myriad mistakes they allowed me to make. Every single experience, good and bad, has led me to this exact moment, where I can be a guide for others from an honest place of knowing.

As with all addicts, and in particular, opiate addicts, I started self-medicating due to a fear of pain. Just existing in the world every day was painful. Having to wake up, get dressed, and be a human. Having to go to school and deal with people I didn't like, didn't trust, and felt isolated from. Watching the news and feeling helpless at the injustice and violence in the world. Enduring the constant venomous stream of my own inner dialogue. I was fully submerged in the darkness, looking for the light, for solace, with those who were just as damaged, hurt, and confused as I was.

Getting high was such a relief. I romanticized the notion of having a gentle nap in the arms of Morpheus and was ecstatic that it was achievable. I didn't understand what was driving my behavior at the time, but I now see clearly: I was building an escape room, a place to hide from everything, including myself. But over time, that escape room becomes your prison. We are told this will happen. We are warned. Yet still, we gather every brick eagerly and mortar ourselves inside, not knowing there were other paths, other choices that could bring in the light.

By twenty-five I had been hard enough on my body— multiple car accidents and living a generally hard-partying lifestyle—that I had lower back pain. Back then, I didn't know that emotional pain manifests in the body. So this ignorance created the perfect excuse for me to stay high on opiates. All day, every day. It felt easy and plentiful, and I didn't think too hard about how much money I was spending, or how much physical damage doing IV drugs did. I was just scared enough of dying—I had enough people I would have been ashamed to know I was an addict—that I was meticulous about keeping track of my usage. I researched how many milligrams a day was the least likely to kill me. This was easy if I was crushing up pills but extremely difficult if I was using heroin. As the years rolled by, the prices of the drugs skyrocketed. When the war on opioids began, suddenly I was buying medicine from people who really could use it but wanted the money to fund their own addictions.

And the funny thing about chronic pain and painkillers, is it creates a vicious cycle of pain that spirals out of control. You have pain, so you numb it. You have more pain, you numb it more. And it works—you get blissful relief and euphoria. As you chase those first magical highs, as you chase the dragon, you don't notice just how much the quantity increases, and your body's *need* for it accelerates. The biggest joke on you is that when you try to cut back, the pain comes back with a vengeance, worse than before. You have a real attack of panic attached to the start of withdrawals, so you give in to your body's demands for medicine. And thus, you are now an addict.

There are many scientific articles about this exact cycle of pain. How chemicals transform the brain, how the liver transforms the drugs, but this is an incomplete picture. Here is my understanding: Every single one of us is carrying our own traumas and pain, and we are taught to fear our pain. Just look at your social media feeds—the number of advertisers selling ways to avoid emotional pain, physical pain, the pain of social isolation is nonstop. Take this pill to lose weight, this diet to avoid depression, this exercise for back pain. The missing piece is *why* are we feeling these symptoms in the first place? Our reaction is avoidance instead of addressing the pain and trauma from an emotional perspective, to follow it back to its origin. Instead, we simply shy away from any and all pain, recoiling as we experience it. We run from it. And I will be clear: I might have had the struggle with opiates, but this is true of anything you use to mask your pain—it all works the same way.

I was a secret eater and binge eater since I was about nine. Honestly, I would have been bulimic except I hated throwing up. These eating-disorder traits were inherited from my mom. I have a vague memory of her telling me she had felt the same way about vomiting as a teenager. That was why she was anorexic in high school. She was a yo-yo dieter all of my life. I knew her as someone who hated herself, not just her body, but herself internally, and this energy transferred to me, and informed how I chose to treat myself and my body.

"What was the pain and trauma you were masking?" I hear you ask. The concise answer is, "My true nature." In longer form, I was a super softhearted child, attuned to everything around me, including spirits and unseen energies and entities. I had nightmares starting in preschool and through my teen years. My parents would have to wake me up because I was crying or screaming. By the time I was seven, I was pulling the blinds down at night. I told my mom that I didn't like the lights in the trees watching me, studying me. I complained about the monsters in my closet, under my bed, hiding in the shadows in my bedroom. But growing up in the Midwest in the 1980s Bible Belt, there was only fear and confusion surrounding the things I experienced, and the reaction from my parents and family was to ignore it, to deny it. I was trained to conform to normal societal standards and told to stop being dramatically overimaginative and a daydreamer.

Both my parents were shutdown, emotionally immature in the exact opposite ways. Dad is a cerebral and intellectual academic. He had learned early to retreat to logic and the ways of the mind to deal with the traumas he was carrying. This served him well in his lifelong career as a lawyer. But the ability to see all sides of a situation isn't the same as *feeling* all sides of a situation. I remember feeling constantly confused when he would ask me to explain my position on some subject—the Cold War, God, heaven and hell, poverty—and would then play devil's advocate and argue the exact opposite position. It felt as if the rug had been pulled out from under me; no stance was safe. My fear of him seeing me as stupid fed my insecurity about being worthy of his love. This was my experience starting in elementary school. I understand now that he was grooming me to have the flexibility of mind he valued, the ability to take myriad stances and argue effectively from those positions. And it has served me well. But in those moments, when I was trying to be the intelligent and eloquent daughter he wanted me to be—and I desperately wanted to be—it felt like I was being shamed for my argument when he would reverse sides. It felt like he was laughing at my childish ineptitude. I retreated to the position of trying to read what was the "correct" opinion and espousing that—and therefore, never trusted my own. I do understand he was trying to help me. His view of the world was that it was a cold, dark vacuum without morals or integrity, and one in which God doesn't exist. People were awful and violent and untrustworthy. Intellect and flexibility, a sharp tongue and wit, were the best armor against all this he could give me. And this world construct was created from the fears and traumas he experienced and inherited.

As for Mom, she was, at heart, a deeply spiritual person. She believed in God and enjoyed the community at her Methodist church, the community of her childhood. I found out, only on her deathbed, that she did sometimes experience spirits and the Unseen. We shared a beautiful moment of her being comforted in her hospital bed by a ghost cat. Her joy and surprise that I could also see bonded us in a new way. But during her life, her own mother's fears of witchcraft and magic forced her to bury that part of herself. Mom's own shame and self-doubt, her own lack of confidence, didn't allow for such a large variance from the normal societal ideas. She endured emotional abuse at home, the most insidious being the silent treatment. Her mother would go for as long as a full week refusing to speak to her when she was a "bad girl."

I am convinced she had body dysmorphia, created by her mother putting her on a diet at six. We both struggled all our lives with food and the control of food. Mom had lost 250 pounds about five years before she died, and was down to two hundred pounds. She showed immense strength and willpower, conforming to a two-year liquid diet supervised by her doctors. But in the end, she chose the freedom to feed her trauma, for comfort, and she died at over 450 pounds.

Mom was also adopted, but she only found out, by accident, at age sixteen. (The main reason I was told as young as possible.) It explained why her extremely petite five-foot mother was so insistent on trying to make Mom's physical stature match hers. Unfortunately for Mom, she was destined to be five foot six inches and towered over her mother. Mom also carried the trauma of a rape that remained buried and unseen until she confessed it to me when I was sixteen. She said it was the main reason she worried about me being out all hours of the night, worried who I was trusting with my life.

Her greatest defense mechanism was to shut down. When she was angry, instead of protesting and fighting for her position, she would go silent. When she was sad, she would hold in the tears and swallow her pain and remain silent. She would unintentionally carry forward the ancestral baggage of the silent treatment, the thing that left scars on her.

This paradox of personalities created the perfect situation for their highly sensitive child to learn how to be the diplomat, the fixer, the communicator. As early as I can

remember, as soon as I could speak in complete sentences, they would come to me when they were upset with each other. Not so much to explain their emotions but to criticize the other, to ridicule whatever behavior was upsetting them. In turn, I would try to explain to them the other person's point of view and how they were feeling. By the time I was eight or nine, I was pretty good at smoothing out the arguments between them, except for the times I couldn't.

Dad had an amazingly scary temper. Because he was a well-respected lawyer, and my home looked so suburban and normal, most people didn't realize the fear I lived in. It wasn't until I reconnected with a friend recently—my best friend from preschool to ninth grade—that she confirmed that my memories were not exaggerated. When she asked how my dad was doing, I said, "Really well actually. He's fairly jolly these days." She almost spit out her drink and looked at me with disbelief, "*Jolly? Really?!* That's crazy! I was scared to death of him!" In that moment, I felt a validation I didn't even realize I needed. Yes, my dad's anger was a force of nature, and it wasn't just my imagination.

I stopped being spanked around the age of ten. I was "too old" to spank. But it wasn't the physical punishment that left the scars. My parents didn't use anything but their hand. I knew many kids who weren't that lucky. No, it was the overwhelming emotion that would punch me in the chest, like being consumed in the fiery breath of a dragon. And it didn't just dissipate once the initial torrential rage subsided—it would stew and simmer and occasionally boil over again. I would practice walking around the house as silently as possible, hoping that no one knew where I was. Maybe if I was silent enough, I could avoid waking the sleeping beast.

The strange thing that many people experience in a violent household is that we learn to embody the rage we are attacked by. I remember years of standing in front of the mirror from about the age of six, yelling at my reflection to "Stop crying! What do you have to cry about?! So what if you're sad? You have a good life—you aren't homeless. You have food and a roof over your head. You know your parents love you. Stop being such a crybaby!" I would then harness that voice I internalized, that rage, and feel it course through my body. I tried to make my eyes glow like embers. I would growl in a deep and ferocious tone and try to blow fire out my own mouth. I had learned to protect myself by embodying my inner anger dragon. Once I read Stephen King's *Firestarter* around age nine, I tried to set my enemies on fire with the power of my mind. I desperately wanted to be able to control my environment, so telekinesis was a natural desire.

In third grade we had an assignment to take two pictures from a magazine and write a story about them. The teacher had cut out the pictures in advance. I chose a tranquil sailboat on the water and a matador avoiding a bull in the ring. I wasn't able to express my emotions freely in my house because, if I am honest, my parents didn't have any way of showing me how. They didn't know how to deal with their emotions, how to talk about them, or how to channel them in a healthy way. So the result was I only understood emotions from an intellectual perspective. So

I wrote one story about an alien matador who ended up getting gored by the bull, including detailed descriptions about the wound and the blood and him dying. The sailboat ended up being attacked by mechanical sharks that destroyed the ship and killed all the people on the boat. Needless to say, my parents and I were called into the guidance counselor's office, and I defended myself with the same denial of my nature I had been taught: I wasn't angry or upset or hurt . . . I was just dramatically overimaginative.

This mantra of being overimaginative has followed me for most of my life. I was consistently and repetitively told by those around me they didn't see or hear the things I did. They didn't have a clue what I was talking about. The only respite from this was in college. It was the most free I had ever felt to be myself. It was a time of connecting to other beautiful souls living as best as they could. I still am in touch with my core circle to this day. But even in that more open time, I felt pressured by my insecurity to keep these things to myself. As best as I could. Until I couldn't ignore it anymore.

I was lucky enough to meet my husband, Andy, during this period. I graduated from college with a double major in voice and viola in 2000. I started working at a music school run by a woman who I now consider my professional mentor and sister. Andy and I married on my family farm in 2002—the house my grandma had died in. The place where my mom grew up. The place my parents lived out nearly all the rest of their lives. But I was living in Maryland by then, so Andy and I bought a house there and started our lives together. Our families got along. We adopted two kitten sisters, and we lived a full and social life. It was good.

Fast-forward to 2008, the year Andy's father died. The entire year before he passed was brutal. He was diagnosed with stage IV kidney disease. Andy was the baby of five sons, as well as a decade older than me. So his parents were more like grandparent age to me; they were both about eighty.

We lived about fifteen minutes away, so we made it our mission to help as much as we could. Taking his mom on all her errands (she couldn't drive), taking his dad to doctor and dialysis appointments. Cooking and cleaning as much as his mom would let us. I was working full time teaching. Andy had pursued an art career a few years earlier, and we were grateful he could spend his days with his parents. We survived as best as we could. It was my first exposure to an intense caregiving situation outside of a nursing home. His dad wanted to die in his own bed, and we wanted to honor that wish. I am grateful this was possible.

The interesting thing about his passing was how . . . quiet it was. About a week before the end, he just didn't wake up when we tried to rouse him. The hospice workers had told us that was to be expected for those who quit dialysis. We set up camp at his parents' house so we could all rotate who sat with him during the nighttime. All three of us sat vigil, just waiting for the final breath.

At night his light snoring was all we would hear as we sat next to the bed. It felt unnervingly calm and peaceful. His desiccated body slowly shriveling like a grape dying on the vine.

And even then, even in that most sacred of spaces, my addiction would not be quiet. I would skim as much morphine from the hospice kit they provided as I could get away with. And then some more. My practice of sneaking around the house as a child came in handy. As I would creep past his bed to the bookcase the drugs sat on, I would silently, sometimes out loud, say, I *am so sorry, I am so sorry, I am soooo sorry* . . . Please forgive me . . .

This wasn't my first experience with the death of a loved one. I was terrified at age three to walk into the hospital room where my great-grandmother lay dying. My body still remembers being placed on the bed and not being able to scream, cry, or move. I was so scared and confused, and for some reason my chest hurt. I lost my grandfather to lung cancer when I was five. I have fond memories of his shining face, like the sun, smiling at me as he played with me as best as he could while lying in bed. When I was sixteen, my beloved grandma suddenly died, carrying a box of oranges up the stairs of my mom's childhood home. (The timing of when I started my descent into darkness isn't lost on me.) My other grandma passed in a tiny nursing home surrounded by staff, neighbors, and family who cherished her, while I was away at college.

So Andy's father's death was the first time I was there to witness that delicate moment when the soul leaves the body. That palpable shift from here to gone. This death also showed me that physical death can be calm and peaceful. He was ready and wasn't fearful; he had lived a wonderful life and had many wonderful memories. He wasn't fighting the inevitable; he was in the home he raised his family.

He was resting in peace.

Andy and I sold our house and moved into the upstairs of his mom's house, and she occupied the mother-in-law apartment in the basement. We began a new journey of caring for an elder, a duty we chose willingly with our hearts. But as is the case with most things that change the course of your life, the path wasn't easy.

My mother-in-law, May, was a warm and quintessential mother. In fact, over the decade we lived together, I started calling her Mom. She and my mother had a lot in common in their histories, in their mothers, and I was very aware of the parallels. Their mothers had had a mean streak and treated them poorly, for different reasons, in similar ways. Their fathers were kind and protective and connected to the land. They both had a strong connection to God, although they both knew God beyond the constructs of their Christianity. For me, the biggest difference was May's warmness. She gave the biggest and warmest hugs *all the time*. One of the most frustrating things about my mom was I constantly asked her to hug me "better." I could only explain this to her as "harder." I now understand I was feeling her walls between her heart and the world around her.

May was connected to her heart in a more open way. As an empath, this was a great comfort to experience, and we quickly bonded to be mother and daughter. Luckily, my own mom appeared to understand and accept that I now had another mom in my life. Andy was the youngest of five boys, and the story she told was that she wanted a girl so badly she kept having babies until Andy's birth nearly killed her. So I was now "adopted" again.

As May slowly declined, my life shrunk and my addiction grew. Anyone who has provided care for an extended time, especially in their home, will understand when I say there is an insidious thread of need that runs through everything and can choke you. The earliest example is Halloween 2009. I was thirty-one when we moved in with her, and I had a lot of goth friends, so Halloween was always a big night. The first Halloween living with her, I was told by May, last minute, we were expected to stay and hand out candy for her at the upstairs front door. I was furious but sucked it up and did what I was told. *It's just one year. There will be other parties. This isn't forever . . .* No one really understood at that moment why I was so angry, including my husband. At that moment I didn't understand fully either. I felt petty and childish. Now, I can recognize there was a part of me that saw where this was going, that knew the path we were headed down. A path where our life was not ours—our life and focus were hers. And I wanted to throw off the shackles and run away. As a couple who intentionally didn't have children, who chose not to be responsible for another life, I eventually realized that was to allow us the space in our lives to have this experience instead.

Three years before May passed in 2019, she was admitted to the in-home hospice program. Andy was doing all the physical work of cooking and cleaning for her as well as for us. I was working a brutal six-day-a-week teaching schedule and doing all the errands outside the home that needed to be done. I had also become tacitly in charge of her emotional well-being. Since she didn't leave the house anymore, just as with my parents, I took her happiness under my charge. I felt the pressure of that responsibility building because she was more negative and complainant than ever. This stemmed from grief, frustration, fear, and a stronger attachment to my husband than any other human. He was her security blanket. I realized that I was destined to fail in keeping her happy. Instead of recognizing her happiness was not my responsibility, I doubled down and started doing everything I could think of to make her feel loved and wanted instead of a burden. In a strange twist of fate, I can now see that she knew how hard I was working to care for her, and it only made her feel like more of a burden. It was a catch-22.

During the winter of 2015, I saw blinking lights in the trees behind the house. There was a red radio tower a few miles away that I assumed I was seeing. But then I would see the lights in the wrong part of the trees. And then, wait, why did they randomly change to white? Why were there now orange lights? Why were there three where there used to only be one? I noticed that the more drugs I did, and the later I stayed up, the more I could see them. I would spend hours obsessively trying to take a video or photo, staying up until the sun rose or dragging my husband outside to try and see them. Over a year of frustration passed without any evidence or understanding.

And when spring hit again, suddenly I was seeing all kinds of colored lights, mists, figures, orbs—and not just at my house. The phenomenon was spreading to anywhere I was, especially the houses I taught at in the more rural parts of the suburbs. One night I was sitting on the back porch (like every night), and a group of small blue orbs drifted onto the porch. As they surrounded me, I felt them brush my skin and heard the chirping of crickets loudly in my ears. I blurted out, "Oh my god, are you crickets?" The chirping intensified, and I knew they were, in fact, cricket spirits. It was the beginning of reconnecting to the spiritual side of myself, the ancient part of my self, rebuilding my connection to my soul.

I could spend pages describing all the encounters with all the different beings, light and dark, terrestrial and higher dimensional, lost and powerful, but that would be a book in its own right. That spring I was waking up from my long sleep since I'd come to this earth and started consciously feeling my own connection to the energy around me. I discovered I could see, feel, hear, *smell* them. And the more I talked to and connected with them, the more that showed up. I rejoiced at rediscovering a part of myself I didn't know I missed—my childhood wonder of the world, my own magic.

"I rejoiced at rediscovering a part of myself I didn't know I missed—my childhood wonder of the world, my own magic."

During these years, May was also having her own experiences. She complained about the blinky lights outside her window keeping her up. She would ask why we hired people to sleep next to her at night. On the baby monitor video screen, I would see sparkly clouds of energy in her room. I took a few photos of figures that were standing or sitting in the room with her at night.

We all had experiences of hearing her husband's ghost walking down the hallway and pushing the buttons on the microwave. (He was a terrible cook.) Occasionally I would hear his voice—sometimes he called out her name. For those years May had a constant "cold draft" above her head. We spent months trying to debunk the ghost theory, but in the end we capitulated. We accepted he was waiting for her on this side of the veil, the ever-loyal husband. This acceptance activated both May's and my deep-seated fears of the unknown, of the darkness, and of heaven and hell. My excitement of discovering faeries, cricket spirits, and angels dissolved into a fear of all things dark.

I was now living in a constant state of anxious panic and exhaustion. I was strung out, overtired, and scared of every new supernatural thing that touched me. I began waking up in the middle of the night, repeatedly, while having sex with . . . something. On more than one occasion, it poked me with its claws. It felt like rape. I felt terrorized. I would see orbs and colors and shadows and shapes enter my room at night and scan me, touch me, hover in the corner. I determined that something was trying to take my soul from me. As I heard it growling, I would feel my body spinning and lifting into the air—but I would twitch and feel the snap back into my physical body. My bed would shake like there was an earthquake, with intense growling and howling under the bed. All the fears from similar experiences in childhood returned with a vengeance, and I no longer felt safe in my home or anywhere else.

I was able to maintain my teaching, although I had to

cancel a lot due to withdrawals, hospice appointments, or a need to try to get some actual rest. If you are high, opiates don't let your brain get enough deep REM sleep, and you cannot stay asleep unless you take enough to make you pass out. But even at that time, I would tell anyone who inquired that teaching was the highlight of my day. I was an in-home piano, voice, and guitar teacher, so I traveled to visit each of my forty-five students. Breaking free of the house every day, being forced to focus on something else, something I enjoyed, was important. My students were my lighthouse, helping me navigate the murky waters of my depression, addiction, and stress. Because I recognized how much I needed them, I pushed myself to maintain my sanity, I wouldn't survive losing that outlet.

I was living a double life.

May's decline was excruciatingly gradual. In fact, Medicare tried to kick her off hospice at least twice and threatened it again every few months. Her response was to have another ministroke, and they would relent. Therefore, death had been a constant topic between all of us and something we did our best to address openly. Honestly, I was thinking about and hoping for it every single day. The end of her life was the end of a prison sentence, the moment my life would be my own again. So when Andy and I got the word she likely had only several days left, I thought I would feel a sense of relief. Instead, the weight of life and death, of my guilt and shame, descended like a yoke around my shoulders. I remember not being sure if it was real, if she would *ever* die. But the next day, I arrived home from work to find a dead crow on the front doorstep—face up, wings splayed open, neck broken. I stopped short. Time ceased, and I burst into tears.

When I was younger, I had engaged in some witchcraft as a solo practitioner, but my fears of doing something irreversibly wrong caused me to stop after a couple of years. But I continued to learn about other cultures and their spiritual practices; my limited knowledge encompasses the globe. Many cultures talk of crows as the messengers from spirits—they traverse time and space to deliver these messages. This one was clear. I needed to accept that her death was finally imminent. I called off work indefinitely, and we sat vigil. Her other children stopped in to say goodbye.

That night I watched a spectacular display from the universe. From the back porch, I stared in disbelief as hundreds of different-colored faeries, orbs and mists of all sizes and colors, angels, and spirits gathered in the trees. They then began to parade through May's window in the basement. It took a few minutes of contemplation before it hit me. It was a funeral procession. Myriad beings wanted to pay their final respect to the woman who loved them, the woman who spoke to them when she didn't know who she was really talking to, the woman who was a faerie and whose time on Earth was about to end.

The moment that made me believe my eyes, at least for a while, was when a large bright-orange orb, the size of a large party balloon, drifted from the trees. In a shaky voice I asked, "Roger, is it you??" A translucent *R* floated from the orb toward me, dissipating as the orb disappeared through the window. I couldn't breathe as I waited for it to reemerge. It eventually reappeared from visiting May, and now it was vibrating. Suddenly it broke into three faerie shapes, holding hands and dancing gleefully around in a circle. They spun faster and faster until they spun back into an orb shape and floated away into the trees. I cried and laughed, feeling something weird in my chest. I now know that feeling very well—it is my heart full of gratitude and release.

In 2000 May and her husband had lost their second son, Roger, to aggressive leukemia. His favorite color was orange, which they saw everywhere after he died. The first Mother's Day after he passed, an orange balloon just happened to get stuck in a tree outside the window where May was being celebrated. After that, they would release a single orange balloon on his birthday. The signal was given and received. And the cycle was nearly complete.

The next couple of days, May was mostly nonresponsive. She stared into the air, focused on something far in the distance. I had heard that this was the time spirits come to prepare the soul for departure. Stories abound of people having conversations with long-gone family and friends. Her lips moved sometimes, but mostly she just sighed or grunted. She had stopped eating, and we just did our best to keep her physically comfortable.

Sometime during the afternoon, she started speaking, which was startling. "Who's coming? Who's going to stay? Who's coming? Who's going to stay!" Over and over for what felt like forever. I kept thinking, *I am not sure who's coming, but I know you won't be staying.* Eventually she quieted and resumed staring. Just a few hours later she spoke again, "No no no no no. NO no NO NO NO no no NO no NO noNONONONONONONONONONO." Over and over, and no amount of trying to comfort her seemed to give her any peace. I felt more helpless than ever. I just sat next to her, quietly sobbing, exhausted and just holding her hand. There wasn't any more to be done.

The following day, she didn't open her eyes except a bit as we shifted around her body weight to keep the blood circulating as well as we could. This was the first time I noticed a clear orb with a blue center hovering in the corner of the room. A part of me recognized it as my father-in-law, her husband. I figured the time must be very near indeed. I had never seen a physical manifestation of him before.

Later that evening, she started grunting, agitated. "Uh-uh. Uh-uh! Uh-uh! Uh-uh!" over and over. I called down to Andy because she was grunting so forcefully that I was worried she would throw herself out of her hospital bed. "Uh-uh, uh-uh, UH-UH!" The protest was so clear. May had endured a lifetime of grief and loss. She'd had a near-death experience she talked about with wonder and comfort. She chose to come back and had been warned the path would be challenging. But she still chose to come back. But now, in this moment, *now*, as the final grains of time were running out, she said NO! What happened next during this, her final night, was proof that there is a point at which letting go is no longer a choice.

The last few nights I had watched as tiny faerie/angel beings pulled fluffy white energy out of her nose, mouth, and ears and created an orb just in front of the tip of her nose. On this final night, it had grown large enough I could see it was clear with a light-pink center and the same size as the blue orb still just hanging out in the corner of the room. Facing her with the window to my back, I felt a flurry of activity behind me, and before I could react, I felt something land on top of my head. Hard. I recoiled and brushed my hands over my skull, my heart pounding—what the fuck just happened?! I heard low background noise. All my life I have heard music where there is no reason to. I used to say I could hear FM frequencies in the air. Just typing that sentence makes me laugh at my own amazing self-denial. How is hearing spirits less likely than randomly hearing FM frequencies? But my fears were tied to being a crazy person, a spiritual kook, and a freak science-based answer felt easier to accept.

At that moment, I sat down and strained my ears to hear. The drums came into focus first, tribal and rhythmic, the tempo increasing with the clarity in which I heard the sounds. I looked out the window into the trees that towered all around the house. I noticed six large orbs, all different colors, sitting on a single branch of a giant tree, like birds on a wire. They swayed in unison, dancing to the same music I was hearing. As the music intensified into a driving beat, I heard the chanting begin. "Ma Ra Na, Ma Ra Na" over and over. I pictured the scene from *Galaxy Quest*, where Tim Allen's character wakes up in a gladiator's ring and the alien crowd is chanting for the beast to tear him apart. It felt like a call for a monster to appear and destroy me. The orbs swirled into a 2-D stained-glass figure. A familiar-looking wolf, fierce, in attack posture, teeth bared. It swayed and growled to the music for a minute, and then swoosh! The orbs rearrange and the same wolf is sitting at the feet of an old lady in a cloak. It is obviously her familiar magical companion. Swoosh! An Asian-style dragon, undulating to the beat. Swoosh! Three human tribal dancers with grass skirts, bare chested and wearing ceremonial spirit masks . . . swoosh swoosh swoosh.

I had no idea how many forms the orbs took, as my human brain couldn't contain it all. Time had stopped. But the message was strong and clear—the opinion I had held for many years, that cultural representations of different deities, including death, were simply the lens that culture chose to see it through. But it was all the same being, the same energy. Death was dancing for me, to confirm I was seeing correctly, that I understood clearly.

After the orbs floated away and the music died away, the room seemed darker than ever. I called Andy over the baby monitor and said, "I need you here. I just saw something crazy!" He came down and sat with me as I attempted to explain what I'd seen. And then I noticed movement outside the bedroom door that led to the basement. I was frozen in the fear of what might come next. I crept to the doorway and peeked around the corner. I saw a solid black tentacle shape, or snake, but in midair, making its way toward us. I backed up to the wall, keeping as much distance between me and it as possible, and watched as it entered the room. It crawled up onto the bed, over May's belly, and entered her eyes, nose, mouth, and ears. It slowly slithered back out, carrying a white fluff with it, and disappeared back the way it came. It was the reaper releasing her last spark of energy from her body.

I slept in a recliner next to her so I could hold her hand and give her morphine by mouth every two hours. I awoke suddenly and heard a gurgling sigh. I jumped out of bed because I had slept through my alarm. I grabbed the morphine and rushed to her side, worried she was struggling due to pain. I stopped and listened. No gurgling breath. Silence. I placed my hand on her chest. No beat. Stillness.

Ear to her chest. Silence.

At 6:30 a.m. I woke up her son. "Andy, come down. I think your mom is dead."

It was later in the morning that I saw the blue and pink orbs ascend to the sky, a cloud figure descending to escort them up to . . . heaven? And they both sent me cloud drawings, more detailed than I can believe even now. I rejoiced at her being with her loved ones, knowing she was in the light, even though she had a huge struggle crossing over. I cried when they showered Andy in tie-dyed light, showing all their love for their child in a clear and dramatic way. I was numb and exhausted. And the next day, I began a battle with fear, a full-scale war with darkness and grief.

I felt malevolent forces all around me. Dark mists and invisible entities pressing up against me, poking me, tormenting me all day every day. Lurking in every corner, ready to claw or scratch, trip or knock me off balance. I felt like the house was full of deep mud, and I couldn't breathe. The demon that I had felt was dragging May into negativity and despair was now trying to attach to me. I shouted and raged at it, begged and bargained for it to leave me alone. Every time I left the property, it would stop. I started teaching as soon as possible, just to get away. For the next week and a half, I couldn't sleep or had nightmares and terrible, gory visions. I spent money I didn't have to stay a night in a hotel just so I could get some rest.

Feeling certain this was spiritual in nature, I googled "Shaman near me." This was my first brave step to shedding the overly analytical mindset to which I had developed a fanatical devotion to. I searched through many websites, looking for someone who didn't appear to be fully entrenched in the spiritual world. After hours of reading biographies, I landed on a shaman close by who also happened to have a neuroscience degree. That was all the excuse I needed to trust her.

I was super nervous when I met with her, but she promised she could help me fight whatever monsters were bothering me. I was reaching for something I didn't really feel like I understood but had always wanted to. Something that felt forbidden but necessary.

Long story short, she freaked me the fuck out. She said she had mostly blocked my ability to see spirits. She said her guides did brain surgery on me because I had a rift in my mind. She explained this rift made me enticed to go to the dark side, to play with dark spirits. She talked about me vomiting up black goo, streams coming out of my nose and mouth, leaking out of my eyes during this surgery. She validated that I was surrounded by energies of all kinds, but mainly a lot of dark spirits, including the demon toying with me. She straight up told me to get psychiatric help immediately because this demon was going to cause me to hurt myself and/or others. It would *make* me.

Sitting in the car after the session, I called Andy and explained the message she'd given me, crying and terrified, pleading to get me help because I didn't want to hurt anyone or anything. We spent the next few days calling psychiatrists, my parents footing the bill because my addiction meant I didn't have any money or health insurance. As those of you who have tried to get mental health help quickly can attest to, the only option was a crisis center or the emergency room and declare you are going to kill yourself. For those of us struggling but determined *not* to do that, all you can do is make an appointment with a psychiatrist. So I did, but I had to wait almost *three months* to be seen. Most of the offices I'd called didn't have an appointment for four to six months. I was dumbfounded. No wonder suicide rates are high. So hoping to get help quicker, I asked my husband to take me to the Maryland Crisis Center.

Sitting in a claustrophobic white-walled room, I tried to explain to the doctor about the spirits and demons and all the stuff I felt and heard and saw. After I finished my outpouring, she looked at me and said, "What you are describing sounds like a spiritual awakening."

I froze in confusion. Not the response I was expecting. "What?"

She looked at me. "You are too well spoken to be having a psychotic break and are too old for schizophrenia. You know that you are seeing things and that they aren't part of this reality. So we can't help you. Maybe find a priest or something? I'm sorry." I tried arguing, but she wouldn't budge and simply gave me a list of thirty more psychiatrists in the area. Defeated, confused, and burned out, I left with a stack of paperwork and no better off than when I had started. For the next three months, I counted down the days, trying unsuccessfully to ignore all the spirits around me, waiting for help to finally arrive.

My new psychiatrist was willing to listen and proposed the same suggestion I heard from my parents. "Grief does weird things to people and their minds. You are probably just seeing things because your brain is overwhelmed by grief." However, he did diagnose me with major depressive disorder and anxiety. I was thrilled to be walking out with a prescription that might change my daily experience.

Over the next months a cycle emerged. He would ask me how I was feeling. I would say not better enough. "I think I need a slightly higher dose." He would tell me I didn't need it, harass me about all the real-world stuff I was ignoring by thinking about spiritual things, and then up my dose. It was sort of helping, but honestly just having a place to vent was probably what helped.

Then COVID-19 changed the world. March 2020 the world came to a halt, and so did my ability to process my grief and depression. I gave up on the doctor, feeling more and more judged and therefore combative. I was just existing, numbing what I could with drugs. I didn't enjoy it at all anymore. I could feel the damage I was doing to my veins and my skin—my soul.

Suddenly, pain patients couldn't get their prescriptions refilled, and there was a worldwide pharmaceutical crisis. The prices skyrocketed again, and I finally had to move to the more affordable option of Suboxone, something I said I would never take because of the potential health and side-effect risks. It is a drug used to get people off opiates, like methadone. The upside was it was taken as a film on the tongue and absorbed much quicker than pills. The huge upside of injecting drugs is the immediacy of the effects. So this drug hit me quickly enough I could stop stabbing myself with a needle finally. It was a big step to stopping the cycle of self-harm.

The next year was a holding pattern as the entire globe waited to see if the pandemic would destroy humanity. The days blurred to months, and suddenly it was the end of July 2021. For the fourth time, Andy had caught me shooting up after I'd said I had quit. He again found me in the choke hold of drugs. I had quit, for real, each time. But then something would happen, and I would be triggered and return to all my habits secretly, including using needles again. This final time it was two things: Andy's best friend suddenly dying in March and my mom moving permanently into a skilled nursing home in April.

I knew that Andy would divorce me for real. It was no longer a threat to try and change my behavior. The man I loved more than anyone or anything was going to abandon me, and I deserved it. And yes, I loved him more than the drugs, but I hated myself more than I loved him. I was disgusted by the lying, stealing, self-harm, and the wasteful use of money and time. Only a drug addict will wait for hours for a dealer in a random parking lot. There were many times I called off work, student by student, just waiting, waiting, waiting, desperate to numb the panic and the pain. I hated myself every time for being so weak, making such terrible choices, being so pathetic. So once again I promised to quit, for real and forever. And after puking my guts out for almost two weeks, *click*. Just like that my heart shifted, and every fiber of my being screamed NEVER AGAIN!

I had promised myself at sixteen that the *one* thing I wouldn't do is kill myself. And here I was, dehydrated, weak, with a bladder infection, my body purging from all ends. I couldn't keep anything down. I knew I might die. I had never had withdrawals this severe and persistent.

I went to the doctor because of the bladder infection and was given an antibiotic. Three days into the prescription I was winded by walking to the bathroom—panting, heart pounding, and dizzy. I went back to see the doctor, and she sent me to the ER. I had developed mild long QT syndrome from the antibiotic. A cardiac enzyme test showed there had been a bit of heart muscle damaged. Luckily, I had skipped the most recent dose, as I suspected it was the cause, and was sent me home several hours later.

And several long weeks later, I was clean and recovered from the worst of it. It wasn't difficult to stay clean this time. Almost dying will make your choices crystal clear. I deleted all my dealers' contact info. I scoured my car and bedroom for hidden needles. Surprisingly, I didn't have cravings or dreams of using drugs. This seemed odd, as each time I had quit opiates before, my dreams would be full of looking for, finding, and shooting up drugs. So why was this time different? It was a different experience because I was different. Because I suddenly felt my heart align with my body—I heard the plea from my soul to live differently. *Click.* And thus, I was no longer an addict.

While I was now clean, I was also shuffling around like a ninety-year-old. Every iota of my body was in agony. I could barely make it up my own front steps. My whole body buzzed, lower back burning. I had tinnitus and vertigo. I felt like shit all day every day and was still steeped in grief from May's death two years earlier and from losing Andy's friend Kerry half a year previous. Still avoiding the only working shower in the house in May's apartment—still having physical pain and panic attacks walking through her space. I started seeing my behavior for the dysfunction it was—I had PTSD. So once again I started the monumental effort of getting mental health care. This time I only had to wait for two months. So I waited.

This time I was doing it for Andy. I needed to feel worthy of his love and being his wife. To be okay for this man who cared for me after giving his life to his mom. He was also a son feeling like an orphan, and he was a man whose wife had lied to him repeatedly. His best friend was dead, for God's sake, and *still* he took the time to make sure I was taken care of. I felt like a burden, just as his mom felt. I finally understood all the myriad feelings that arise from being an invalid. I felt worthless, helpless. My life felt unimportant and a burden for the limited people around me. I barely had the energy to make it to work. I would sleep every free minute I could—go to bed as soon as I got home from work, sometimes waking up for dinner and sometimes sleeping through it. I tried to shower at least once every two weeks, but several times it was an entire month. I was doing everything I could to appear like a normal human being.

One thing I was grateful for during the pandemic was the prevalence of masking. It was an excuse to not wash my face and not brush my teeth—two less things to worry about. I distinctly remember the fear of what I looked like returning to me as people stopped masking. Did I look to others like the filthy hag I felt like?

And in this state, a crack in my right upper molar became a hole. The achiness I had experienced for a year in my jaw became a constant pain. I cried every day before and after work. Not just weeping, but full-on uncontrolled sobbing, wailing in sorrow and pain. After living in this torture for weeks, I finally overcame my dental phobia and made an appointment for a dental consultation while I waited for the appointment with my new therapist.

Something had to change, or I wasn't going to keep my promise to myself to stay alive.

In November 2021 I had my tooth extracted and finally met my new therapist. She was a nice lady, in the early stages of pregnancy, who seemed to understand me. It was a relief to find someone in the field who validated my feelings and experiences. She helped me realize how much anger I carried regarding my parents, how deeply scarred I was by being adopted, and suggested that I was a highly sensitive person, not a broken one.

I will forever be grateful for one simple suggestion she made. We were a few weeks into our sessions, and I kept bringing up the spirits and orbs and faeries. I said, "I just want to *understand* what all that is about!"

She tilted her head. "Well, if it doesn't cause you too much anxiety, maybe you can explore the spiritual side. I can't really help you, but maybe you can find someone who can?"

My heart skipped a beat. Maybe I could find someone. Someone different than before. Just a few days previously, my college friend Lyra, one who listened to many hours of my sobbing on the phone, had mentioned a medium she knew. It felt important, so I followed through. Just a few days before I met with Karyn Crisis, I had an encounter that I still can see clearly in my mind's eye.

I had slowly allowed myself to see the little blinking lights and small orbs again since working with my therapist. One night, lying in bed, I was watching their subtle display, when my head buzzed in a familiar way. I took a few deep breaths to try and control the panic and fear welling up in my chest. A single point of pure white light appeared in front of my face, at eye level. It then drew a symbol of an eye in the air. My mind said, *Is that the Eye of Horus?* It hung in the air for a full minute or more. I didn't want to blink for fear it would disappear. It was an electric neon sign daring me to accuse it of being a figment of my imagination. Then it finally disappeared, and all that was left were the blinky ones.

I jumped onto my phone and did my googling magic. It wasn't the Eye of Horus, but similar—an Egyptian symbol for Sleep Traveler. This is a title for a high priest with the ability to astral travel and gather information to help the pharaoh during his rule. The term hit me hard in the heart. Yes, yes, yes! OMG it makes sense. Like a film on fast-forward, all the nightmares and lucid dreaming and unexplainable nighttime visions . . . all were clues to this lifetime puzzle and flew through my mind—the pieces finally made sense. I *was* astral traveling; I was visiting new realms in my sleep. It was the first moment I was ready and willing to start trusting my own experiences, even if my fear of being crazy, a loony, a crackpot weirdo was still triggered. After all I had seen and experienced, how could I not believe myself?

"After all I had seen and experienced, how could I not believe myself?"

When I worked with Karyn on Zoom, she validated my experiences and gave me guidance on how to start asking my guides for help, how to feel more empowered on this new journey. I read her book *Warrior of Light* and noticed many of the descriptions of beings she talked to were eerily similar to mine. It's all real . . . It's all real . . .

Breathe, Sara, breathe . . . As I was just starting my fledgling journey back to myself, back to magic, I received a panicked phone call from my friend's wife. One of my favorite people on the planet, just a year older than me—Dave Vissari—was dead.

It was about a week before Christmas 2021. I was in the middle of teaching at my student's house when I got the call. When she sobbed, "Sara, Dave's Dead!" I responded blankly, "Dave's dead?? What? Dave's *dead?*" She started wailing, and I was dropped into a bucket of ice. I was frozen in place, and my student looked strangely at me. I whispered hoarsely, "I need a moment please. Go tell your mom I can't finish your lesson."

Sitting in a random student's living room, I processed her words. Hyperaware, I couldn't freak out, because I didn't want to upset the family. It took every morsel of strength to not disintegrate into tears. I knew that once I started, I wouldn't stop.

I made it outside to my car before I lost it. I called Andy and screamed, "Dave's dead! Dave's dead! Fucking universe!! Why? I fucking hate God! First Kerry and now Dave?! I am so fucking pissed! Why? Why?!" He, of course, was bewildered and then overtaken by emotion. We cried on the phone together for at least fifteen minutes before I said, "Okay, okay, I need to get home . . . I have to try and keep my shit together so I don't kill myself driving home."

This was the last straw for me. I was furious at the world. I raged for days, randomly screaming, crying, and then feeling guilty. Guilty because, from the outside, he didn't look like a best friend. We spoke one or twice a month on the phone, and after he'd moved to South Carolina, we only made it down there once, just a few months before he died. But I couldn't deny that a new and huge hole had been cut out of my heart. I had an emptiness so profound it was confusing and scary . . . It took months until I realized that I was grieving the loss of my soul brother. We were in a band together for a few years after I graduated from college. I'd known him for two decades. He was the first person I created music with who didn't make me feel judged and small. In fact, he made me feel confident and capable. His smile disarmed any defenses one might carry, allowing him to touch your soul. He saw me, in all my damaged glory, and loved me, not despite it but because of it.

I cried out to his soul for over a week before I connected to his spirit. I met him in what appeared to be an all-white waiting room in some kind of spaceship. He was dressed in an all-blue uniform. I was surprised to see how tall he appeared, full head of hair and the same unkempt goatee. He looked more vital than I had ever seen him.

I hugged him hard and long, the warmth of his body familiar and comforting. "Dave! Why are you so tall?" He smiled his signature crooked grin. "Well, when you are carrying the weight of the world on your shoulders, it literally crushes you." I pondered this and remembered his hunched shoulders, his extremely wide stance, and thought, *I am seeing him in his true form, undamaged by living.*

We talked about a lot of things that night. He promised he would be around for a while. He asked me to help him keep an eye on some people for him. It was the first time I felt confident about my personal magic, and trusted what I was experiencing. I saw there could be another way to exist in this world. We hugged, and I cried some more, and he consoled me. But I now understood *why*—why then and why it was time. But it took a while to release that anger at myself, the universe, his wife, and him. But this communion was a good first step.

The next couple of weeks were super intense, as his death created another vortex of energy, and I was seeing more orbs and fairies and ghosts again. The fear was deep in my heart, and I felt daily panic again. I was still talking to my therapist, but the spiritual stuff just wasn't something she could help me with. I was feeling attacked again—something was trying to rip my uterus out of my body. After almost a week I was desperate for relief. I could see a spiritual mist/being as it was happening, so it didn't occur to me to see a doctor. I was losing hope that my life would ever feel livable and pain-free. I had needed those two meetings with Karyn to start believing in myself, and this pushed me to find a way to dive to the bottom of my being and start finding another way to live. I had to find someone I could see in person. Someone who could do reiki or energy healing or I didn't know what, but someone who could help me make permanent change. I was desperate and terrified again. I took a leap of faith that I would hear the "chime" of my guides in my ear when I clicked on the right website link. Holding my breath, I once again googled "Shaman near me." And who popped up immediately? Atousa Raissyan. *Ding!* A name I had not encountered in all my previous searches. The person who would save my life. Literally.

I was in such a state of fear that I can't even imagine what my original email inquiry must have been like for her to read. It was a mishmash of the last many years, and I was so confused about what was happening and what I was asking her to do to help me. She called me, and I babbled about all my stuff again. She said, "Listen, I can help you, but it's going to require you to do a lot of work." I said, "I don't care what you want me to do, but I cannot live like this. Just please help me!"

We met for the first time about six weeks after Dave died. Walking up to Atousa's front door, I had no idea what to expect, but it wasn't the person who opened the door. I had seen her photo on her website, but it didn't capture the power of her presence. Her bright eyes see directly into your soul, but they hold a surprising softness. A gentle, curious love.

At our second session, I confessed that I kept seeing her as a tree. I said, "At first I thought you felt like stone—cool and solid and strong. But you also have a heartbeat . . . so I finally realized you are a tree." I was startled when she chuckled. "Yes, my main guide is a tree spirit." I didn't know yet that seeing people's essence is part of my magic.

The work that we did together was deep, and intense, and life changing. I saw her once a week for nearly six months. Sometimes I would schedule an extra session if something really challenging was happening. I was so surprised at how physical my reactions to the energetic/emotional releases were. In the beginning I would feel sick for two or three days after each appointment. I would be clammy and weak, have a headache, nausea, diarrhea, congestion, sneezing, you name it. She assured me these were normal symptoms for the type of shifting I was doing. I still COVID-19 tested regularly, just in case. A few times I had I felt so sick I couldn't make it to work afterward. But

I knew I was changing, and fast. She helped me shed the toxic programming I was holding on to from childhood, from society, from my trauma. She gave me mantras and tapping, meditations, and homework. I spent all, day every day working on finding myself, my highest and truest self—excavating my ancient self, connecting to my soul.

It's difficult to fully explain the work Atousa does. It is so expansive and covers so many modalities. Yes, it's talking and meditation. Yes it's shamanistic. She uses reiki, sound, movement. Her adaptability is what makes her perfect for this client-based work—she does whatever needs to be done in the moment to help you see what needs to be revealed, healed, and released. Atousa wrote *Change Yourself, Change the World* in August 2023, and it is a perfect description of the work she guides us to do in her sessions. If you want to know more about what she does, it's the perfect place to start.

I have continued to do the healing work with and without her. I am growing and shifting every single day. I am a medium, a channel, a healer, and shaman. I know myself and my guides. I am pure magic and have learned that by simply being myself, I help light the way for those around me. I love myself completely—every single part. But it doesn't mean I don't still shed and grow and find new parts to integrate. That is the amazing and beautiful part of this path—it is continuous. For example, I also seem to be very attuned to the transition of death. This skill of helping others prepare for death spiritually and physically is something I am still learning about myself and my magic.

It is a double-edged sword being able to see death coming. It is a gift to know and see the transition happening. It creates an understanding around certain behaviors or problems that arise in the individual I witness it in, human or animal. But the difficulty is that I see it coming, often many months in advance. It takes effort to remember to breathe, to allow the changes in its own time without trying to control the process.

I have a trauma girl—a part of myself—who sees death approaching, but no one else around her does. She is then so scared of what she sees she just cries and cries, wishing it to be over. Over for her as the witness and over for the person transitioning, who many times is fighting and struggling emotionally and/or physically as the changes occur.

And this is the perfect example of divine timing. I had worked intensely with Atousa for almost six months, and we were done for the moment. Just a month after we stopped, I woke up one morning covered in a soft white fog of energy. I asked, "Oh? Who is this?" And then I felt the answer. My mom.

Mom had been in a nursing home now for over a year. I had seen her in December 2021 for Christmas and knew, even then, it would be the last Christmas I would have with her, although I only had my own knowing to explain why I felt that way. It was now July 2022, and Mom had been struggling with an undiagnosed illness for the last several months. Dad and I were constantly fighting with the nursing home to do testing and to give better care to my mom. Remember, I am still living in Maryland, and my parents were in Missouri. So over the last four months, I had spent hours on the phone trying to get answers about my mom's nausea, mental changes, pain, dizziness, lack of appetite, depression . . . a long list of symptoms that felt disparate and mutable. I knew her symptoms well because I called her at least once a day, often a few times, every single day. Dad drove forty-five minutes to see her every single day. This was not a situation of a family allowing their loved one to languish in an institution. This was a family pushing for their loved one to receive the level of care they deserved. That they paid an outrageous ten thousand dollars a month for.

Mom had gone to the hospital the night before I awoke covered in her energy. So when I realized I was feeling my mom, I asked, "Mom, are you okay?" She replied, "No, I need you. You need to come. Now." I bolted out of bed and started making phone calls to the nursing home and hospital, trying to track down where exactly she was.

After two hours I finally got a nurse on the phone. She explained that my mom was lucky her night nurse had brought her in, because she was extremely sick. At that moment she was in cardiac intensive care. That knowledge didn't make any sense to me, but I said okay and asked to talk to her.

As soon as I heard her voice, I knew this hospital trip was different. This wasn't even the first time she had been in intensive care. But it was the first time I heard her voice oozing with weakness and fear and pain and confusion, so I responded, "Mom, hang on. I am flying in as soon as I possibly can. I'll leave today."

Four hours later I was at the airport and started an excruciating journey to her. Every possible delay due to weather occurred, and every mechanical issue you can imagine. I should have made it to her by 8:00 p.m. that same day but didn't arrive until 5:00 p.m. the following day. Funny thing is, I now know that it was because there was a lot of spiritual preparation required for me to be able to do the work I was going to need to do. But of course, at that moment I just didn't want her to die before I got there.

When I finally made it to her, she was hallucinating spiders and clouds of gnats. I didn't know how to explain to my dad and the doctors that she was seeing spirits—I could see them too. The best I could do was calm the fear she felt about them, reassure her they weren't going to harm her. I had never seen her so sick.

It turned out she had developed sepsis in the nursing home. So over the next two days, she received lots of meds by IV. I was shocked when they abruptly moved her to a regular floor. I didn't understand. She was definitely still really sick but apparently stable enough to leave the ICU.

I questioned myself. I thought this was the end? Did I hear wrong?

It was about 7:00 p.m. when they moved us into her new room, a tiny space that her bariatric bed would barely fit into. There was a tiny little couch next to it. I had dropped Dad at home hours earlier because he wasn't comfortable sitting in a hospital. As soon as the nurse left, Mom looked at me with her scared little girl face, a face I was very familiar with, and said, "I don't like this room."

"Why not, Mom? I know it's a little cramped, but it's okay . . ."

She pointed at the wall in front of her. "I don't like *that*."

I was confused at first and then realized she was seeing something. I squinted my eyes, trying to see what she was seeing.

"It keeps telling me that I am supposed to follow it, but the door looks scary. I don't want to."

I took her hand. "Mom, you don't have to go anywhere you don't want to. I'm right here with you."

"Don't leave me."

"Okay, Mom. I'll spend the night."

Thus began a two-week odyssey. I spent every night with her. The first two nights we were like teenage girls having a slumber party. It was the most fun we had had together in a few years. Watching silly movies, laughing, listening to the radio and singing along. But soon the discussion turned to May and her death and why it was so difficult. We talked through all her fears about death and the other side, and I gave her all the limited information I had at that point. It was a moment when our highest selves were talking. And it saddened me that we managed to have this level of conversation only a few times in this lifetime.

Mom was done with her life. She had been talking about being ready to die for a few months, and I didn't see that sending her back to a place where she would repeat this cycle of hospitalization was a solution. So I fought for her right to *not* have treatment. It was a fight that took every ounce of strength I had. I told my husband not to come until I was sure when she would die. Honestly, I was struggling to manage myself and both my parents, and I just couldn't feel responsible for anyone else at that moment. I was able to explain to Mom why he wasn't there and express that he did love her very much.

We finally got her admitted to hospice in the hospital. But when she didn't just drop dead, they started discussing moving her back to the nursing home—and I was surprised to discover that Mom was scared about that idea. I finally figured out it was because she didn't want the health aide she loved dearly to watch her die. And in another twist of divine intervention, the morning they tried to move her, she tested positive for COVID-19. She couldn't be moved. We both silently rejoiced.

As I had been sleeping on the couch for ten days in her room, and spent every day with her, I knew I would catch it. I did test positive a week later and missed her funeral, but that day I tested negative and was allowed to stay. The next week was rough, as she went through all the changes that happen to the body as it prepares to release the soul. I had hoped that it would be easier to watch this time, but it will always be difficult. I took comfort knowing that she was safe and protected by spirits. I had guides standing vigil at the end of the bed. I saw all kinds of spirits drop in to pay their respects. I even was privileged to hold my late grandfather's hand, a man I had never met, and watch behind my closed eyelids as he connected with Mom through me. He showed us a field with all her ancestors waiting. (This scene became a reality for me when I performed a house healing on the family farm a year later.) She sighed and cooed as he explained things, and I could feel her starting to release.

The next day was the last day she spoke. Dad and I were leaving to go to lunch, and he said, "I love you, Sally." She weakly nodded and said, "I love you too." I said, "I love you, Mom." She said, "I know." Dad and I chuckled together as we left, not knowing at the time that we both were envious of the other's answer. I said, "Well, at least you know she loves you *too*!" He said, "At least you know she *knows* you love her!"

And this is a perfect encapsulation of the love I share

with both of these people. People who may not have always understood me but who loved me dearly. People that I love with all my heart and soul. And I am so grateful to be able to help them in this very special way. But I have to do my best to remember that while I am a witness and a guide, their baggage isn't mine to carry. I can help people lighten through energy work, but I cannot carry it in my body anymore. It damages me too much and isn't my place to do so. The part of me that desperately wants to hold on to that energy is the girl who thinks it is her job and the only way she will be loved by her adopted parents. She says, "I carry them because it is why I exist—it is why I was born into this family." But this girl doesn't understand that she was born into this family to *be herself.* That is *all.* To share the amazing wellspring of love that floods her heart, to sing and be joyful, to show others it is possible to live in freedom from fear and connected to a loving universe. And while it has taken us a while to reach this place of safety and joy, this place of loving and understanding ourselves and our true nature, it is our wish to be a lighthouse for those around us. To share our light, love, and soul. To walk our unique path.

I know this story isn't pretty. There are many details I wanted to erase as soon as I typed them. Certain sections took much longer than others because of the need to cry in shame over the hideous acts I have committed for my addiction and self-hatred. In those moments I allow the dark and pain to sweep over me and allow the tears to flow. I apologize to all those in this story that I have wronged. And now I work on forgiving myself. But I have the hardest time forgiving myself for all the thousands of wrongs I have enacted upon my steadfast partner, my constant support. Even now, as I type this, a part of me is disbelieving that Andy stuck with me, that he endured me. That I didn't damage him to the point he gave up on me. And a larger part of me—the rest of me—rejoices that I was gifted such a wonderful support during my time within this vessel. Almost like it was planned out.

"Change is always possible."

However, the overriding reason I wanted to write this chapter, these words, is to show that change is always possible. There is another way to live aside from fear. We do not need to languish in terror inside our prisons. Many paths lead out of the darkness and into the light—into a space where you are consciously aware of the loving and tender arms of the universe embracing you. All those paths are lighted by your heart. You are the medicine. Your heart is your guide to reconnect to your Divine Humanity so you too can embrace both your shadow and light.

About Sara Cronan

I am a heart-centered private music teacher and shamanic practitioner, and provide holistic music lessons and coaching for piano, voice, and guitar. In July 2024 I relocated to Surfside Beach, South Carolina, and opened Heart Song Healing Music Studio. HSH Music Studio also offers a variety of healing services, including tarot guidance readings, sonic energy cleansing, and custom magical objects. Magic is available to each of us if we connect to our hearts and trust in ourselves and the world around us. Love is always the answer.

Website: https://hshmusicstudio.com/
Facebook: https://www.facebook.com/
heartsonghealingmusicstudio/
Instagram: https://instagram.com/hshmusicstudio/

PATHWAY

By Shonna Perkins

For my soul a hundred years from now, in your new body—may this book as a whole bring a smile to your face. And to those just finding this book—may it help you on *your* journey. Before I share my chapter, the question I have for you is what defines a *healer*? You may write it down or not—that's your *choice*. Let's see if it stays the same . . .

They baptized her in a river of fire, not realizing her soul was of the phoenix.

Crossroad. I saw myself holding a rope to a familiar place—darkness. Not any darkness, but the dark arts. I held this rope tight while playing a game of tug-of-war. With what? I wanted to be a healer, but I craved control and vengeance in the form of validation. I gritted my teeth, caught in the in-between. Gray zone. I saw my light, but I allowed this darkness to coat it. How did I get here? But there is a pivoting point, there is a choice. Busy hands leave you empty handed. I had to let go. Of what?

During my adolescent years, I was warned to not speak of my past due to it being *bad.* Or hard to digest. But I see now it's triggering. So let's pull that *trigger.*

Prior to my birth, my mother had a miscarriage—eight months into her pregnancy with my brother, he was crushed accidentally. This was her sixth pregnancy, and she only had two live births before him. After this physical trauma, my mother was advised that due to damage to her uterus the chances of pregnancy were dropped to a 1 percent chance. But when science challenges the universe, life finds a way.

A year later she met my father. Her pregnancy with me was not easy—I was a dry-birth risk. Adding to the mix, my mother was left single due to my biological father's scandalous ways.

My mother wanted a boy—every son she ever had never got to take his first breath. But on every previous ultrasound, I stayed curled into a ball—and stayed that way until the final ultrasound. I uncurled—it's a girl . . . Seventh chance and a third life.

I fought for this life before I took my first breath. Fighting would be my greatest strength and my greatest weakness.

I can recall from my very early years my mother worked two jobs tirelessly to support me. Though she had two other daughters from a previous marriage, she did not have sole custody of them. My mother had a troublesome past of experimenting with drugs in her adolescent years and into her early twenties. Thus, leaving us with only weekend visits when allowed by *their father.*

My mother and I lived with my grandfather for a time.

Her goal was to provide a home and gain custody over my sisters.

During this time I was being bounced between family members while my mother worked. Until a coworker of my mother suggested watching me through the daycare that she ran out of her house. Within a week I was being dropped off without a second thought.

I learned very early the cruelty of racism and that my skin color stood out like a star in the night sky.

It was three against one or five against one. Either way, I was having the shit beat out of me at the age of four to five years old by the other kids in daycare. I would hide under the table, layering myself in blankets, stuffed animals, or pillows to soften their blows. My mother would be told, by my sitter, that the bruises were from playing and my crying was due to me being tired from refusing to nap. Only then to be advised by my mother that if I wanted to *play* with the boys, I had to get tough. I tried to fight back, but the odds were never in my favor. The abuse came to a breaking point when one of the boys decided to throw a piece of brick at the back of my head while outside playing. I lay on the lawn, crying, as it started to rain. I asked, "God, why are these kids so mean? I just wanted to be friends." After several minutes of sobbing in that cold summer rain, I rose and went inside. After this, my mother stopped taking me.

The first year of grade school, I struggled with dyslexia and had this overwhelming feeling of *anxiety*. I did not fit in. So I remained quiet throughout class. I was made an example by my teacher regarding my poor studies and was considered a *distraction* for defending my ability to draw. My mother was brought in on multiple occasions because of my poor academics and my "lying" regarding my art. The school was in disbelief that the child they labeled with a "comprehension issue" could have this level of drawing. The final straw came when my mother was called by the guidance office because of the graphicness of my artwork. My class was asked to draw the difference between ourselves and our parents. Needless to say, I drew my mother and me nude—highlighting the maturity differences in our bodies. Mind you, I was only six years old. My mother defended my creativity and perspective of the world. The guidance counselor was not happy regardless. I was pulled from the school—they had failed me and added salt to the wound by trying to have me create a how-to-draw book for kids.

Once I was older, I fully understood that the school was attempting to have me create this book behind my mother's back and without her consent. I can recall telling her that my teacher kept trying to have me do extra artwork and explain how I was able to create these images. After my mother pulled me from the campus and threw this information in their face, they sent her a more formal letter asking if I could provide my talent to "help" other children. She declined their offer.

Within the next month, we were moving into what would be my childhood home and I was to be enrolled in my new school. Here my creativity was welcomed by the teachers, and I was placed in after-school classes for my dyslexia. At this time my mother was also going through a custody battle with her ex-husband over my half sisters from her first marriage.

One afternoon I came home from school expecting to see them, but I was met by my mother slumped at the table, crying. When I asked if my sisters were home, my mother blurted, "They no longer want to be a part of our family and do not wish to speak to us."

I tried writing letters to them that my mother would help address, only to receive them back with *return to sender* written across them. I was heartbroken at the age of six.

Following the next couple of weeks, our house seemed to have more than just myself and my mother in it. There were countless nights of me running to my mother screaming that there were people in my room. Three men would walk around talking of construction or watch me watching them. One of the nights while I was crying, a hand touched the side of my bed, then a man's voice asked, "Hey, kid. Are you all right?"

I was horrified because of now realizing *we* could interact consciously.

My mother assumed it was just me processing the loss of my sisters. This went on for weeks until my mother decided to switch our rooms. Within the first night, I woke up to my mother scooping me outta my bed as she whispered, "Shonna, you are right—there are people in your room. You are seeing spirits."

And for several weeks we slept in the living room, and every night you could hear them stomping and walking down the stairs. It was nothing to have items crash on the floor and doors shutting on their own. We were terrified and tired. My mother, as a last resort, reached out to her friend who is a pagan, and we learned how to share a home with the Unseen. I learned that the paranormal would be my unspoken second normal.

I can remember watching shows about hauntings,

ACTIVATING THE DIVINE HUMAN

Jesus, aliens, things about other religions, and folklore—thinking how all of it is strangely connected. But how they talked about it was as if it was a foreign language.

As the year went on, school became easier, but my mother was having odd behaviors. She would send me outside due to being unable to look at me, or I was being left home alone. I found myself outside often, talking to animals and nature. From the time that I could walk, I was catching lizards, snakes, frogs, or anything else that I could touch. It was abnormal to see me without some type of animal beside me. By my third-grade year, I had my own zoo—fourteen rabbits, a cat, two dogs, a wild ridgeback boar, and a ferret. I took care of all of them, waking up early to feed them. All these animals were either gifts or had followed me home. My mother did not fully fathom how, or why, these animals came to me—she just went with it. She supported my passion for art, animals, and nature.

Until, that is, her boyfriend at the time decided I had too many rabbits, stating that we should start eating them. I grew up hunting and understood the cycle of life from an early age. But because of the graphicness of how one of my rabbits was mishandled and poorly dispatched with a hammer by my mother's boyfriend, I set my remaining rabbits free one afternoon . . . My mother also ended her relationship with this man a year later.

During my fifth-grade year, my mother met her second husband. I told her from the start there was something off about this man. She disregarded my statements.

My stepfather was an alcoholic narcissist. He had all forms of abuse down to a science. When he was not assaulting my mother, he was coming after me verbally. His words were like a whip against my skin. Claiming that I was the best *son* he never had and that I should have been a boy. Or he would comment on my weight as he poked at my arms and abdomen. As time went on, he became bolder with his physical assaults on my mother. While intoxicated one evening, he became so belligerent that my mother rushed into my room to hide me under my bed while he threatened her with his pistol. She had him arrested, and after that he promised to become sober, but the verbal and mental abuse did not stop.

One afternoon while walking to my room, my stepfather stopped me. "Just so you know, you are not special. These gifts, magic, and whatever bullshit are not real."

My mother became reclusive during those years, and I am uncertain when she started abusing methamphetamine. It was after my twelfth birthday when she took me for a car ride to confess and apologize for abusing drugs in our home. She explained that she had gotten ahold of a bad cut of meth that made her partially blind in her left eye and deaf in her left ear. (I see now how the years of domestic violence and drug abuse affected her in many ways, then how I reflected this.) Soon I became anorexic—I felt no desire to feed myself. *My soul, this life.* I tried talking to my mother about depression, only to be met with fearful outlashings by her and mockery by my stepfather

A shift in our home soon followed. The spirits became more active. My stepfather would "trip" down the stairs, and objects would be thrown at him. My mother would experience scratching down her back or arms. Certain other family members and friends would also experience similar situations. I was left untouched. *Seeing now that I*

*had attachments that became protective and stepped in where
I lacked a shadow.* Nearly eighteen years later (present),
I was recently able to connect with this particular being
(lost soul) and release her.

Midway through my middle school years, both my older half sisters, now adults, reached out and reentered my life.
I suffered separation anxiety and panic attacks often. My
sisters tried to help me the best they could. But my parents
were blind to me because of their constant fighting.

It was grad night of my eighth-grade year. My class
went to Universal on a hot June afternoon—I drank very
little water and had not eaten in three days. My world was
spinning. I sat on a bench in front of one of the roller
coasters; it was almost 10:00 p.m. I had dry heaved earlier
and was now suddenly freezing. I looked at my friend as
I choked, "I cannot feel my heart." My vision went black.
My friend's concerned voice became a slur. I was in the
stars for what felt like hours. Weightless. I was not alone—
there came eyes meeting mine. *It's not time.*

Free Fall

I sprung up, as if thunder echoed through my body.
I was in my friend's arms as she was sobbing and trying
to call for help. Other classmates were now around us. I
gasped for air—my lungs were on fire, and my abdomen
was in knots.

A man dressed in dark clothes was on the back side of
the bench, and our eyes met. "Hey, kid. Are you all right?"

I nodded my head, closing my eyes for a hard blink.
He was gone.

I didn't know my name when the EMTs came. I

couldn't name my parents or any information. I found myself on a stretcher. After a ride to the Orlando ER and five IV bags of fluid later, the doctor informed us that due to my malnutrition and dehydration, my body was consuming itself. Both parents now saw that my spine and ribs were visible. The following morning my mother explained how she'd felt my death that night—saw the unfolding. I was on a brief strict watch. I spoke nothing, virtually mute for several days—processing what I had experienced.

> Parallel: mother explained that she has been able to see death since her teenage years. She lay in bed at 10:00 p.m., feeling as if she was having a heart attack, trying to speak to my stepfather breathlessly and could only hear my name being screamed by multiple voices. She added she was certain of my departure minutes before the ER called her cell phone.

A month later I was with my older sister and collapsed. Once at the ER, an ECG and other tests were done, revealing I'd strained and tore the muscles around my heart due to my body still recovering from anorexia. My stepfather disregarded the doctor's concerns, and my mother tried her best to understand. I would simply be reminded that I just needed to calm down.

Due to my natural curiosity and after my near death, I searched for a spiritual teacher. No luck. I studied on my own. My family is a mix of Baptists, but I read about other religions and practices and saw no difference between them. Understanding there is a connection. All hands pointing in the same direction. But this "man-made" life did not make sense to my heart, and I questioned it often.

During my freshman year of high school, I came out queer. My mother seemed accepting until, during one of her raging fits, she dragged me into her vehicle and drove me to family members' and friends' homes to confess my sexuality like a *sin*. She then gave my number to young males she met, advising me that they just wanted to be *friends*. "If you are a *lesbian*, then it does not matter" was her response. At certain points, my mother would jokingly sexualize me—even going as far as to describe my breasts as "knockers" to her male friends. Commenting on my "beautiful" appearance as her success.

The day after Christmas, my grandfather had a massive heart attack, and my mother became his caretaker.

I was left with my stepfather. Leaving me to do much of the home care while going to high school and working on the weekends. I was already being bullied throughout school, and now certain family members alienated me. I was told by classmates that I did not look like a lesbian, then one teacher commented, in front of the class, that I was a waste because of my sexuality and appearance.

I clung to life, demanding a lot from my body and my mind. *Control.* I continued to work part time to pay for myself. I pushed myself hard academically—honor and AP classes while also enrolled in the junior police program. I was not involved with sports, but I exercised like an Olympian. By my junior year, I was running the track and the bleachers, doing weights, and executing seven hundred crunches a day. I see now that I was numbing my emotional pain. And blocking out so much more. *Denial.*

My mother was not present, and my stepfather was still verbally abusive. My body could not keep up, so I tore the majority of the muscles in my back. My doctor, being a man of good physique himself, was horrified by my routine. Bed rest and medications were prescribed. However, I learned quickly that I have reverse reactions to sedatives and muscle relaxers. Instead of putting me down, my body went into fight mode with each dose. With no drugs allowed to ease this pain, I was to heal on my own accord. I lay in bed, my back feeling like it was fileted open.

Once I was able to go back to the gym, I caught MRSA from the school equipment. I became septic. I had a dangerous fever over 105 degrees Fahrenheit, and my heart rate was through the roof.

My mother growled at me beside my hospital bed to "Calm the fuck down so that we can go home." The doctors warned my mother and me that the infection was close to my heart, advising I should probably stay.

Needless to say, she opted to have a drain placed in my chest, and I was prescribed antibiotics. I fought my blood infection at home. My body felt as if it was on fire—any movement I made left me breathless and trying not to aspirate.

During this time lying in bed, unable to move, I heard *God.* There was an unhinged understanding that I needed to go through this. I was doing something regarding my family. I lay confused and in a daze. I was left with my thoughts and looking back at my past; rage built inside me. The rage was a buffer from my emotional pain. I cried, *Why? I don't understand!* A deeper voice simply replied, *But you will—one day . . .* I lay in the dark.

After going back to school, now anemic, I took the time to find a school counselor whom I could speak to about my home life and how I was feeling. I tried once again to speak to my mother about my depression, only to be threatened with a psych ward.

I often took to books on lightwork and dark arts. I read about Christianity, Wicca, paganism, Native American practices, the occult, demonology, other cultural practices, and much more. I was involved with my artwork intimately as a form of communication. I was recognized by the local museums, and a pastor took to some of my biblical references. I thought nothing of it . . . just silent speeches from a muted world.

I was familiar with migraine attacks since my middle school years, but now I was having them a few times a week. And my menstrual cycles were terrible. I see now it was my body's response to my denial of self. I was addicted to physical pain. *I can't see the rope wrapped in my hands too . . . this familiar place.*

The summer before my senior year, mother went through a separation from her husband—I was house-hopping between friends and family to avoid both my parents. Until my uncle offered to have me live with him and my aunt. It was quiet.

After my mother removed her ex-husband from our home, she convinced me to move back in. She still was not *present.* But I could see that she was trying to recover herself from the years of domestic violence. Trying to find her path.

I was halfway through my senior year when she reconnected with an ex-boyfriend from her very early years.

What seemed to be a mellowing point in our lives, was only the calm before the storm. He convinced my mother to have us move in with him and his son while she rented out our home.

My mother's boyfriend lived in a trailer. I had no bedroom, so I slept on his son's old twin mattress beside the back door in the living room, where the roof leaked when it rained. My mother shared a small room with her boyfriend, while his son had the master bedroom. I was forced to keep my clothes in my soon-to-be stepbrother's room, which he would lock me out of. This boy had dropped out of school by his sixth-grade year and did whatever he wanted without repercussions. I was reminded daily by his father that my past was nothing compared to his son's and that I had it easy.

Due to the demands of my classes, I needed access to the internet. His son being a dropout was excited for this so he could game with his online friends . . . After a month he decided to cut the connection cord to my computer when no one else was home. Then rewire the internet to his room only. Stating that my online studies slowed down his gaming. I was forced to have him type my homework while I spoke, because of his refusal to let anyone use his computer. Thus, I started staying after school to use the library computers. Only to come *home* expected to cook and take care of my stepsibling. The word no was not an option. I was this seventeen-year-old's nanny.

Seeing now, his son and I were similar in age and both shared similar traumas. How we chose to grow from those traumas highlighted our paralleled truth. Dark. Light.

After I graduated from high school, my mother remarried, and we moved into my grandfather's home so that my mother could care for my grandfather full time. He was suffering from Alzheimer's.

I had quit my part-time job so I could go to school full time. I was struggling to get grants and loans for college, even with my excellent academics and top GPA. Being underage, I had to use both my mother's and my new stepfather's information. It wasn't until I went to the financial aid office that I was informed that due to my stepfather having financial discrepancies, I was unable to get loans or grants. Adding that I couldn't apply on my own until I was twenty-five years old. I was crushed. I came home to talk to my mother about this, only to have her confess that my grandfather did have a college fund set aside, but her ex-husband had used it to buy his new vehicle. Promising to pay it back. He never did.

I fucking lost it. Snapping point. I lay on my bedroom floor, unable to move, as I had a full meltdown. I didn't know *what* I was going to do. I planned to go to school for veterinary science and possibly continue to study law. I applied to random jobs like crazy in the meantime. *No luck.* Then I saw an opening for a position at a local veterinarian clinic and applied. I got the job.

Even though I could not go to college, I asked the practice doctor for books that I could use to study on my own. I worked my way up from kennel staff to surgical prep. After a couple of years, I started training new staff and was sent to other clinics as an aide.

I once again started looking for a spiritual mentor. No luck. Druids. High priestesses. Wiccans. Even asked my own pagan granny. I frequented all random New Age shops. Each told me they were not the *one*. But I contin-

ued my spiritual studies. I wanted to be a healer, whether I comprehended the meaning or not. But I also wanted control. Rope held tighter.

I was still living with my family. And the abuse still did not subside. Verbal. Emotional. Mental. And my stepfather was not shy about his homophobia either.

There came one day when my stepfather was threatening my mother. Being sick of his behavior and this pattern of the men my mother chose, I stepped in the middle. Using myself as a shield. *Oops.*

I found myself being slammed into the wall. My stepfather squeezed my arms until I could feel my veins popping as he slid me up the wall. I saw red. Before I knew it, I had kicked him in the groin, and as he dropped me, leaning himself forward, I grabbed a handful of his hair and then busted his face into my knee.

My mother defended him at this point. I went to work the next day with two large purple handprints on both my arms. My manager and practice doctor pulled me into the office. Both cried with me as I explained.

I tried not to get involved with their fights after this. I only stayed to help watch over my grandfather and my mother as she cared for him. Walking around on eggshells, and I was no ballerina—I had a southern mouth, and I was not afraid to bite back when provoked. But my stepfather never touched me again, or my mother in front of me. He would warn his son, "She might be small, but don't be blind."

The disease my grandfather had now left him dependent and immobilized. He had reverted back to his child self, forgetting who everyone was. There were moments when I would help feed him, and he would whisper "I am

ACTIVATING THE DIVINE HUMAN

sorry" or ask about my art, remembering who I was. I still painted when I could.

During this time, I found myself working up the courage to practice house blessings.

However, I was practicing from a place of fear and banished many things—messages and visions. My mother would talk to me about the women in the family having a *sense* but then would sweep it under the rug once the words slipped her lips. She would remind me to not speak so openly about what I could see and do.

My first house blessing experience occurred with my own family home. *Practice what you preach.* While all family members were out for the day, I took the time to bless our home. I started at dawn—opened all the windows and anything that had doors. I burned sage, washing myself in the smoke first, and asked God to guide me. I started at the entryway of our home and went room to room, wall to wall. Asking anything that was stagnant to release and go back to where it came. Once each room was complete, I then burned a mix of sweet-smelling incenses. Meditating on love, communication, and flow. Once I felt ready, I marked each door/window with a trinity knot, using eggshell chalk. The once gray home became lighter. Later that evening my mother, grandfather, and stepbrother came home. All were chatty and playful. We were all sitting at the kitchen table, when my stepfather came home. He stated that the house felt uncomfortably hot. We were all puzzled. His behavior became more agitated and aggressive into the night. During dinner, my stepfather was still complaining that he was on fire while sitting at the kitchen table, now only in his gym shorts and a tank top.

The rest of us were in jeans and T-shirts. The house was set to 74 degrees. Suddenly my stepfather threw his fork across the room, and it pierced the wall as he screamed, "Is no one else fucking hot? I feel so unwelcomed and uncomfortable!" My mother yelled back, "What the fuck is your deal? You are acting possessed!"

For three days this went on, until I spoke to my mother. I advised her that I did a blessing and prayed to God while everyone was out the other day. Looking her in the eyes, I told her that I felt that her husband had something dark within him. She looked at me and told me to immediately undo what I had done, adding that he goes to church. I looked at her and said, "Just because he goes to church does not mean Jesus is in his heart." Later that day I washed my trinity knots off every door and window, other than the ones in my room. That evening my stepfather came home and acted as if everything was normal. When asked if he felt hot still, he was confused by the question.

I understood that due to the backlash my mother received from our family regarding a particular vision she'd had as a teenager, that became a nightmare in reality, regardless of her desperate warnings. She feared for my outcasting. Being called the devil's child . . . Never speaking of those three days after my house blessing and my stepfather's reaction.

Regardless, she would often complain to me that due to my line of work in veterinary medicine and my "practices," there were more animals in our home. Lost pet souls. She also noted the people who would pass through. She'd express that I needed to send them away. When they were ready, I would ask them to leave. Where? I had no idea—clearly, there was a door, but I could not see it. *Yet.*

293

Months passed and I did not have much of a dating life until a friend convinced me to join a dating app. Within a couple of weeks, I matched with a woman, and we hit it off. She and I had similar goals in mind. And soon we started dating. We understood that we each had a past. Both desiring control and healing . . .

During this time my stepbrother was picking up on his father's behaviors and one evening started physically assaulting my mother over a verbal argument. I stepped in as a shield to his blows. I *allowed* my stepbrother to punch me in the face full force twice. I was unfazed physically, but I saw red. I don't remember pinning him down while punching him, but I can recall his father pulling me off his son. Then he tried to hold me down so his son could attack me back.

My mother stopped *his* son before he could land a blow on me, but in turn he blacked both my mother's eyes.

The next day I had two goose eggs on my forehead, like horns. While my stepbrother . . . needless to say, moved out to live with his grandmother.

His father stated it was an unfair fight for his son and that I should be ashamed.

I being a five-foot-three and 135-pound female, while his son is a six-foot-one and 175-pound male. Fair? Ashamed? No.

A year later my grandfather was in hospice and his days were limited. Granted, I dealt with death every day in the veterinary field, but clearly this was different. I can recall hearing what is called the "death rattle" coming from my grandfather as he watched me and my mother with concerned eyes. He looked unhappy that I was present while I helped my mother put him in his bed. As I departed his room for only a few minutes, my mother screamed for me. Rushing back, I locked eyes with my grandfather now, his facial expression one of fear at seeing me watching him pass. Time froze. I mouthed to him, *It's okay.* What I can only describe as relief was on his face, eyes locked as I watched him transition. He was one of the first people I saw after I entered this world, and I was the last person he saw as he departed it. An oval of light opened as his soul left his body—I watched in shock.

Within the next few months, I moved into an apartment with my girlfriend. I would soon be breaking and re-wearing my rose-colored glasses for the next eight years. There was a bond, and we did love each other. However, we would both be teaching each other hard lessons. My problems were my problems and her problems were also my problems. Our relationship would be a dialed-down version of both our pasts—until it wasn't. I may not suffer from a form of substance abuse, but I was my personal sadist.

We would both experience spiritual activity kicked in overdrive during our time together. Orbs, flashes of light, disembodied voices, doors opening/closing on their own, and items being thrown.

I also noted a shift in my personal energy while at work. The first case—a young dog came in simply for her yearly visit. I held this pet. Suddenly I heard *I'm sick*, while the doctor, upon examination, stated the pet was healthy. I reached for the pup's popliteal nodes, finding a small growth the size of a pencil eraser. In silence I guided the doctor's hands to this location. Samples were sent out— the dog had stage III lymphoma.

After this I would simply guide doctors to areas of concern from the animals in silence. This went on for years.

Only one doctor picked up on what I was doing. She, being an atheist, admitted that if she did believe in God, then I was surely touched.

After Hurricane Irma, my fiancé and I decided on a fresh start in 2017 and moved to Virginia in 2018.

Before our move, I scheduled an appointment with a seer. I did not ask any questions while this senior woman simply watched me watching her. Her words, I see now, held more truth than what I could comprehend. "You are stuck, and it seems that you need to make a choice. You'll be moving soon, and there will be a lot of changes. But this is needed. You'll also reunite with someone from your past that you love, and it's going to be healing . . . But what makes this hilarious is that you've already known this and yet you keep denying *you!*" She laughed at my confusion.

Within the next couple of years, COVID-19 followed. What seemed to be a time of resolution for my fiancé and myself showed me how I'd taught her how to manipulate me. When things didn't go as planned, she then hit me with soft objects out of her personal frustration. I would ask her to stop, but she disregarded this. She ended up working her way up to using a phone charger cord on me one evening—until I popped her back. I cried, seeing a part of myself I never wanted to see again. After this there were many nights that she would smack/hit me in the face while I was deep asleep, due to *our* life, *her life*, not being where *she* wanted it. I did not fight back. I would ask re-peatedly that she stop. I tried being the perfect partner, but I ended up allowing myself to become her servant and emotional pincushion. She would explain that I could never understand her parental loss and trauma. She would add that I needed to do more and she "believed" in me. Thus, I kept re-wearing my broken rose-colored glasses.

I worked like a dog when her form of employment shut down during COVID, and I allowed everything to be placed on me. Supporting her in the best ways that I could and providing a home while she went to school. But I was reminded by her often that it was never enough. I was at a loss and struggled with intrusive suicidal thoughts. During many of my shifts at the previous clinic where I'd been employed, I'd fought the thoughts of walking into traffic. Wishing many days that I would never wake up. Or maybe I would have a hiking accident.

However, I started finding clovers, four-leaf clovers. Not one, but ten or more a day. *Magick.* I had so many that I just started sharing them with random strangers. Seeing the spark in their eyes brought an innocent joy to me.

Then in mid-2021, we found ourselves living in a hotel for roughly two months until we moved into our last home together. I pushed myself through an EMT program during this transition while also studying herbalism on my own. I hoped that not only healing animals but people too would be a great resolution. I gave out what I needed from myself—I needed me. If I aided in healing others, it surely must mean I would be healing myself. Denial. Fear. Repeat.

" In order to heal our world, we must take the steps toward healing ourselves first. "

To do what is good solely by others, we are, in turn, not being fair to our individual selves. And in order to heal our world, we must take the steps toward healing ourselves first. We can either be our healthiest or our most toxic relationship.

> When we hit our lowest point, we are open to
> the greatest change. (Aang)

Rising Up

Now settled, I started meditating more often and found myself considering searching for a mentor again. During several meditations in this parallel, metaphysical plane, I communicated with guides. I was still battling thoughts of self-hurt and having infrequent migraines. But started to *see* more clearly. Then came one meditation vision in 2022.

I was trying to meet my Higher Self for guidance—I was battling my thoughts of suicide. I was brought to my soul. A large tree, and within the trunk was a spiral room that reached the heavens, decorated with countless photos. Men. Women. Children. They were echoes of time so long ago. *Me.* Then entering a tearoom where I met an Iranian woman with white curly hair and eyes of gold that would change colors. She greeted me with a familiar grin of *Where have you been?* in the room filled with hues of greens and blues. We spoke of my past, and she advised that everything needed to happen to get me ready for my purpose and this moment—adding that I was protected throughout most of it. I came out of this final meditation with tears streaming down my face while I sat in the middle of my living room. Confused. Angry. Saddened. But there was a sense of love. My fiancé at the time tried to console me.

Few weeks later I found myself on Atousa's website.

Identical. Minus the white hair and changing eye color. But I am sure you can imagine my shock. I shut down my computer and logged back on. then revisited her page. *This is it. I have fully lost my marbles—the woman in my head is a real person and a shaman.* Time for me to go out on a limb and reach out to touch fate. Message sent.

A Zoom meeting later and a month after, I was standing at her door.

" I braved through every blocked memory and met myself at each moment, letting go of the fear."

I asked the universe for a teacher, and I received. The moment we met physically there was recognition— not from this life. My past was the greatest master, and *she* was my guide. We sat in my uncomfortability for countless sessions. I blocked most of my past memories. Atousa advised me during one of our sessions that I have a stronger connection to my past live*s* than this lifetime. Trauma. Denial. Judgment. Anger. Rejection. Fear. I needed to face this. I needed to face *me.* I braved through every blocked memory and met myself at each moment, letting go of the fear. Seeing that I had unmet needs/wants from myself. But this was not easy. I preferred torture, as I was reminded. *White knuckles holding this unseen rope.* For a year Atousa and I worked together. During this time, I saw how much of me I gave away and how little I left for myself. And that I was hiding from myself. *Playing games.* Through our work, Atousa had me go in and find the answers—much of her teachings were second nature for me. Like a forgotten journal that I misplaced years ago.

" Then my second and hardest breakup was with my toxic self."

Within the first four months of working with Atousa, one of the biggest Band-Aids I ripped off was my engagement. Neither myself nor my partner was happy. But this only came to a head once my fiancé was caught trying to plan an affair with a friend. I had enough of her patterns and my choosing to roll over out of fear. I woke up to smell the bullshit. *Goodbye.*

Then my second and hardest breakup was with my toxic self. I saw how poorly I was treating myself and how this reflected out.

With this overdue break came my resolution in layers. These layers of healing and releasing took nearly another year and guidance. Presently still working on this. I saw both the dark and the light within me. I was beaten by and now healing by my own hands.

Witnessing my patterns and personas. Then how this reflected in my life and how I was choosing these things because of being comfortable in my *chosen* hell with my unspoken rules. And that I was afraid of myself. Breaking away from this cycle. I become the observer. Gnawing within me was this twisted game I'd denied for years. Now mirrored by this woman who listened to me when I couldn't hear myself.

I was holding this rope tied to a familiar place. I wanted to be a healer, but I held on to this wrath and vengeance that was controlled by my fear and judgment.

I tugged and nothing seemed to budge. I thought I needed both. Lightwork and the dark arts.

Not understanding that I was falling apart.

I saw the dark goddess smiling back at me from the shadows—never acting, just watching.

Why me? I'd been here before. I'd made that comforting choice or stayed in the between.

I saw all those that I love, and wished I could be embraced.

Busy hands leave you empty handed.

Glancing down, seeing that the rope I clutched was the very noose I placed upon my own throat that only I could cut loose.

Releasing my hands of this senseless game and it began to rain, clearing the skies to lighter days.

The rope soon decayed as I saw my life clear as day, never to be ashamed of where I came.

Opening my arms to the greatest change.

I saw in this meditation reflection the cycle, my *tireless* battle. I did not trust in Source, Universe, or God. I was not trusting myself. I became a people pleaser, trying to box myself in and run away from my past. I chose to be blind out of fear. Not seeing that I was never alone. I also played all the parts in my story. Victim. Hero. Foe. Understanding that I did not have a terrible life. I was holding on to so much baggage—mine and everyone else's. That was my choice. There is no wrong or right. Only lessons . . . Like a seed buried, I could either let the soil consume me or take root to grow toward the sun beyond me.

> " Like a seed buried, I could either let the soil consume me or take root to grow toward the sun beyond me. "

I wanted control and justice. Swaying ever so slightly toward the darker side (my thoughts of self-hurt) but never staying. I needed to make a choice.

The in between—half a glass. Dark arts—empty glutton, lost within. Lightworker—following a path beyond *me*.

I came to Atousa to become a shaman, not seeing I was already there. Transformed. Accepting myself for all that I am. Still practicing this daily. Universe gave me the tools and knowledge, but the deep waters I was so terrified to jump into was the river of my life. Sink, float, or swim. I plunged. Letting the water wash over me, I did neither. I surrendered.

My past is simply that. I let go, seeing where I am at presently and how everything happened as the foreground to show me who I have always been. Shedding those layers, uncovering that woman buried under all that armor, then holding that terrified inner child. Forgiving and grateful. I needed to embrace myself. *I am a healer. I am still learning. Always grateful as I start to see myself.*

When we heal ourselves, we also heal the generations before us and after us. We heal our past lives, and we heal those who enter our lives, with or without knowing. Leaving this world (our life) better than how we found it.

God does not have a defined shape or name. God is the unconditional love that is within us all. Unconditional love is not to be confused with lust or desire, but loving yourself (the world) fully and respecting those healthy boundaries. Shadow and light. Divine and human. I chose to walk a path of light so that I could see my shadows and say "hello" to those parts of me, then "goodbye" to the illusions of fear.

As Edgar Allan Poe once said, "Never to suffer would never to have been blessed."[5]

During my healing journey, I witnessed the ripple effect that my healing has had on the world around me and within me. And that continues as I work up my pathway, as I shift toward my sincere self, not hiding my past while reconnecting to Source. I saw loved ones shift as well on their own. My family grew in ways I never expected. In my vulnerability came my community.

On my birthday in 2023, I held two photos. One of my child self and one of my teen self, then touched every physical and unseen scar. Grateful for every time that it did not work.

I share with you a personal favorite poem that a wise friend wrote:

I come to you shining the light
Parting the path to heaven
Yes it may cut
It may bruise
It may hurt
But it will lift
It will bring joy
It will bring love
I guarantee if you trust
You will clear your path for good

---

5 https://tinybuddha.com/wisdom-quotes/never-to-suffer-would-never-to-have-been-blessed/.

Life is calling you
I'll keep shining the light
For you to heal and clear the path
To remember you are supported in the wings of grace
To see the heaven inside

The light is within
Just be witness
To hear and see
I'll guide you
And will be with every step of the way
By clearing and letting go of layers of self
I can see the light
The light is inside of me
I am perched in the wings of grace
I am safe
I am supported
I am loved
I am love
I am grace
~Atousa Raissyan

Our pathway may never seem clear. But see through the illusions of human fears. Your life is a growing seed. Reaching out in all directions but never straying from its true destination. Rising above and becoming one with all that is creation.

Made with love,
Shonna

About Shonna Perkins

Her intention in sharing her chapter is that this life is worth living. Life is not meant to be easy or hard. It's meant to flow. Like water and how it changes current with each obstacle. The air that we breathe . . . giving and receiving with every breath. Or like fire—when fields are burned, it creates others . . . The horizon might seem tall, but it's because we need the best view to see the bigger picture: us as one. Magic is real, you are never alone, never stop creating, and you are loved.

Artwork: https://fineartamerica.com/profiles/shonna-perkins

THE FOUR SEASON

Message of Love
By Sue Rahmani

Your duty is to be . . . not to be this or that.
~Ramana Maharashi

I decided to write these small stories to heal myself but also to make a difference to those who might be going through the same.

It is so true what the air hostess in the airplane says regarding safety procedures—in case of an emergency and lack of oxygen, first fix your own oxygen mask before attending to someone else. I am trying to learn to do that without feeling guilty.

Between all these words and pages, my lack of oxygen is translating to many different emotional traumas and circumstances that I am trying to deal with in my head and in my body.

It was a strange feeling, trying to organize my thoughts on how I wanted these words to manifest, form, and be read by someone else rather than myself. I had to go back and watch all the chapters of my life from memory and relive them again, but this time I was the observer and not engaged. I watched my life from outside and all sorts of emotions came to the surface, but I was not involved. I was watching my life like a movie, so I got myself a large popcorn and a box of tissues and just sat with it. I surrendered to what was about to come and I held myself tight and lovingly and started to watch.

What I came to realize was my role changing throughout this motion of life I now call "The Movie." I noticed there are places in my life where I am the hero of the story and other times I am the producer, the set designer, the demon, the sound engineer, and the director. I made the choice even if sometimes it didn't feel like I had one. The truth is I *always had a choice*, and sometimes I made the wrong choice. No one to blame.

Here is how I decided this to unfold. Instead of just telling my life story, I decided to write vignettes that are not attached to each other so the reader can choose them separately if they don't want to read them back to back. In each section, depending on my mood and subject, I added some of my own poetry and that of others who've inspired me. Occasionally I added a meditation technique I found useful, with full step-by-step instructions. There will be space for even shouting inside a pillow or crying under the shower, if that helps anyone. (It helped me).

My intention is not to tell anyone how to do their life, nor that I managed mine super well. That would be a lie. I have daily struggles too, and life continues to give me lemons. How I deal with it has changed. How I approach life is different. I live a fuller life, so I doubt my life changed so much, but change came from me and my mindset toward living fuller and making it more enjoyable and whole. I still get those moments where I shout inside my pillow or take a long shower and cry, but not as often.

So this is what I want these pages to feel to you:

I want these pages to feel like a gentle kiss on your hidden open wounds.

I want these pages to feel like a tight, genuine hug with no judgment.

I want these pages to feel like a breeze of fresh air on the heat of your emotional struggles.

I want these pages to feel like you are enough, loved, and protected.

I can honestly say, I lived a good life and I certainly know how to laugh and keep my sense of humor. We can be creative together and come up with crazy ideas and dreams. Freedom in a safe space is the key objective here. We can share however we like to express, release, unlearn, and surrender, and I hope you relate to what you read and that these pages give you the space to *be*.

Ready to face yourself? Let's go . . . I have you and will hold you when it gets tough. I promise, my delicate love warrior. Don't forget love always wins over fear.

Worthy of love, I am,
When I am touched, heart will weep,
The warmth of a delicate soul, heals me,
The praising sound of a clap, brings me courage,
The clarity and roundness of my tears,
promise me the feelings,
To be told "I love You" promises me divinity.

Dancing in the wind,
Holding hands,
Making love,
Shouting with excitement,
And praying with hope,
Brings me blissful dreams.
My dreams mark my way,
My way is clear,
My steps firm,
My mind sharp,
My hands strong,
And my heart is full and leading.
I am leaving the past behind,
All the heavy attachments I carried,
The self-sabotage games and blames,
Those who did me wrong,
The self-pity and victimizing spaces I refuge.
I start fresh,
Painting a new version of myself,
With acceptance, joy and no regret.
Worthy of love, I am.
~The Gayatri Mantra

I want to share this mantra because it was my life companion since my self-discovery journey began. The mantra has power and remedy to all circumstances. Sit with it and chant it for a while until you feel the energy of it running through every cell of your body and being.

Among all mantras, the Gayatri is called the essence of all mantras. All spiritual powers and potencies are contained within it. The Gayatri meditation on spiritual light. In all the teachings and scriptures, Gayatri is called supreme in bestowing light. In all the teachings and scriptures, Gayatri

is called supreme in bestowing enlightenment.

It is practiced by Hindus and Buddhists alike. "For pure spiritual potency in the accumulating of the highest light, there is nothing to compare with the Gayatri Mantra."[6]

The Gayatri Mantra—sometimes referred to as the "guru mantra," has been chronicled in the Rig Veda, which was written in Sanskrit, about 2,500 to 3,500 years ago, and the mantra may have been chanted for many centuries before that.

According to the Vedas, there are seven realms of spheres or planes of existence, each more spiritually advanced then the previous one. It is written that through spiritual awareness and development, we can progressively move through these realms and ultimately merge with the Supreme Being.

It is said that by chanting this mantra, divine spiritual light and power is infused in each of our chakras and connects them to these seven great spiritual realms of existence.

The full Mantra:

> **Om Bhur**—1st chakra, Muladhara—Om and salutation to the Earth plane
>
> **Om Bhuvaha**—2nd chakra, Svadhisthana— Om and salutation to the Atmospheric phrase
>
> **Om Swaha**—3rd chakra, Manipura—Om and salutation to the Solar region
>
> **Om Maha**—4th chakra, Anahata—Om and salutation to the first spiritual region beyond the sun
>
> **Om Janaha**—5th chakra, Vishuddha—Om and salutation to the second spiritual region

6 Thomas Ashley-Farrand, *Chakra Mantras* (San Francisco: Red Wheel/Weiser, 2006), 158.

beyond the sun

Om Tapaha—6th chakra, Ajna—Om and salutation to the third spiritual region beyond the sun, sphere of the progenitors

Om Satyam—7th chakra, Shasrara—Om and salutation to the abode of supreme truth

(Feeling the next three chakras above the crown of the head)

Om tat Savitur Varenyam—Om and salutation to the realm that is beyond human comprehension

Bhargo Devasya Dhimahi—In that place where all the celestials of all the spheres have

Dhiyo Yonaha Prachodayat—Received enlightenment, kindly enlighten our intellect

(Translation from Thomas Ashley Farrand's *Chakra Mantras*)

In the War Zone with Madonna

The lights would cut off, but the radio remained on with battery, so we could hear the sirens to go to safety, usually the basement. I always wanted to watch the bombing from our rooftop, and instead, despite my mom shouting, would run upstairs to the roof with my baba (dad) and hide behind the cooling system, taking shelter in my baba's arms and looking at the sky, waiting with curiosity.

The adrenaline of fear and whether it was going to be near us was part of this sick game in my head. The ability to look at the planes and see them drop the bombs and the falling . . . EXPLOSION. Phew . . . didn't hit us this time and couldn't be that close if the windows were not shattered. Back to the darkness of the night until the next siren.

This was the routine for a while, and bombings could be any time of the day or night. No one knew where to go next. Many people left their homes or lost them. Some schools were closed, but some were still open if they could provide shelter in case of bombing. Mine was open, but my parents were not too bothered if I didn't go, and I would only go if I liked the teacher or the subject for that day.

The war of Iran and Iraq lasted eight years, parallel to the Islamic revolution overtaking the monarchy. It started when I was just ten years old and ended when I was eighteen and an adult! From primary till end of secondary school.

After primary school I decided to go to a school that was not the norm. I was studying art. People perceived kids who went to art schools as dumb and lazy, but that was not true. Iranian culture believed and celebrated the high IQ but not so much creativity.

Persian culture had more respect for children who were good with math, science, and literature than art. Art was considered to be a hobby. Something you did on the side after you mastered all the academic requirements. Mothers would boast about their children's grades at dinner parties and daydream of a future doctor, lawyer, or accountant for their smart children.

We were a different tribe. We were too cool for school and rejected by parental societies outside the school. They would warn their beloved children to avoid us. We were a bad influence and, quite frankly, losers in their eyes. However, we endured this and loved this separation. We formed our own pack, and since we were all artistic, it was fun to

313

rebel and stand out even more. Gave us more substance to express in the form of art, poetry, and performance.

The war was coming to an end, and so was school. Most people learned how to live with the war. Interesting, how humans adapt and adjust to everything and find beauty within the ugliest. The number of used bullets we found and collected from our gardens and making them into necklaces and jewelry pieces were a basic trend among the youth my age.

The urge to be like Western kids was something we aspired to. We didn't want to look backward and disconnected. We hated the fact that our government wanted to keep us isolated and cut off from the rest of the world. With no exception, everyone had friends and families who'd parted from Iran and now lived in the United States and Europe, and they kept us in the loop with Western ideas, fashion, music, and trends. We would pay big bucks for a pair of Nike or Adidas trainers to look westernized.

The Islamic regime was against many things young people strived toward, and there came a big price if these restrictions they called "Islamic laws" were broken. Having mixed parties, music, dancing, showing hair, tight clothing for girls, makeup, perfume, hair color, and looking westernized were on the list of what we couldn't do.

None of this stopped us. My room was full of posters of Michael Jackson and Madonna that I'd bought from black market. We used to buy bad-quality and scratchy cassette tapes of their songs and played them in our mixed in-house parties, dressed in our cool Western clothes and makeup, dancing.

Many of our parties would be broken into by morality

police, resulting in capturing us and taking us into cells, with slashing and insults as punishment, unless we managed to escape by running away and jumping into neighboring gardens and nearby fields in the dark. Our parents would get the unforeseeable call to come and collect us, which usually involved large cash penalties and lots of preaching on Islamic laws and what a disgrace we were to our society and those martyrs who'd lost their families in the war.

This was our norm and our opportunity to create amazing underground art, music, and literature. Everything else, including vodka, could be bought easily on black market.

Looking back, I still feel, despite the traumatic circumstances my generation experienced growing up in Iran, we thought we had a happy childhood. But for those more fortunate, like me, who left the country and lived outside, they realized that actually how we grew up was absolutely limiting, torturous, and unfair, especially for girls. Adapting to a new way of life outside of Iran, at the age of twenty-one, felt like a new beginning. I had the freedom to fly but never learned how to use my wings.

In my comforting sensation of existence,
Joyous tears of greatness of this freedom,
The reality of the weakness of human betrayal,
The generosity of Divine forgiveness,
The sound of quiet whisper of the earth,
The delicate kisses of the eternal breeze,
The childlike excitement for life,
And me.

Sanskrit Mantra: Prasada hum (I am divine grace)

Radiating grace, I share my divine blessings

You can repeat this mantra for feeling whole 27 times or one full mala of 108 times.

Getting Out of My Head

Lying on the bed next to him and listening to his breath. Was deep and a bit noisy, and I didn't like it, but I didn't do anything. I had been tossing and turning all night, thinking. My thoughts were mixed up with haggling with myself, guilt, and resentment. I was kind of blackmailing myself to stay, but my heart was weeping, wanting to leave.

What about our children? They were still very small, under ten years old! Suddenly I felt selfish. The voice in my head judged me for even thinking of leaving. I reasoned with the voice and said I will take the kids with me and look after them. The voice slapped me with the question of *Without their father?* I shut up again and tried to go back to sleep. Many nights passed with me thinking in bed while he slept. He had no idea what was going on in my head, nor asked.

Everything seemed so wonderful from outside. Perfect life with the house, healthy kids, blossomed careers, proud grandparents, the cat, the car, and the rest of it. Only, I felt empty. Completely empty and sad. I was not speaking about my feelings, as they were conflicting internally to myself, and I didn't want to sound crazy or ungrateful.

On one of those sleepless nights when I was watching him sleeping and myself thinking, I felt something was happening to me inside and out. It was like a rise of energy all over me that carried clarity. I didn't know what it was, but it was certainly powerful. So much more than me.

Did I conquer my fear of leaving? The facts and consequences remained, but my fear was gone. There was this surge of self-love that held me close and was kind to me. It understood I was not a bad mother nor a bad wife nor a selfish woman. *I must leave and that is the right thing to do.*

I had no answer why it finally was confirmed in my head and heart that leaving was the only good option. Finally the two aligned and understood something I couldn't explain. Somehow, no explanation was required. The heart knew, and the head followed, and I felt free.

I knew it was going to be messy and painful. My husband's reaction when I told him, my parents trying to put sense in my head, my children feeling unsettled, and everyone trying to blackmail me to stay because of them. Plus, all the labels I needed to wear with the badge of "dishonorable wife and mother." None of it would stop me. It was the right thing to do. Doubt did not manage its way in again. Call it faith, God, energy, or whatever you want, but I felt safe, and I knew I would be fine and so would my children, and I went ahead with it.

I called my best friend to let her know I was leaving, and I was certain about my decision. I asked if she would accompany me to see a family lawyer for support, and she said yes. My husband still slept soundlessly and deeply every night, thinking life was perfect.

The lawyer asked, "What is the reason for wanting to divorce your husband?"

I looked at my friend across the table and paused. For a few seconds, which felt like a long time, I reviewed all my whys with all the emotions they brought up. All the hurtful

317

nonintentional comments he'd made popped into my head.
Are you going to wax your upper lips?
Would you consider a breast lift?
Is the diet working at all?
At the family and sex counselor's office, he'd boasted about his high sex drive to the therapist, but I knew we hadn't been intimate for months and months. No initiation from him, and when I tried, he would either refuse or put a sheet between us to not feel my skin.

Suddenly the rise of sadness and anger flushed in my face, remembering how little and unworthy I felt then and how much I was trying to be better, prettier, sexier, thinner, funnier so he could find me attractive. But that day, at this lawyer's office, I was finally strong enough to stop it. I told the lawyer, "The reason for me wanting to divorce my husband is inappropriate behavior." And she wrote that down in my file.

It took around a week for the letter to reach my husband by post, and in the meantime I let him enjoy his sleep, knowing it was not for long. At this stage I was angry at him for so many reasons, but mostly for not seeing me. It was convenient, and our relationship had become like a parenting contract and nothing more. All that feeling of sadness and worthlessness turned into fury after my visit to the lawyer. It was fascinating to see the change. How did this vulnerable, little, unsure woman switch into this roaring, angry tiger? My determination gave me strength, and despite the negative emotion anger brought, I admired it. I wanted to be angry.

He received the letter, and shit hit the fan. He told me he would not go ahead with the divorce and it was not something he was willing to negotiate or even talk about.

He was in shock, and his reaction was impulsive, but I understood. It was hard to keep calm and not fight back or start with the blame game and victimizing. Now we both stayed up in bed, and instead of his heavy breathing, we were listening to each other's heavy sighs.

A few weeks passed, and we walked on eggshells around each other, and I could see the heavy pain on his face. To be honest, my emotions were getting mixed up from moment to moment, and I had a lot of self-talk to keep my focus and not be distracted or manipulated to change my mind. I reasoned with myself and permitted myself to have contradictory emotions from moment to moment until the dust settled down. So the emotional roller coaster began.

He finally talked to me and suggested that we stay married but have an open relationship. He expressed that what he "doesn't know can't hurt him, and our children won't be affected." I was insulted with this offer. I wasn't leaving because I'd had an affair or wanted to. I was leaving because I was invisible and worthless in my own home, even if it was done to me unintentionally. So I refused.

Battle continued, and it became a cold war. No one would say anything, but the fighting resumed in silence and through expensive lawyers' letters. We were still sleeping in the same bed, and our children were clueless. We became actors going through the process badly.

This was when I learned how to truly pray. I was talking and pleading to something I felt was hearing me and giving me power to cope. Cope with the judgment of my family, who could not understand why I wanted out if my husband was not cheating on me. My husband, who

could not understand why I felt leaving was the only option left for us. And our friends, who were choosing sides.
The look of pity for my children on people's faces made me
want to puke but gave me more determination to succeed,
so I prayed harder and wholeheartedly.

Life continued like this for eighteen months before my
husband finally left the matrimonial home and our divorce
was finalized. What was left was me with my prayers, asking for strength and focus to be able to move my new and
unfamiliar life with my two minors forward.

What I knew deeply was, no matter what, this life is a
flux of movement, and that is inevitable, and I am part of
this change. I had two choices: to sink and feel sorry for
myself and take my life down or to swim with the motion.
I swam, even if I had to swallow heavy water and cough a
few times.

I decided, for a change, I was the only one in charge
of my life, and I took full responsibility and started taking
baby steps. I could choose for myself without worrying if I
upset anyone or about being disapproved of, and the moment I realized this reality, I was liberated. This was my
most glorious moment. I smiled at myself and trusted my
God to keep me and my children safe.

He did not disappoint, because through this hardship
I learned love is stronger than my fear, and I loved with my
whole being.

Fast-forward to now.

Today I am at peace with everything that took place,
because it made me the woman I am today. I still don't
approve of anything that happened in my marriage but
accepted that my husband didn't know how to love and

never had the intention to hurt me or break us up. He was simply deprived of love and loving. I have forgiven him and myself. My anger and sadness then turned into compassion today.

May we all be happy,
May we all be Loved,
May we all be in peace, within and around.

Sanskrit Mantra: Aham Rema (I am Love)
I am made of love and love is me.

You can repeat this mantra for feeling love 27 times or one full mala of 108 times.

Holy Whore

I was standing completely bare in front of the full-size mirror and forcing myself to take a good look at myself, top to toe, every detail.

I was cringing and not finding this easy. So much body hate and self-criticism. In my head I was physically ugly, and now I confirmed it inside this mirror. I couldn't look at my body for any longer. The fat thighs, the saggy boobs, the round and bloated belly, the extra-thick calves, the cellulite and stretch marks, my painful bunions, funny-shaped fingers and nails . . . *Is there anything decent looking in my body?* I asked myself. It made me lose more confidence. I *am ugly, undesirable, disgusting, and unattractive.* It was a fact.

For fourteen years I was invisible to a man I once loved. I found courage to end it and walked into a new life, which I was getting the hang of quite well, but this aspect of me was still quite starved and needed to heal. I was feeling deeply worthless as a woman, and to overcome the void, I was shining bright in all other areas of my life as a way of compensation. Only I knew of my deep-rooted trauma and how far it had dug emotionally. From the outside world, I created an image of a confident and high-achieving woman with a lot of energy and wit, but the melancholy aspect of myself was an old wound I continuously licked when in hiding.

I decided to fix it. "I always fix things and take control, and this should not be any different. I am in charge." *After all, I have my yoga and spirituality to save my soul and end my suffering* were my initial thoughts.

So I increased my weekly yoga classes and got better and better at it. It gave me a boost getting into some funky poses. I felt better about the quality of how my physical body was serving me. Lost the weight by eating very little, and since I was doing a lot of yoga, it was natural to become vegan.

I continued my yoga journey further and created a hippy community for myself that I felt was trendy enough to be a part of and separated me from the norm into eccentric. If I was a hippy doing funky yoga poses and eating vegetables only, I became interesting because I am no longer average.

This went on, and in the meantime, I dated men. Men I met online, on Facebook, in the bar, and at work. I learned how to flirt again, and since I kind of was worshipping this new feminine, lean, and thin body of mine, I oozed sensuality. Wow, that felt great. I became self-obsessed and totally besotted by my beauty. Men liked me. They found me attractive and desired being with me. I'd never felt the same with my husband, and this was giving me my confidence back . . . but only on the surface.

Every time I bedded a man, I was left heartbroken and

empty afterward. The few relationships I made after my divorce all ended up in heartache too. What was funny but sad at the same time was, they still wanted to sleep with me but not to be with me, and I so longed for love. So much so that occasionally I agreed to remain a friend with benefit in the hope that love might blossom if I hung about a bit longer, but it never did for them.

The more my heart was broken and shattered, the more I had to let the light in. Today, I know taking yoga classes to form a sexy body were not a coincidence, and its purpose was not to make me feel sexy but to patiently wait until I broke down and put my soul back together, teaching me real life lessons.

" I became honest to myself. "

In parallel to my heartaches and men issues, I dove deeper in other yoga practices. I began to explore different schools and teachings until I was introduced to Mandala Yoga Ashram in Wales, where I became a regular visitor and resident. Going there made me feel safe, and I began to face my darkness with light. The Tantric teachings at the ashram and my personal practices and research brought me to a place in myself that I became aware of myself and the reality. In a nutshell, I took away my mask, at least for myself. I became honest to myself. Nothing was fixed, none of my issues were resolved, I was still emotionally scarred and damaged, my moods and feelings were unstable, but I didn't lie to myself anymore.

I didn't want to hide from myself, and because by this time I had learned to sit still and meditate or breathe, I could easily keep myself company without resentment and possibly reflect.

One thing was for certain—I wanted to become a better person. I wanted to do good and be peaceful. I was seeking joy and grace all the way along, from the beginning of my adult life, but only now was this evidently clear, because I let all the dust settle and cleared out the mud at my soul level with regular meditation, Tantric lessons, and becoming still.

Stillness is not equal to perfection or becoming a saint. You can be still and imperfect. Stillness, for me, works like the windshield wipers of the car when it is raining. I can only see better, so I drive myself properly, but like the car, sometimes I crash into a wall, a tree, or another car.

"Soul-seeking practices are a lifetime journey, and I am still learning every day."

Soul-seeking practices are a lifetime journey, and I am still learning every day. My karma of the past, my current ones, and my ancestral karmas I am carrying from previous generations must be worked and cleared at this dharmic dance of human existence.

Knowing is the key surrounding the power and love of the path.

What is life?
Perception of events?
The question arises when we are challenged,
Although we survived all the events of life so far and still living,
We ask ourselves every single time,

Why we, as humans, want so much?
Even when we only need the basic,
Judgment and doubt . . . internal questioning,
I am no victim to my thoughts,
My mind is to serve me and not me being a slave to it,
I rise above my thoughts,
Above the chatter,
And all the bloody gremlins,
It is what it is,
And this shall pass too,
Is called the dance of Dharma & Karma,
A human process for growth.

Sanskrit Mantra: Satyam Vijayate (Truth is victorious)
I open myself to the truth and light.

You can repeat this mantra to open yourself to the magic of the universe and trust it 27 times or one full mala of 108 times.

Burnout to Balance

Sitting in my office chair and staring at the same email I was trying to read for the past fifteen minutes, repeatedly reading the same line and not understanding it. I burst into tears.

Suddenly it became too much to bear. My body and brain weren't complying with my demands and were shutting down. I was exhausted, ashamed, and feeling useless. Physically and mentally shutting down without me having any control. *I always have control and this can't be happening to me.*

So I tried again to read the email and push myself against the odds. "Damn it," I said, and sobbed harder. It wasn't working, and I was no longer in control, my brain not grasping the meaning of the words I was reading I cried hysterically, and my body shook with a high level of stress. It was here, at this moment, when I knew this time was different and I needed to ask for help.

I was sent home that day and didn't return to work for another three weeks. My doctor signed me off due to high levels of stress and started me on medication.

I stayed home and tried to get better. It was not easy. At first my head was still on a race and couldn't switch off work. Lots of emotions were rising up, and I was not necessarily well enough to deal with them effectively, which would lead to panic. I was up and down all the time. Totally lost in my belief that I failed not only my job but my family. I saw myself weak and useless, unworthy and incapable. Even my body and head didn't want to cooperate with me.

This was how I saw it from the grip of my depression and burnout. I am worth nothing and best being dead!

Like everything in life, time passed, and with my medication kicking in, plus the start of a weekly psychotherapy, I was getting stronger again. I was being helped to first settle and ground and eventually review the cause of all this mess I'd brought to myself unknowingly. This was when the real work started.

Looking back at my career history, I was always a reliable and willing employee. Responsible, creative, and adaptable. Basically, the typical "yes" girl who strived to achieve and be seen, so I made sure, at any cost, that I shone.

All the missed bath times or bedtime stories with my little children are a few to mention that I still regret. Attending school plays, football matches, and almost all weekends and Christmas holidays were out of the question because I was working in retail and those were the busiest periods, so I was needed at work.

I believed I was hurting more than my children, as they didn't know any other way, and this was how they were growing up, their norm. Mommy was always at work! But in my heart, I felt more useful at my job, and because it was a job, I had a great justification to defend and justify my absence, saying my job needed me more than my children. I couldn't say no to my boss or let the team and the business down. I blamed it eagerly on my gambling husband, who was having the time of his life watching our children grow up at every stage, until we divorced a few years later.

This feeling of being more productive and needed and successful outside the family life and in a corporate world stayed, and I think it might have come from something much deeper that I carried from generation to generation. My sister was the same. It might have come from a cultural rebel against the belief that Iranian women stay home and become trophy housewives. So we were doing both in equal measures—two full-time jobs in one, and of course, that has its toll on you eventually.

My managing director at the time of my burnout was a chatty, bubbly woman I liked and trusted. I worked for her like I would do for a friend and was still the same "yes" person in that I was agreeing to take on more and more, and she did not deny it either. I was at my desk by 8:30 in the morning and left after 7:00 p.m., eating my lunch in front of my computer. Otherwise, I was on an airplane or train traveling to Europe on business. I would take an early flight there and the last flight, same day, to come back if it was a short stay. During peak season, I was away for almost two weeks at a time, working in the showroom, meeting and presenting clients with new collections. I was the omnichannel operation manager for this French fashion house, and my role covered diverse responsibilities within different departments, and we were growing faster than anticipated. At the same time that the business was growing, my children were also growing. After my divorce, they lived with me, and we were clashing, especially me with my son. He was fifteen and experimenting with drugs and being destructive.

I can firmly say this was one of my most difficult and traumatic periods. So many valuable lessons I am grateful for today, but so many emotional scars to go with them. To paint the picture a bit better, I was in this high-demand job that required my attention and would keep me away from home for weeks and had a boss who piled more work on me, abusing the friendliness and trust I thought I'd built with her. At home I had two teenagers in a tiny two-bedroom flat, along with their childhood nanny (she slept on the sofa), who watched over my children while I was at work. My former husband was no support and lost in his own mess. Financially I was earning a decent salary, but the lifestyle I'd built before did not match my new one as a single mother of two. (Just noting that I didn't have any financial support from the father.)

Plus, emotionally, as a woman, I felt lonely. I missed having someone to love and hold. Therefore, I piled the game of dating into my busy schedule to find the special man who I thought was out there. As a result, I kissed many frogs, and none turned to a prince.

I remember crawling into bed, tossing and turning,

thinking of everything and praying. Sometimes I stayed up trying to find my son, who was not answering his phone and was meant to be home a few hours ago. I called the missing person's number to report him missing and once walked to the police station for assistance. When he would show up, we would get into heavy and abusive arguments and say things to hurt each other. I was angry and felt tired and alone, and so did he. Plus, he was the child, yes, but a mouthy one who wanted to fight.

It was getting difficult to manage my children, and I shared this with my boss, asking if I could pile my total hours into four days instead so I could be more present with my son, who clearly needed my presence and attention. Her reply was "You already do these extra hours when you are here early and leaving late, and if I let you work four days instead of five, business loses one day!" She was right, but I was giving these additional hours because she was giving me more and more tasks, and I never said no. She suggested taking my request to higher management and reassured me that she would do her best to help me. I believed her.

Three weeks later an official HR letter came that my request was refused. However, the date of this letter was from three weeks ago, a day after she'd reassured me. I called HR, and they confirmed this was a decision made by her at the time the letter was written, and I realized she'd never taken my request to higher management but made me wait three weeks in anticipation so she could go on her vacation. My world crashed. I died inside with the betrayal. I was unable to look at her or smile or pretend. My tears rolled down, and I tried to find my center again. Being lied to had hurt, but the realization that my family life didn't matter hurt more.

I was not a new employee. I'd been there for five years, with two major promotions, and she could trust me.

This went on, and I became detached and more distant, mixed with disappointment and anger. It was heavy to carry in addition to everything else. It was the uninvited guest I could not accommodate. On the surface business was as usual and my manager was still as chatty and bubbly as before, unaware of me finding out about her lack of sensitivity to my situation—until I shared it and my disappointment. I remember vividly that I was crying in her office, seeking an acceptable reply from her, and she told me to stop crying because this was business and not an appropriate space to show emotion. I cried more because I knew it was time to leave, but I couldn't be rational and just walk out. I still needed to pay my mortgage and bills. So I tried to buy some time and continue with my work. My relationship with my son, however, was breaking up and becoming more and more unmanageable, and my daughter, who was a good girl, felt neglected.

The three weeks I had at home made me realize I needed to trust my higher power and do what was right, even if risks were involved. I knew I was unable to continue working for someone who was dishonest, and our life values and morals were a world apart. I was scared and still in recovery. I asked the universe to help me get out and keep my family and me safe. I asked God to show me ways of doing it. I remember saying, "Show me signs and give me the ability to recognize them."

I returned to work on shorter hours, at the request of my doctor. The expectation of my boss was to deliver a full week's result in my part-time hours, which I knew I couldn't do. I decided to have a chat with the HR manager, and I did. What came over me to fully unveil what was going on and my situation at home with money and at work with my manager? She was the earth angel. I was asking the universe to come and rescue me. She heard and understood me. I lasted at this job no more than a day after our conversation. She told me to go and grab my bag and go home. "You will be fine and don't need to stay for a day longer."

Thanks to her I could leave and have a few months to breathe, recover, and figure out what I would like to do next. I am always thankful to her.

Burnout happens all the time to a lot of people. It happened to me almost a decade ago, but the side effects of it are still quite raw. My body recognizes the triggers and tenses and goes to defense mode immediately. I know a lot of what happened to me was my own doing and allowing and attracting it to myself unconsciously. The lessons I learned and stick by and the values I built are so worthy that I am thankful. My trauma became my best asset and taught me self-love, self-value, forgiveness, and facing my biggest fears knowing I am always protected. I just needed the clarity to see the signs and the magic.

It is not numbness that I don't feel the pain anymore
It is Consciousness
It is not carelessness that I don't react anymore
It is detachment
It is not confusion when I no longer chase
It is trust within
It is not lunacy when I say I found myself again
It is self-realization.

Sanskrit Mantra: Vedo hum (I am pure knowledge)

My being is wise and knowing.

You can repeat this mantra for reaching your answers 27 times or one full mala of 108 times.

Battle of Aging Gracefully

Have you ever felt misaligned? This aging business was very misaligning for me. They clash and contradict each other!

In my head and heart, I felt I was still young and would daydream about exciting projects and activities that required a youthful and fit physique, which I no longer have.

It took me ages to come to terms with this. It began with early signs of menopause—hot flashes, mood swings, and slowing down of my metabolism. I suddenly couldn't reconnect and recognize my physical self, and panic took over. I began to look at it as the process of decay and dying. I'd lived most of my years already despite feeling mentally youthful. How long was there left even if I lived long? Twenty or Thirty years, max. Then I would remind myself how short twenty years was and how little time was left in my life, and this body of mine was slowing down when I needed it the most—to fill the remaining years catching up with everything in my bucket list. Frustrating, isn't it?

I had to share and discuss my frustration with my psychotherapist, whom I had been seeing for years. Telling her I could not understand, nor was I ready for it. We had so many sessions discussing different stages of life and the cycle of it. How to embrace aging and the wisdom that it brings. How this wisdom translates into this new chapter of life and how, as an older person, it's possible to still having a fulfilling life and enjoy it too. It was not easy or in my control . . . aging was happening, and eventual dying inevitable, so get on with it and make something of it or watch yourself decaying to a slow death. I chose living, but with that I needed acceptance and adjusting.

I am still walking with death side by side, and it has always been that way. I just never acknowledged the presence of it, and now I do because it gives more reason to be alive while I am still here.

I guess what I am saying is, through the dark side of life, which is equally death (in many aspects), I understood living or the light . . . whatever you want to call it.

Therefore, I began accepting and then loving my aging, knowing so many people don't get to experience it. I started to sit in silence and send love to my osteoporosis and aching bones. Give thanks for being able to still walk and move on my own free will.

After each shower, I oil and moisturize my aging skin, hands, and feet, sending them love for being faithful partners in this life cycle, taking me through all the years we grew old together.

Getting involved and taking part in this writing project is also giving thanks to my life by looking back into the dark sides as well as the light to embrace the journey I have come so far, calling it my life. The healing process of unloading, unfolding, and arriving, plus dropping the heavy baggage at the door and entering.

I want to enter this freeing space in my heart. It has nothing to do with aging or youthfulness. It is neither life nor death either. It doesn't care if you are overweight, have cancer, or are poor. I experience it sometimes but am aware of it all the time after a lot of practice and internal work. I remind myself of it knowing it is there, and I can run to it if I want to. This is a sacred space within me that welcomes and loves me regardless. Is a space of total BEing, with no attachment and labels. Is a place of soul. It is nothing but everything. It is active but is still, is male but also female energy . . . It just IS.

" I am accepting the flow and cycle of life, as it comes with knowing beyond this realm. "

So I now love my aging process. I am not tied to explaining myself so much. I can afford and choose what my heart seeks. I love openly and with plenty. I am accepting the flow and cycle of life, as it comes with knowing beyond this realm. I am I am I am . . .

I have cholesterol, but I am not cholesterol,

I have osteoporosis, but I am not osteoporosis,

I have extra weight, but I am not the excess weight,

I have fifty-three years of life experience, but I am not the age.

I have droopy aging skin, but I am not the skin.

I have dreams and desires and demands, but I am none of them.

When you really understand this aspect of your being, aging becomes a privilege, along with all the aches and pains and limitations it gives you, because none of it defines the real you.

Magic is always around us, and dreams can come true when freedom is the essence of every soul.

Isn't it magical that one will only see its true light in

complete darkness?

It is pitch black here . . .

Shine on me, Ma

Sanskrit Mantra: So Hum (I am)

I am the consciousness.

You can repeat this mantra to experience oneness and state of Samadhi (consciousness) 27 times or one full mala of 108 times.

Inner-Smile Meditation

I want to leave you with this old favorite meditation and visualization I learned years ago and that still, to this date, serves me.

The inner-smile meditation is a technique traveling the awareness through the body in a specific and clear path based on the distribution of neural pathways throughout the body to balance consciousness. The attention moves the sensation of a smile from the physical body to the inner body and to the consciousness.

- Sit or lie down in a comfortable way and become still. Limit your bodily movement to the minimum.

- Smile gently and notice: How does the smile feel on the face?

- How does it feel on your jaws, tongue, lips, eyes, forehead, skull, and temples?

- Move the feeling of this smile into the upper body: neck, shoulders, arms, hands, fingers.

- Move the smile into the torso.

- Move the smile into the lower body: pelvis, hips, legs, feet, toes.

- Bring the smile throughout the internal organs, from the top of the torso cavity down to the pelvic floor. (To keep this simple and easy, you might simply focus first on the heart and lungs, then the digestive organs, and finally the genitals and reproductive organs).

- Bring the smile into the nervous system: brain, spine, and nerves.

- Finally feel everything smiling together.

- Move the awareness beyond the physical body: The smile moves into the energy body and your chakras and glowing.

- Continue to sit or lie down: let your consciousness absorb the healing energy of the smile.

This mediation is taken from my advanced yoga teachers training at Ishta Yoga—London

About Sue Rahmani

I am Sogol, but here in the UK, they call me Sue.

Born and raised in Iran and moved to London at the age of twenty, while attending university. I remained in London after my education and have made my home here ever since. I live with my two children, Cameron and Yasmin, who are about to fly the nest.

I started my career in luxury retail and fashion. I currently serve in learning and development, helping people find their best selves in their jobs.

I am also a five-hundred-hour certified yoga therapist, meditation teacher, shamanic healer (level 1), and motivational public speaker.

You can invite me to speak or run workshops or bonding activities for your organizations, retreats, and groups.

Follow me on my social media sites.
LinkedIn: linkedin.com/in/sue-rahmani-05237740
Instagram: sue rahmani @suerahmani
Facebook: Sue Rahmani
Email: sue.rahmani70@gmail.com

THE GOLDEN PATH

By Victoria Stattel

You are real. You are precious.
And you matter so very much.
~Jonathan Hammond

When I was little, I would lie in bed every night and talk to Mother Mary and a spirit named Micheal. According to Christian beliefs, Mary is the mother of Jesus Christ, who is considered by billions the Son of God. Mary is said to have conceived Jesus by the Holy Spirit. I knew Michael to be my older brother, whom I had never met in physical form, as Michael died when he was a few days old, never leaving the hospital. I have memories of talking to them as friends. Visiting casually, with ease, and feeling safe. That changed instantly one night, around the age of eight.

Lying in my bed, I saw it. In the corner, a dark fiery pillar about four feet tall, glowing red and pulsing. I heard, "Those who are closest are the greatest prize." My chest tensed, my eyes swelled, and fear ran through me. Remembering this moment still gives me goose bumps, and I can feel my blood racing.

It didn't occur to me to pray—reach out to Mary or Michael. Scared and frozen, I said aloud what came to me, "I don't want this anymore. Leave me."

Though I did not realize it for decades, that was the moment I chose to live my life alone. Solely aligned to my will and mind's decisions on what was best and right. The spirit listened to my request and for the next thirty years was quiet.

From the Outside

For about two decades, from the outside all seemed to be going according to plan: three varsity sports, band kid, top graduate from high school, military academy, helicopter pilot, married to a great guy by twenty-three. I wasn't perfect by any stretch and pushed boundaries and limits, but overall it appeared I was doing well and on the "right track."

But on the inside I was dying. Unhappy, lacking luster, doing what I thought I should be doing with no enthusiasm or energy.

The facade cracked when at the age of twenty-seven, I was getting divorced and felt suicidal. Through the help of many and sheer determination, I pulled myself up and out, emerging into another decade of reordering my life through an exterior lens: a banner military career; promoting ahead of peers; a successful tour in Afghanistan; and a job at a top think tank, followed by a position at a Big 5 consulting firm.

By the age of forty-two, from the outside it seemed I had reconstructed my life back to sanity: seven years into a second marriage and three healthy children—my large white center-hall colonial even had a Volvo in the driveway. The exterior cracks that were witnessed years before swept under the rug, blamed on a military career and time deployed in Kabul.

But on the inside it lingered . . . the uneasiness, the unsettledness, the dirty secret no one really knew, or at least never talked about. When life was quiet, when I dared give myself a second to be still, it was there—the unsettled, the unhappy, the lost. Searching for an anchor, I was like a flag in the wind.

The Spotlight

COVID-19 put a magnifying glass on my life, forcing me to reevaluate what I was trying to ignore. Once in lockdown, the cadence of seeing my husband a few hours a week collapsed immediately into all day, every day. We had been in separate rooms for months, in couples counseling and seeing each other briefly on weekdays, and barely coexisting on weekends. Additionally, I was physically exhausted, as the primary caregiver of a five, four, and two-year-old. A zombie in my own life. I allowed no time to deeply think, reflect, or evaluate. And I certainly did not pray.

Though surrounded by a religious family, having attended sixteen years of Catholic school, and praying with my littles at night, I felt nothing to a spirit. Any remaining faith was diluted to oblivion when in Afghanistan. How could a God exist with such atrocities in this world? So I continued on by my own will.

But then, one early March morning those first weeks of lockdown, something illuminated.

I came downstairs to my beautiful kitchen. My husband looked at me and coldly stated, "Go back upstairs with that attitude."

"I didn't say anything," I quietly pleaded back to him.

"I can see it in your face," he replied without looking at me.

I followed my pattern—lowered my head—and turned to leave. Stating my case would get me somewhere I didn't want to go, and I was so tired.

But this time I caught the eye of my eldest, Edith, looking at me, and I saw yearning in her searching eyes. I thought, *I do not want her to think this is okay. I want better for her and I am teaching her what right looks like.*

I went alone to my room and closed the door and fell to my knees. My mind played out the last words our marriage counselor had said to me just a few days prior to the lockdown. She was recalling a recent session with just my husband.

"Victoria, when he was with me, he got upset."

I replied with all the attributes of a maiden, wanting to retain my life and a fairy godmother to fix it. "Yes, he told me. I am glad. Maybe it was a breakthrough."

Looking back at me, this wise woman spoke with firm love. "No. That's not it. I have witnessed you, and I have witnessed him. And I saw what you saw and what is happening in your home. I want you to lock your door at night and do whatever you need to do to get out of that marriage—whatever it takes."

Circular, confused, and untethered, I was beyond lost, having no sense of my own reality from years of gaslighting. But what I did have was the memory of Edith's eyes and a tiny spark of something that felt like truth from my therapist.

And from that ember something emerged, something from deep inside, and it whispered through me aloud through weeping: "Come back, I need you. Please come back."

The First Guide

When I got off the floor from my watery plea, I looked over to a book I had recently bought, *Lux* by Elizabeth Cook. It was a book about King David of the Judeo-Christian faith tradition. King David was the biblical ruler of ancient Israel and a main character of the Bible's Old Testament. David was anointed as a boy to be God's chosen king by the prophet Samuel. It is believed that the Holy Spirit remained with him for the rest of his life and that Jesus is a direct descendant of David, fulfilling the prophecy of the Messiah.

What attracted me to *Lux* was not the story of David, the unexpected chosen one, the famed giant killer, the city builder, the powerful king. I knew this book focused on David, adulterer and murder. For David not only had an infamous affair with the married Bathsheba but also had Uriah, her husband, killed while Uriah was fighting for David on the battlefield. This seemed grossly paradoxical and called to my cynicism, but when I opened *Luxi*, I found far more than I expected.

Cook's interpretation of David is from within David's own mind. His mind when he sees Bathsheba, when he orders Uriah to certain death, when he looks himself in the mirror and peers over his balcony at what he has created. From the outside, his life presented an image of elegance and allure: castle, kingdom, wives, an army. All with a polished facade gleaming under the sunlight, yet it masked the turbulent currents churning within.

In *Lux* Cook exquisitely describes David when he realizes how far off he had come off his path, how empty he feels. She takes us to David in his cave after he calls back to God.

In his cave, David holds his shadows, his self-betrayal, and his denial of God, who had given so much to him. He spends time with himself and God in the darkness, exploring deeply—forgiving and healing, grappling with his own worthiness. Allowing himself to be forgiven and ultimately realigning with Spirit as a cocreator in his life. Moving into that seeming paradox of surrendering to God's intent through the act of free will and continued action in the physical world.

Somewhere in my own depths, this story blew on my tiny ember and reignited the tiniest flame of hope. Maybe, just maybe, if David, so chosen, so holy, could fall off the road and be welcomed back, perhaps there is a chance for a wretch like me. So I did my best to find my way out by going deep within.

My Cave

Soon thereafter, I fell into months of deep confusion—trying to remember which way was up, unraveling where I was, how I got there, and where I wanted to go. Months and months of blur.

By late 2020 the marriage had dissolved, and we were deep into the divorce processes. And that was when I found it. In the heart of COVID-19, tucked back in a small alley of an old Annapolis street, I had found my cave. And here, like David, I began to heal.

I began the work on embracing my shadow. What is your shadow? It's the parts of all of us that we are not initially inclined to shout off the rooftops about. So we keep it hidden. We keep it dark. It exists, it is always there, and it doesn't leave because you look away. It is the parts that come in the night when you are quiet and feel scary. The pieces of you that you pretend aren't there, the tears you don't shed because you are afraid they will break you. The anger you lead with because disappointment feels too hard. Those parts that we have been told by society are bad. The ones that feel icky and sticky and learn to not talk about because we'd rather not believe these parts exist and what they represent are real.

But it is these pieces that need to be integrated so we can all stop chastising ourselves for being human. Stop kidding ourselves so we can feel better about life when we deeply know we are not being clear about the world around us. From the shadows they call, the wild crazy ones, like John the Baptist, shouting on the hills that you are living a lie.

It was here that I began to recognize, hold, and forgive myself the years for self-betrayal. Self-betrayal so deep that I had almost completely forgotten who I was in my journey to be who I "should be."

I came to terms with the fact that my relationship with my now ex-husband was a mirror to my relationship with myself. That there was an energy there that felt comfortable and right, though it was so very wrong.

> " I began to accept those parts of me that were not perfect for what they were—human. "

I began to accept those parts of me that were not perfect for what they were—human. Those past versions of myself were me doing my absolute best each and every day to protect myself in the best way I knew how to survive and find connection in the world. Ultimately, coming to gratitude for those versions of myself that got me to that cave and doing her best and giving me exactly what she thought I needed.

Spirit Returned

It was then that the flicker of Spirit began to awaken in me. Goddesses fell into my path here, there, and everywhere. I spent time with Kali, Kuan Yin, Lilith, Hecate, Mary Magdalene, Brigid, Hathor. I read books, meditated, and took temple classes. I felt at home and happy with these women. I was ecstatic when I met my first spirit guide during cranial sacral therapy—a beautiful woman in pink who emerged from a lotus flower, who said she would be with me to guide me. I began to feel held, understood, and on a path that made sense to me and my ego.

Goddess Rejection

There was one lady I did not let into my house—quite literally, with all the statues, images, and symbols of goddesses, one was not invited: Mother Mary.

I knew her, or I thought I did, from my years in Catholic school and time in and around American and European culture. And I knew my answer to her: "No thank

you, Ms. Always Looking with Your Head Down Lady.
I've tried your kind of sacrificial love, and really, it's not
for me."

I was enjoying all the other bits, the witchy Hecate,
Kali's destroyer energy, Brigid's playfulness, Isis's wisdom,
Hathor's power. They were welcome.

But to my dismay, Mary persisted.

Blessed with vivid imagery, I have occasionally had
semiconscious visions. Often I will see a golden path—
glowing, flowing liquid, or iridescent lights. When I have
these visions, they are often accompanied by words, insights, or graced understandings. So one night in late
2022, I had a lucid dream, and it did not surprise me to see
a golden path before me.

In my vision I looked down and saw my bare feet on
a glowing path. I looked out into the darkness and saw a
group of three women dancing around a fire in the woods.
*Perfect. This is it and I am going to my ladies—I believe I see
Hecate, Brigid and Morgana.* Great. I happily walked down
this path.

And then there she was—right there on the road—out
of nowhere. Mother Mary.

"Oh, Hello, Mary," I said to her in obvious surprise.

"Hi, Victoria. That is where you are going, but first you
need to work with me," she said kindly

Far more focused on where I "was going," my thoughts
quickly formed into an "Ugh—um, really? I don't think
so." What came out was a hesitant, "Okay."

Then I awoke and generally ignored that short conversation. No special prayers, no mediations, no nothing. Just

kind of thought maybe it would pass. I had my opinion about Mary and her form of love, so I continued on my way, and my ego felt quite good about this decision.

Her Way

About two months later, I was invited to a women's retreat in Chicago. Very woo-woo, embedded in Native American traditional healing practices. Perfect. This sounded great, and I was excited to get there.

When I arrived I encountered the beautiful woman who runs these events, Sam, a force of nature in all the most wondrous ways. Wise thousands of years beyond her age, she exudes incredible grace, talent, and power. Trained in healing and spirit traditions from around the world, I felt at home as she pulled out her copal, an Isis status, drums, and singing bowls. But what was this! A candle of the Virgin of Guadalupe! *You've got to be kidding me.* There she was right at the center of the altar Sam was creating— Mary, looking down and to the right again. I mentioned her during the initial circle and my struggle with her, then did my best to put Mary out of my mind believing she must actually want someone else at this retreat.

The first night we journeyed together, I found myself with usual visions and loving thoughts, being shown things that resonated. I knew Mary was my guide, but that felt okay, as she showed me love for my children and love and understanding for my ex-husband. I gently nodded to Spirit. "Yes, I see, the lessons, the growth. Okay, thank you." Mary was with me, but I was okay. This was all peaceful, lovely, all going according to my expectations.

Then there it was, I began to be shown the faces of

men from Afghanistan. The memories flooded in. The ugliness, the lies, the pain, the violence, and the abuse. My mind raced, my body tensed, and I said my piece: "Oh no, not going to happen. This is what I'm talking about, Mary—love for these people, this kind of behavior, no way, not today. Take this how you want it, Mary, but your kind of love gets abused. I've seen it over and over again in big ways and small ways. This whole empathic, gentle love business is for the absolute birds, and I'm not interested."

I sat up and went to bed irritated and annoyed. *How dare she enter my spiritual retreat? When will she get the hint?* I had seen a lot in Afghanistan, never mind everywhere else, and I wasn't having it.

Then it happened, in a gentle, unending-grace sort of way. The next afternoon we did a heart-opening ceremony. This practice is communal with the intent of women holding sacred and loving space for each other so we can each heal through being seen and held.

Midafternoon in the ceremony room, I was sitting between two women on the floor, all three of our knees touching in crisscross applesauce. A beautiful woman of mixed ancestry—a divine healer in her own right—actively listening to the other across from her speaking, holding hands. I had my hands on both of their shoulders, holding space, nodding, looking down and to the right at the woman telling her story of horrific terrors in her childhood. She shared stories she had never told before. We witnessed her healing tears. Helping her hold the pain she thought would break her, finally feeling safe to cry, to talk.

And then it happened. Something in me said to look up. I looked up at the altar, and there was Mary looking at me. I was perfectly mirroring her. Down and to the right, arms outstretched.

In an instant I understood. Mary holds space so others can heal. You are not too big, too bad, too ugly, too awful, too disgraceful for her. She is not afraid of your dark, your shadow. She welcomes all of you with open arms and tells you that you are worthy. All the colors of your humanity—your irreverence, your hatred, your bitter tears, your anger, your betrayal, she loves you anyway. She knows you are doing your best and that you are human. She reminds you that you are not broken, that you are enough, you are divine, and that you are worthy of love.

" For to completely hold sacred space for others, you must first hold it for yourself. "

In the most gentle way, she showed me not only her love but also its tremendous power to heal. I also recognized that holding sacred space for others is not easy—it requires complete presence for another and an open heartedness that comes only from an acceptance of ourselves and a belief in our own worthiness. For to completely hold sacred space for others, you must first hold it for yourself. Once accepted in self, you can tell the deepest part of another's soul that they are loved, it is okay to be human, continue to do your best, and when you know better, do better, and know you are worthy—just as you are.

Her Story

Though more appreciative, I generally didn't change my ways or actions toward Mary after the retreat. However, about two months later, she came to me. I had another lucid dream. I met Mary again, along the same golden path. This time tears streamed down my eyes as I apologized.

"I am so sorry, Mary. I didn't know. I didn't understand."

She lovingly accepted. She revealed some lessons to me, hugged me, and then sent me on my path, leaving me with some final words: "Victoria, you will tell my story within six months."

Having no idea how to complete this task, I obediently said, "Of course. Thank you."

About four weeks later Atousa, a beautiful woman and shaman, whom I had worked with a few times for energetic healing, offered me this chapter. Here is my attempt to tell you what Mary has shared with me, or at least the tiny sliver I feign to understand.

Dear Mother, help me:

1. She was there all along. Mary told me she witnessed me and was with me all the years I asked her to be quiet. Silently waiting, ever present. When I asked for her to come back, she came back gently and in any form I would accept. Specifically telling me my first Spirit guide in pink was her . . . They are all reflections of her, but she knew if she came as herself, I would resist, so she came in whatever form I would allow in.

2. Every choice is the right one. I was shown a splitting of the golden path into many paths, leading to

many glowing doors. My vantage point changed, and I could see beyond the doors from a bird's-eye view. What I saw was that all the paths merged again on the other side. I was told it does not matter our choices, as Spirit will meet us on any road we choose and is there to guide us all back to our purpose/dharma in this life and will always be there to guide you.

3. Have faith. Your life is part of a bigger, divine plan. You are worthy of all your dreams, life, and talents because you have them. Therefore, my job is to be me and yours is to be you. Holding the paradox where you are incredibly important and not important at all. Meaning we are all playing our parts in a broader human story in which we are all connected—so in that way it is not about you or certainly just you. But you have a vital role—we all do, and your job is to be you. And holding the beautiful reality that this life was created in a manner that you are you, through Joseph Cambell's suggestion of follow your bliss, while continuing to trust that you will be given the lessons, guides, and grace that is perfectly required in perfect time for a greater purpose.

4. Earthly mothers need to look to the Divine Mother for wisdom, guidance, and strength. It is a mistake for an earthly mother to try to be "perfect." This causes perversions of motherhood and stress in families. We can and should attempt to improve each day. However, we are to look to the Great

Mother for wisdom and guidance. We should teach our children to pray to the Great Mother to protect them and guide them, and they should also witness our prayers to her.

5. The relationship with Spirit is meant to be collaborative. Like the Sistine Chapel image of God and Adam, we need to reach back out to Spirit, who is also reaching to us. Once we reach out, our duty is to keep eyes open to find, listen, and collaborate. Holding both surrender (to flow and Spirit's will) and action (our behavior in the physical world) simultaneously.

My Road

What I can see now is that after lowering to my knees, crying out to Spirit on the floor in March 2020, is that over the next four years was a perfect symphony of guides, guardians, helpers, friends, lovers, and synchronicities— many of which I still do not, and likely will never, understand—as so many of these were put in place seemingly decades before.

I'd love to tell you another happily-ever-after story that I listened to, fell into deep faith, and have now found myself existing in a perpetual summer. That has not been the case, certainly not for me. What happened was, I fell into about six weeks of deep spiritual madness. I was given numerous additional guides and miracles, yet I was wrestling with myself and God. Do I put myself on the "trust bus" and believe these moments of ecstasy, understanding, and grace are real, or do I listen to the part of me that was screaming not to go on the crazy train?

In late March 2024, I decided to surrender and hold in my heart that life is not happening to me but for me. Allowing this belief, that Spirit is always present and guiding through words, angels, humans, animals, and all else has led me here.

And where is here?

What came to me during meditation about here are two things.

First is the surprising companion of joy. For though I didn't understand it at all at that time, Mary showed me this perfectly in a dream. For, as I walked past Mary on the path, I was met by the Celtic goddess Brigid. And Brigid told me to remember. Not to remember the pain, the scared, the running through the woods in fear but to remember the fun, the joy, the magic of this life. Though we are always growing and learning, we are not meant to do the work forever of healing. We are meant to accept all of ourselves, let our ego rest, and live as a Divine Human. And there lives joy—so we can stop working on ourselves and our own egos all day (protecting it, nurturing it, saving it) and get into collaboration with Spirit and do the bigger work, which requires you to be fully alive, present, and aware so you can be an instrument for the Divine—as a perfectly imperfect human, the creature you were created to be. And this only happens when we believe we are worthy—and what a tremendous and unexpected joy it is. For without the fear that unworthiness and disbelief bring, you can enjoy life as an adventure and a journey, knowing it will all work out as Spirit intends because life is about far more than just your individual existence living through "thy will be done."

" For without the fear that unworthiness and disbelief bring, you can enjoy life as an adventure and a journey. "

Second is the reminder that here is a journey, not a destination, constantly unfolding and weaving through living. What I can promise you, this path is not linear nor the easiest, but it holds the most magic and the greatest of partners.

May we all have ears that can hear, eyes that can see, an open heart, and a clear mind.
Happy loving—start with self, you're worth it.
Amen, A'ho, and so it is.

Victoria

About Victoria Stattel

Victoria is dedicated to serving heart-centered, high-performing individuals who aspire to live extraordinary lives.

Victoria specializes in bridging ancient wisdom with modern methods, giving her clients grounded and practical approaches to unlock the extraordinary. A certified life, body mastery, and executive coach, Victoria is also a recognized intuitive, spiritual alchemist and crystal healer. Victoria's practice is further enriched by her own life experiences as a successful executive, strategy consultant, entrepreneur, military officer, and helicopter pilot.

Victoria serves individuals in-person in the DC metro area and remotely through her company, Golden Path Partners, www.goldenpathpartners.com.

Email her at victoria@goldenpathpartners.com.

About I.AM Publishing

Atousa started I.AM Publishing after being an author in two multiauthor books and publishing her solo book. She felt that the hybrid self-publishing companies were not properly meeting the needs of emerging authors or those who just wanted to share their healing journey with the world. I.AM publishing is transparent in the process, invites the author to be a part of the publishing process, and simplifies the mysticism behind the Amazon self-publishing world.

The biggest advantage of I.AM publishing is that Atousa helps the author to activate their chapter or book by bringing out the desired energy in the pages, cover art, and what the book will feel like to the reader before it is birthed into the world.

I.AM publishing customizes the service based on your needs. You own the right to your book, art, and sales from the book.

To get in touch please visit AtousaRaissyan.com/iam-publishing.